Bounds of Their Habitation

BOUNDS OF THEIR HABITATION

Race and Religion in American History

Paul Harvey

ROWMAN & LITTLEFIELD
Lanham • Boulder • New York • London

Published by Rowman & Littlefield
A wholly owned subsidiary of The Rowman & Littlefield Publishing Group, Inc.
4501 Forbes Boulevard, Suite 200, Lanham, Maryland 20706
www.rowman.com

Unit A, Whitacre Mews, 26-34 Stannary Street, London SE11 4AB

British Library Cataloguing in Publication Information Available

Library of Congress Cataloging-in-Publication Data

The hardback edition of this book was previously cataloged by the Library of
Congress as follows:

978-1-4422-3618-9 (cloth : alk. paper)
978-1-4422-3619-6 (electronic)
978-0-8108-9625-3 (paperback)

∞™ The paper used in this publication meets the minimum requirements of
American National Standard for Information Sciences—Permanence of Paper for
Printed Library Materials, ANSI/NISO Z39.48-1992.

Printed in the United States of America

For
Rob Sackett and Christina Jimenez, colleagues
Kathryn Gin Lum and Edward J. Blum, friends and coauthors

And
Andre Johnson and Andrew Manis, preachers and scholars

Contents

Acknowledgments   IX

Introduction: Religion and Race in American History   3

1   Red, White, and Black in Colonial American Religion   11

2   Religious Freedom and Religious Repression
     in the Early United States   43

3   Religious Ways of Knowing Race in Antebellum America   73

4   Religion, Race, and the Reconstruction of Citizenship   99

5   Race, Religion, and Immigration   129

6   Religion and Civil Rights: The Color of Power   159

7   Liberation Theologies and Problems of Religious Freedom
     in a Conservative Age   183

Epilogue: Contemporary Dilemmas of Pluralism   205

A Note on Sources   217

Index   241

About the Author   253

Acknowledgments

THIS BOOK STARTED AS A CONVERSATION with John David Smith, general editor for the *American Ways* series; he and Jon Sisk helped throughout the process of shaping and then finishing this work, and I thank them. My teaching home, the University of Colorado at Colorado Springs, provided me support and intellectual comrades who have enriched my life and writing career. Too many colleagues to list have conversed with me on the theme of race and religion in American history for more than a quarter century; I hope to thank all of you in person. Those to whom the book is dedicated have been especially inspiring and uplifting, in ways impossible to describe, at various points in my life. So, as always, has Suzi Nishida.

Bounds of Their Habitation

Introduction

Religion and Race in American History

And hath made of one blood all nations of men for to dwell on all the face of the earth, and hath determined the times before appointed, and the bounds of their habitation. (Acts 17:26)

This book is about the relationship of religion and race in American history. It starts with the premise that both "religion" and "race" are categories invented in the modern world, for particular purposes. The specific ways in which we understand these terms have some roots in antiquity and the medieval era. Yet, as full-blown categories, they are relatively recent creations. Once conjured up, these categories took on lives and realities of their own. From there, they deeply shaped social hierarchies, cultural expressions, and political power.

Starting around the Renaissance, "race," the term referring to the organization of social power according to the cultural meanings given to accidents of phenotype, became deeply inscribed in Western thought. It quickly permeated religious beliefs, fables, and mythologies. And around the same era, "religion" came to be demarcated as a separate sphere of human life referring to the human relationship to a transcendent being. Since that time, definitions of and controversies about both terms have proliferated. But in everyday discourse, they have clear and uncontested meanings. They have become "commonsense" terms. Everyone knows what they mean without having to think about it. Since those meanings changed over time, tracing their usage and interconnections will illuminate much about American religious history.

People know what the terms "religion" and "race" mean, even as scholars debate them endlessly. Yet these terms are useful not so much when defined but when analyzed for what they do and how they work in societies. In the modern Western world, "religion" works as an expression of individual belief generally in some transcendent power. That way of conceptualizing the term excludes a considerable terrain of human behavior from being captured by it. The word thus distinguishes denigrated cultural practices from honored sacred expressions.

Scholars speak of religion and race being "co-constituting categories." This is scholarly jargon and shorthand meaning, essentially, that religious concepts formed racial ideas, and racial concepts infused religious ideas in American history. The two worked in tandem to create deeply held notions of where people came from (including origins, myths, and migration stories), who they were *as* a people, what they as a people were to do with their individual and communal lives, and how they would define themselves among the others around them. Religious ideas created racial categories and *imposed* race upon individual human bodies—what scholars refer to as "racialization," or "the imparting of a cultural meanings to human bodies of particular appearances." That process also helps explain the hierarchies that emerged out of them. But religious ideas also helped undermine racial hierarchies. Likewise, ideas about race created the categories of religion by which people imposed order on the chaos of ideas and practices swirling around them. But as ideas about race came to be seen as human inventions serving social purposes, the religious stories undergirding them also were subject to the same scrutiny.

This book traces the long interaction, construction, deconstruction, but continued life of race and religion from the seventeenth century to our contemporary world. In doing so, I hope to convey, through historical narrative and biographical vignettes, some sense of the complicated story of that interaction. The title of the book, from Acts 17:26, tells both sides of that story—how God made "of one blood" all nations (always a favorite verse fragment for religious liberals and pluralists), and how God had then determined the "bounds of the habitation" of those people He had created (the favored fragment for those interested in proper religious order and hierarchy among diverse peoples). This book develops these ideas through a series of thematic chapters, each focusing on particular individuals and events. There is an "American Way" to religion and race unlike any other place in the world. The rise of religious pluralism in contemporary America (together with the continuing legacy of the racism of the past and misapprehensions in the present) makes understanding it crucial.

* * *

Religious diversity characterized the Americas before Europeans or Africans came, and their arrival reinforced regional religious variety. A riot of religions has been a reality, a "fact on the ground," in American history, not through intent but simply through the historical processes by which people from all parts of the globe met on the continent. That story began in the sixteenth and seventeenth centuries, when peoples from Europe, Africa, and the Americas first interacted throughout the American continent from Canada to Peru and Brazil, and everywhere in between. But while a de facto pluralism (perhaps better termed as the "reality of human religious diversity") was always a reality, so was the de jure religious rule of those who defined themselves as having the right religion, over those defined as not. As the story progressed, this increasingly took the form of Euro-American Christians defining the terms, orders, and daily realities for non-Christian peoples, and eventually for Christian peoples who were of other-than-European descent.

Religiously diverse, colonial America was not pluralist in any modern sense. Different varieties of the Christian faith were (sometimes grudgingly) tolerated, if not in the same colony, at least in the same region. While this may seem a paltry parody of pluralism to contemporary eyes, it was, for seventeenth- and eighteenth-century viewers, a remarkably motley array of religious sects and beliefs jostling against one another, an Atlantic world of religions. Euro-American migrants, and sometimes Indians and Africans as well, could find worship within a Puritan, Congregationalist, Presbyterian, Baptist, and Quaker meeting house all within the same day in some locations (especially in the middle colonies, always the most religiously diverse of North America). By the mid-eighteenth century, Americans heralded this religious ferment, what we might now see as diversity among the Christian sects, as a crowning glory of life in the New World. Later, in the revolutionary and constitutional era, American philosophes such as Thomas Jefferson allied with evangelicals to push forward revolutionary ideas and practices of religious freedom that found their way into state constitutions and eventually into the First Amendment, the crowning glory of religious freedom in the United States.

Religious diversity was a fact of life in colonial America. Religious freedom, in its modern sense, was not. Defining religious freedom remained a struggle to be waged over centuries. Colonial-era residents of North America—Spanish, French, Dutch, German, English, Native American, African, and others—struggled to comprehend the facts of diversity on the ground while defending their own notions of faith, doctrine, and practice within their own communities. Religious freedom, then, was limited and ethnocentric; for many, it meant the freedom to practice the one true faith and repress all others. For Euro-Christian colonizers especially, religious freedom certainly did not extend to non-Christian practices, which were by definition heathen and thus suspect.

A complex of historical factors (such as the gigantic global enterprise of colonizing the New World and then populating it with Europeans and African slaves) and mythic groundings (such as stories from the Old Testament and diverse indigenous American and African traditions) influenced the construction of modern racial categories. Euro-American Christianity was hardly the sole or even primary force in this process. Yet religious myth, originating from interpretations of biblical stories as well as speculations about God's Providence, played an important role in the formation, revision, and reconstruction of racial categories in the modern world. In short, *religion* played a significant part in creating *race*. Yet if Christianity fostered racialization, it also undermined it. Biblical passages were powerful but ambiguous, and arguments about God's Providence in colonization, proselytization, the slave trade, and slavery were contentious. Christian myths and stories were central to the project of creating racial categories in the modern world, but the central text of Christianity, the Bible, was also amenable to more universalist visions, and in that sense it was not a fully reliable ally for theorists of racial hierarchy.

For much of the eighteenth and, even more so, nineteenth centuries, race and religion were joined in the project of civilization. Christianizing others involved civilizing them. Sometimes this involved brutally stripping colonial subjects, especially Native Americans, of their own civilizations. This included language, religious belief, and cultural practice. "Kill the Indian, Save the Man" was the motto of nineteenth-century white reformist groups devoted to Indian education. At other times, the joining of Christianization and civilization underwrote idealistic crusades of bringing formerly enslaved peoples into American civilization, as in the abolitionist movement and, later, in the creation of black schools and colleges during Reconstruction. In other instances, the intertwining

of Christianity, civilization, and whiteness justified the complete exclusion of peoples from the American Republic, notably in legislation such
as the Chinese Exclusion Act of 1882. Progressive Christian writers such
as Josiah Strong articulated a Christian nativism, warning against the
dilution of the Protestantism which had been instrumental in forming
American democracy. In short, the connections between religion and race
were complicated; idealism and brutality often went hand in hand, as did
notions of inclusion together with the instruments of exclusion. Idealism
and imperialism often joined in projects both inspiring and ignoble.

In the twentieth century, Christian thought helped undermine the
racial system that it had helped to create. In the twentieth century, ideas
of cultural pluralism that percolated through the progressive intellectual
world of the early twentieth century eventually found their way into an
American discourse of religious pluralism. This was never all-inclusive.
For groups whose spiritual practices did not constitute a discernible
"religion" and thus did not enjoy the benefits of First Amendment protection, religious freedom remained a more distant ideal. Yet for many
others, including those who were excluded by the legacy of racist immigration legislation and others who historically had been dishonored,
religious pluralism as an ideal in public discourse constituted a true
revolution.

In the 1950s and 1960s, black and Latino civil rights activists finally
penetrated the walls of the segregation. The civil rights revolution in
American history was, to a considerable degree, a religious revolution,
one whose social and spiritual impact inspired numerous other movements around the world.

The contemporary United States is, demographically speaking, a
largely Christian nation. Even after recent declines in those claiming
adherence to some Christian tradition, about seventy percent still are in
that column. In other ways, and increasingly so, the United States is a
religiously diverse place, thanks largely to its history of successive waves
of immigration that brought to these shores (just to name a few) German
Protestants, Central European Anabaptists, Irish Catholics, French
Huguenots, Italian and Eastern European Catholics, Polish and Russian
Jews, Latino Catholics from Mexico and Central America, Japanese
Buddhists, Chinese Confucians, East Indian Sikhs, Thai Buddhists,

Middle Eastern and South Asian Hindus and Muslims, Southeast Asian Hindus and Muslims, African Muslims and Christians, and Pentecostal celebrants from Central America and the Caribbean. Religious conflicts occupy courts and other places in the public square. In recent years, those have often come from religious conservatives who feel embattled, even persecuted, even though they historically created a powerful Protestant moral establishment that effectively governed the country for the better part of two centuries. In other cases, they have arisen from conflicts between particular religious practices (such as Islamic prayer times and rituals) and the demands of the modern workplace. Yet even in the tense environment after September 11, 2001, incidents of ethnoreligious conflict, although sometimes frighteningly violent, remained relatively sporadic in comparison to the consistently violent and intolerant religious and cultural conflict that still characterize many other regions.

The current balancing act of a demographically Christian nation with a rising pluralist population will shape race and religion in the decades to come. The implicit, de facto Protestantism of the American Republic historically has defined public discourse, shaped public ceremonies, and dominated public life in the personage of political officials. Moreover, racial profiling as applied to black or Middle Eastern Muslims affects lives and individual liberties in a way that is simply unthinkable for the dominant Protestant majority. In this way, the nexus between "religion" and "race" has never died. But it undeniably exerts a relatively smaller influence in comparison to the power of that dualism in earlier centuries. Religious pluralism requires an official rhetoric of respect and neutrality. However imperfectly practiced, religious pluralism has opened up spaces for ethnic groups and minority religions that were formerly surveilled and suppressed.

Religion and race remain tied together in the public mind. Although religion is no longer racialized in the ways it was in previous centuries, religious congregations tend to be racially separated, a simple reality of how Americans of diverse ethnic backgrounds have ordered their lives. Race still has a color, and a religion, even while the public rhetoric of American religion is ostensibly raceless and colorless. Thus, in a society sometimes said to be moving into a "post-racial" era, ethnic and racial constructions remain a central ordering fact of religious life. Americans remain united by an unusually high association with faith, with religious belief, but divided by faith since the institutions reflecting those beliefs still tend to be divided by race, culture, and politics. Given the history of race and religion in America, it is hard to see how it could be otherwise. And yet, given that history, it is possible to envision it being otherwise.

1

Red, White, and Black in Colonial American Religion

IN 1723, A PLAINTIVE PLEA from an anonymous group of mixed-race slaves arrived in the letter file of a newly installed bishop who oversaw Anglican affairs in the American colonies. These slaves were, they wrote, "baptised and brouaht up in a way of the Christian faith and follows the wayes and Rulles of the chrch of England." They wrote to complain about the law "which keeps and makes them and there seed Slaves forever." They also criticized their masters, who kept them from following the Sabbath: "Wee doo hardly know when it comes for our task mastrs are [as] hard with us as the Egyptians was with the Chilldann of Issarall." Their letter concluded with an explanation of why they did not sign their names: "for freare of our masters for if they knew that wee have Sent home to your honour wee Should goo neare to Swing upon the Gallass tree." These mixed-race slaves insisted that their religious status gave them rights to freedom and respect. They were willing to fight for those, whether through imploring pleas to imperial officials or in rebelling against governing authorities.

Taking off from this story, this chapter examines the complicated evolution of both "race" and "religion" from the earliest days of Spanish, French, and English settlement to the mid-eighteenth century. We will explore how Europeans deployed Christianity to define racial others, while those others resisted by using Christianity to demand rights and respect for themselves. Ultimately, however, what had been defined as cultural differences, and therefore mutable, eventually came to be solidified into racial difference, and therefore immutable. Race in its modern form came to define the bounds of habitations of religious communities, even if members of those communities challenged those boundaries, as did those writing the letter to the bishop in 1723. This set a pattern for the next two hundred and fifty years of race and religion in American history.

Religion and race commingled from the earliest days of colonization. Peoples from around the Atlantic World struggled for control of their lives in a world that was transforming before their eyes. All of them dealt with a diverse world of bodies and spirits, which compelled frequent religious encounters with peoples of wildly varying cosmologies and practices. The result was a constant cultural conversation, carried on both peaceably and violently.

North America was one of the most diverse religious societies in the world in the colonial era. French Jesuits interacted with powerful Iroquois bands; Spanish Franciscans were more or less powerless to stop Puebloans in New Mexico, including Christianized as well as "heathen" Indians, from practicing kachina dances and other ceremonials of their heritage; Anglicans in Virginia and South Carolina sent out missionaries to preach the gospel to enslaved Africans who came from a diverse variety of religious backgrounds ranging from Islam to Catholicism to tribal faiths; Protestants of all sorts in Pennsylvania interacted both peacefully and violently with natives who often used Christian intermediaries to try to protect their dwindling land base; Puritans in New England leveled charges against "popery" even as Catholics in the originally Catholic colony of Maryland found themselves as minorities even in their own world; and natives from hundreds of different tribes engaged in religious practices that differed from each other as much as from European forms. European observers, most famously the philosophe and wit Voltaire, saw in America, especially among the Quakers in Pennsylvania, a peaceable kingdom of diverse peoples and faiths living in harmony. He publicized it as a model for all to follow.

Voltaire's idea was not totally imaginary. Compared to many places, notably Europe, colonial North America appeared as a thriving ecosystem of religious profusions shooting up everywhere. Yet coexistence did not mean mutual understanding, and contact created conditions for *causus belli* more so than *pax Americana*. Indians living there knew better, for they experienced bouts of violent hostility in the backcountry. Whatever its primary economic and political motivations, the entire colonial project hinged on the conquering of native peoples and the exponential growth of the trade in slaves. Both quickly developed religious justifications and rationales.

Europeans may not have had a fully developed modern idea of "race" in the colonial era, but they certainly brought conceptions of hierarchy based on religion and skin color, and sometimes on "purity of blood"— limpieza de sangre. As one historian has pithily summarized it, there was racism before race. That is, practices of racial hierarchy emerged before a fully developed quasi-biological notion of "race" solidified. Throughout much of American history, European colonizers associated themselves with the sacred, in contrast to pagan others. This was rooted in a European heritage that not only whitened images of Christ, angels, and God but also darkened characterizations of the devil, demons, and witches. Many British colonists imagined themselves as God's chosen ones. In contrast, they envisioned Native Americans as "children of the devil," or as "black dogs," or other objects signifying satanic power. They divinized whiteness and demonized blackness.

Meanwhile, however, those Europeans also engaged in various acts of proselytization, intending to bring others into the Christian fold. When they were successful, they faced questions of how an Indian or a Negro could be also a Christian person. And given that raced bodies claimed Christian privileges, Euro-Americans puzzled over how best to practice Christian proselytization, as was their biblical duty, but deploy it on behalf of racial hierarchy.

This chapter follows a few such stories illustrating the complexities of race and religion in colonial America. Each one contrasts a moment of religious interaction, conversion, or understanding with one of power, dominance, and control. We will begin with the contrasting stories of Popé, leader of the Pueblo Revolt of 1680 in New Mexico, and the "Mohawk Saint," Kateri Tekakwitha, converted by (and who herself effectively converted) a French Jesuit missionary. The French who recorded the life of Tekakwitha began the process of creating the hagiographies which recently have led to her canonization. During the same era in New England, Puritan missionary John Eliot produced the first Bible published in America—in the language of the Massachusett Indians—and created a system of "praying towns" for Indian converts. These early efforts disintegrated after King Philip's War of 1676. Afterward,

New Englanders condemned natives as members of a cursed race, to be overcome by the people of God.

In the eighteenth century, while maintaining close relations with Moravians and other sympathetic missionaries, Indians carried on a "spirited resistance," sometimes resisting Christianization, other times adapting Christian manners and allies for their own purposes. Meanwhile, in the early eighteenth century, Francis Le Jau and the Society for the Propagation of the Gospel in Foreign Parts brought their Anglican gospel to the newly emerging slave colony of South Carolina, setting up a battle between missionaries and planters for the soul of the colony. Through the mid-eighteenth century, the first international superstar evangelist, George Whitefield, found an audience among early American evangelicals, who in some cases brought the message to select groups of slaves. By the time of the American Revolution, early black converts were establishing some of the first quasi-independent black churches in America, aided and protected by Christian slaveholders but frequently attacked and surveilled by white communities suspicious of their motives.

Christianity thus operated to define the bounds of the habitation of racial communities and to explode them. The former happened more consciously, and through the legal system; the latter emerged as a product of those who took the biblical texts about equality at their word. This interaction became fundamental to race and religion in American history.

SPANISH, FRENCH, AND INDIAN WARS

Spanish explorers and settlers from the sixteenth century predated the English, establishing a beachhead colony at St. Augustine, Florida, in 1565, and settlements in New Mexico late in the century. Franciscans followed the soldiers in New Mexico and began to missionize among the Pueblo people. Three quarters of a century later, the Pueblo Revolt of 1680 vividly displayed native anger at coercive Christian proselytization.

In previous decades, early hopes for widespread Christianization, spurred on by millennial dreams of expanding the righteous Spanish empire, had been disappointed. The fabled golden cities of the northern regions were nowhere to be found; neither was the great harvest of souls that had provided the propaganda necessary for funding the struggling New Mexican missions. The more optimistic friars claimed large numbers of converts but fought continually against the reimposition of idolatry. Native dances and ceremonies especially offended their Christian sensibilities; they were the very embodiment of paganism. No matter how many times the fathers confiscated the instruments of idolatry—masks, kachinas, and other icons of Pueblo cosmology—and punished those who led heathenish dances or attacks on the priests, the native gods returned. Further, the friars grew apoplectic at Indians who satirized them and the Christian religion, comedy that entertained even Christianized Puebloans. In the mid-1650s, for example, a resident of the Awatovi Pueblo who had served as a priest's assistant performed his own burlesque on a Catholic Mass for a village of amused Indian comrades. Putting on the absent priest's cloak, he chanted, prayed, and sermonized as a priest would do, to the great amusement of the crowd.

More serious, and deadly, was a pan-Indian revolt in northern New Spain in 1680, now commonly referred to as the Pueblo Revolt. Prior to 1680, on various occasions individual pueblos or nations had rebelled against Spanish rule but consistently had been "reduced and returned to obedience." In 1680, however, in what had appeared as a peaceful time, New Mexican natives "in general rebelled on one day and at one hour, and it was by a miracle of God that they did not destroy everything, as was their intention," as a Spanish chronicler later wrote. He added, "Our return to the kingdom must be in the form of a conquest with men, arms, and supplies to safeguard and garrison it as it is reduced to the yoke of the holy gospel and obedience to the Catholic Majesty."

Beginning August 9 and continuing into the fall of 1680, through the region of the pueblos in central and northern New Mexico, natives killed nearly four hundred of the 2,500 Spanish colonists, burned almost every church in the colony, demolished crosses and chapels, and tortured and killed twenty-one of the thirty-three resident religious. Besieged Spanish leaders first defended their last citadel at Santa Fe, until Indian attacks forced them on a long march southward toward safety in El Paso. The natives followed the religious instructions of messianic leaders. They bathed to cleanse themselves from the pollution of Christian baptism, surrendered their Spanish names and Christian wives, and vowed a revitalization of Indian ways. It was the first of many such messianic and

Popé or Po'Pay, leader of the Pueblo Revolt in 1680
Source: Photo on Flickr from "Dougward," licensed under the Creative Commons Attribution-Share Alike 2.0 Generic license.

violent eruptions that took hold over the next two centuries in areas of white-native contact throughout North America.

Some students of the 1680 uprising have downplayed religious motivations for the revolt. They insist that the specific and horrific conditions of drought, famine, and disease in the years preceding 1680 provided the primary impetus. With modern understandings of human revolution, certainly these underlying factors appear critical. Yet the expressed motivations of the rebels themselves must be considered carefully. They aimed their wrath directly at the symbols of Catholicism, which was, after all, the primary point of contact between natives and Spaniards. At the pueblo of Sandia on August 26, 1680, for example, the delegation led by Governor and Captain-General Don Antonio de Otermín found the convent "deserted and destroyed, the cells without doors, and the whole place sacked. The images had been taken from the church, and on the main altar there was a carved full-length figure of Saint Francis with the arms hacked off by an ax. The church had been filled with wheat straw for the purpose of burning it, and fire had started in the choir and in the choir stalls. Everything was broken to pieces and destroyed; the sacristy was found empty of chests and of all sacred vessels and vestments, and of the carved figures that were there, for everything had been stolen and profaned by the rebellious traitors." As another account put it, the Indians' hatred toward Christian symbols extended to smearing excrement on crosses and communion tables and hacking off the arms of an image of Saint Francis.

Further investigations into the anticolonial insurrection revealed the religious motivations and symbology behind the rebels' cause. In December of 1681, not yet in control of the colony but anxious to learn more about the causes of the debacle, Spanish colonial leaders initiated a judicial inquiry. One early examination, soon to be confirmed by other pieces of evidence, pointed to the role of the Pueblo Indian dubbed El Popé. Native sources indicated that Indians "held him in terror" because of his supposed talks with the devil. As a veteran of earlier Indian rebellions and one who had experienced torture and lashing at the hands of the Spanish governor in 1675, Popé himself envisioned an Indian renewal that would recapture the power of the kachina, who had descended underground and would not return until the Spanish were driven out. Indeed, Popé used both Pueblo and Christian symbology. He told his followers that by living under the ancestral prescriptions, Indians would raise "a great quantity" of their traditional foodstuffs, "and that their houses would be filled and they would have good health and plenty of rest." In planning the revolt, Popé circulated a knotted cord made of maguey fiber among villages. Those who wished to join the rebellion would untie a knot. He selected August 11, 1680, as the day of attack. It coincided with a full moon but preceded the arrival of caravans from the south that would replenish the Spanish supplies of ammunition and horses. However, two Indians captured on August 9 revealed the plan to Spanish authorities, compelling Popé's forces to move more quickly than planned. Along with others, Popé ordered Indians to destroy all images suggestive of Christianity and remove their baptismal names by plunging themselves in rivers and washing with *amole* root, a traditional Indian cleansing potion. By doing so and by imitating kachina dances, Popé had told them that "they could erect their houses and enjoy abundant health and leisure." Another interrogated Indian added that Popé and the leaders "said they were weary of putting in order, sweeping, heating, and adorning the church," and wished to "live contentedly, happy in their freedom, living according to their ancient custom." After the expulsion of the Spanish colonizers, Popé then insisted that Indians reclaim their lands, "enlarge their cultivated fields, saying that now they were as they had been in ancient times, free from the labor they had performed for the religious and the Spaniards." The first century of Christian proselytization in the Southwest thus ended in violent revenge by the very natives who supposedly had been made children of the Christian God. And the Spanish *Reconquista*, when it came in the 1690s, was brutal.

TEKAKWITHA

The Spanish in the Southwest confronted already "settled" Indians in pueblo communities and thus simply stationed missionaries among them. Both the French and the English, by contrast, perceived segregating converted Indians into Christian communities as a key part of educating Indians in the ways of civilization. For the English, this meant strengthening an Anglo-Protestant empire against threats posed by the Spanish Catholic and French, and enlisting Indian allies where

possible in this goal. Mere conversion alone, it was clear, was insuffi-
cient, for Christianized Indians (especially those allied with the French)
were frighteningly capable of launching deadly assaults upon outposts of
English civilization. Thus, over time, missionary idealism merged with
imperial realpolitik in the goal of producing civilized Indians as part of
the project of pacifying the New World for the Protestant king.

Throughout North America, missionaries established missions,
reserves, and praying towns for Indian neophyte and converts who would
be removed from "heathen" environments and placed in laboratories
of Christian civilization. These places produced Indian converts who
attempted to adopt Christian ways, but they also compelled European
settlers and missionaries to establish military protection for Christian
Indians against non-Christian Indians and sometimes military protection
from rebellious Christianized Indians.

Kateri Tekakwitha was a Mohawk Indian who spent the last years
of a short life (ca. 1656–1680) at the Jesuit mission of Kahnawake, a
reserve near Montreal established for Mohawk converts who allied with
the French. There, they constructed a village, grew corn, and hunted in
the traditional way. They also adapted Christian ways of worship and
social practices such as marriage. The French were bent on settlement
and trade. They poured funds into development in the Iroquois regions
of Canada. Disease and alcohol devastated Indian nations. French military invasions compelled a peace treaty in 1667 that cleared a path for
the arrival of Christian missionaries among the Five Nations of the
Iroquois League. The Jesuits proselytized aggressively through the
1670s. Many Indian converts moved northward, allied themselves with
the French Father, and settled along French-controlled areas of the St.
Lawrence River in and around Montreal. A group of French Jesuits who
settled there in the late 1660s recounted their joy in rediscovering "old
Christians," mostly Hurons who had been converted in previous missionary expeditions but then had to be left behind because of warfare with
the League of the Iroquois. They were seen still faithfully carrying out
Mass: "We could not help shedding tears of joy at seeing these poor captives so fervent in their devotions and so constant in their faith after all
the years they had been deprived of all instruction." They saw mothers
making crosses on the foreheads of their children and telling them of hell
and heaven. One father enthused that "their devotion greatly surpasses

One of the oldest portraits of Saint Kateri Tekakwitha by Father Claude
Chauchetière around 1696
Source: Public domain.

that of the common run of Christians, even though they were deprived for so long a time of any help from their pastors."

Tekakwitha was one of these converts. She was the daughter of an Iroquois non-Christian father and converted Mohawk mother. Tekakwitha's story was particularly valued by the Jesuits because she endured persecution among her own people for her Christian ways and lived the life of an earthly saint. Having lost both of her parents and survived smallpox (though with a significant loss of vision as a result), Tekakwitha turned to Jesus. She led a small group of native women who pursued Christian perfection on earth. In 1682, two years after her death, a French Jesuit recounted, with admiration but also some hesitancy, the "austerities practiced by certain Indian women," which possibly involved "some indiscretion." Beginning by engaging in acts of penitence with switches and thorns, they then increased the divine agony with the use of iron girdles and other practices picked up from nuns in Montreal. "Thus have man-eaters," as one Jesuit described it, "which they were in the past, become lambs through the grace of Jesus Christ, to such a degree that they are now exemplars of virtue and of religion for all of Canada." The indoctrinated faithful (or so the Jesuits portrayed it) confounded heretic Dutch Calvinists who had come to convert them but instead found themselves theologically overmatched.

The sensitive French Jesuit Claude Chauchetière, on his own mission of self-examination, used Tekakwitha's story to resolve his own personal crises of faith. The Indian saint's narrative became an international sensation. Translated into several languages, it circulated through Europe. After receiving baptism, she seemed to be not a "neophyte needing to be confirmed in the faith, but a soul filled with the most precious gifts of Heaven who had to be guided in the most sublime spiritual ways." Her perfect purity, in fact, issued a challenge to the young men of her village, "and laid many snares for her with the sole view of dimming a virtue which dazzled them." The missionary "thought he could discern that God had great designs as to that virgin."

Kateri's death at the age of twenty-four in 1680 created an ideal hagiographical subject. Soon, the invocation of her name became associated with miracles and healing. Kateri Tekakwitha personified the noble savage turned ideal ascetic Christian. She appealed to European visions of the New World as both virginal territory and souls awaiting the word of Christ. The Jesuits took her as an icon of the ultimate triumph of true religion among the savages they struggled to understand. Tekakwitha's story, once presented in hagiographic form, ultimately served as hand-maidens to the reorganizing of Indians peoples and nations in New Canada.

Everywhere, the Christian-Indian contact was complex and contested, as both sides assimilated and synthesized the ideas of the other. Perhaps the most important lesson learned from a continent-wide survey, how-ever, is that missionizing was never simply a one-way street. "Converts" never simply left behind older ways. Conversion and domination were never bound inextricably together even if the two were sometimes rein-forcing. The experiences of praying Indians in New France and New England show some of the complexities of the religious dialogue carried on throughout the continent between European newcomers and dispa-rate groups of natives whose religions, dependent as they were on local ecologies and on a natural balance of forces, came under severe stress in the age of colonization.

MASSACHUSETTS AND METACOM

Protestants in New England faced, if anything, an even greater challenge than had the Jesuits in New France. Puritans found it difficult enough to discern the movement of God's grace in the souls of their fellow church members or even themselves; in the seventeenth century, they set about searching for such a movement in the souls of natives whose ways were otherwise inscrutable or terrifying. They operated from a mixture of proselytizing and civilizing motives, from both idealism and realpoli-tik. As one Puritan told the educator Eleazar Wheelock, "Nothing can be more Agreeable to our Christian Character than to send the Gospel to the benighted Pagans," and "Nothing more Conducive to our Civil Interests than to bring them to a Subjection to the Religion of Jesus."

Christian missionaries, Catholic and Protestant, filled the pages of their journals, pamphlets, and books with their hopes and visions for conversions. This was signified in the seal of the Massachusetts Bay Colony. It shows a classic noble and winsome savage saying "Come Over and Help Us," designed as much as anything to inspire funders at home.

They wrote just as extensively about their frustration at the seeming inability of the Indians, even of the converts, to adopt Christian doctrine and practices. In not doing so, Indians clearly not yet been "reduced" to civilized ways of thinking and living.

In New England, John Eliot translated the Bible into Algonquian, intending to teach Indians the word and train up their own ministers. He published that Bible in 1663; it was the first Bible produced and published in North America. Meanwhile, beginning with Natick in 1651, Eliot and his colleagues created a series of some fourteen Indian praying towns. They eventually held upward of 2,300 individuals in a string of villages around the Massachusetts Bay and into Martha's Vineyard. Eliot hoped to concentrate the work at Natick, which was to be the centerpiece of the New England strategy of reducing Indians to civility. However, a number of other praying towns soon sprouted in the region. Indians migrating to them sought to remain as close as possible to their own homelands. The praying towns themselves merged the division between those such as Eliot, who sought to reach the Indians in their own languages and through the idioms of their own customs, and other Puritans such as the Mather family, who insisted that converting the Indians into Englishmen was the only sure way to banish barbarism from their souls. "Some of them began to be seriously affected, and to understand the things of God," wrote Puritan leader John Winthrop in his journal, describing the effect of Eliot's preaching, "and they were generally ready to reform whatsoever they were told be against the word of God, as their sorcery (which they call powwowing,) their whoredomes, etc., idleness, etc."

Besides working on his Bible in the Massachusett language, John Eliot prepared manuals for Indian missionaries who sought to preach among their own people. Included in them were fictional "dialogues" between native ministers and skeptical tribespeople. In these works, unconverted kinsmen of the Christianized Indians respond in wily and sophisticated ways to Christian pleas. The unconverted Indians in these fictional discussions resemble Satan in *Paradise Lost*—obviously in the wrong, but yet more interesting and in some ways wiser and sharper than the formulaic language in which the Christian message appears. As a kinswoman ends one message, after acknowledging that the convert had wearied himself with "long discourses," she urged him to "stop your mouth, and fill your

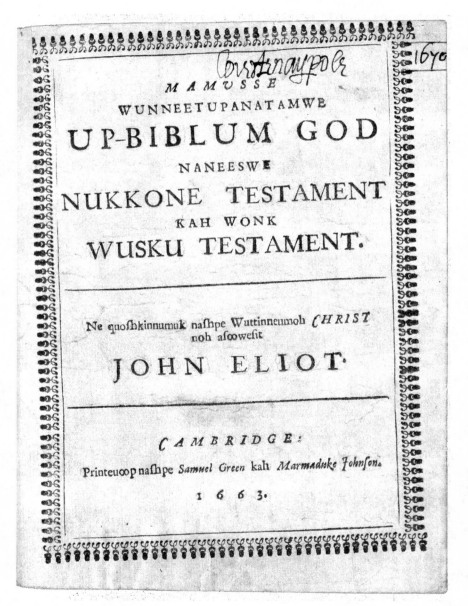

Title page of John Eliot's Bible
Source: Courtesy of Dartmouth College Rauner Special Collections Library.

belly with a good supper, and when your belly is full you will be content to take rest yourself, and give us leave to be at rest from these . . . heart-trembling discourses. We are well as we are, and desire not to be troubled with these new wise sayings."

In the Massachusetts Bay region, Eliot's work failed to persuade one important leader. Metacom, the Wampanoag Indian later christened King Philip, was a member of a tribe in which, by the 1670s, a majority had made their lives in praying towns. Metacom employed as his assistant a Christianized Indian named John Sassamon, who had briefly attended Harvard College. Later, when Sassamon mysteriously turned up dead, apparently drowned in a river but upon closer examination clearly clubbed in the head before being tossed into the water, three Indians were tried and executed for the murder. The violence and vengeance clearly exhibited the tensions leading to King Philip's War.

In this 1676 uprising, Indians attacked half of all New England villages. The death toll was staggering, for both sides. Approximately 5,000 Indians (or about forty percent of the natives of southern New England) lost their lives, as did 2,500 New Englanders (around five percent of the English population). Captives on both sides numbered in the hundreds. While a substantial number of Indians, praying and otherwise, remained loyal to (and even fought for) white New Englanders, the sheer destructiveness of the war itself deepened white New Englanders' animus toward Indians. Those who wore "the Name of *Praying Indians*," as one contemporary tract put it, had "made Preys of much English Blood." The war also broke up and destroyed most of the praying towns and forced the relocation of Christian Indians into a consolidated group of smaller villages which, even when reestablished after the war, struggled along with relatively few members. The surrounding English population increasingly suspected that good Indians were dead Indians.

The entire enterprise of Christianization and the establishment of praying towns, effectively collapsed after King Philip's War. This East Coast debacle of destruction paralleled the contemporaneous Pueblo Revolt in northern New Mexico, as regional tribes banded together, launched ferocious attacks on white colonists in the hinterlands of their respective empires, and self-consciously sought a revitalization of Indian ways and a destruction of Christian symbology. Meanwhile, during the war, Eliot's praying Indians huddled on Martha's Vineyard, without

food, clothing, and fuel. The preeminent Puritan divine of the late seventeenth century, Cotton Mather, rejoiced at the victories of white New
Englanders, convinced that God's plan called for less proselytization and
more subjugation.

Mather wrote in reflecting on the brutal event: "These parts were then
covered with nations of barbarous Indians and infidels, in whom the
prince of power of the air did work as a spirit; nor could it be expected
that the nations of wretches, whose whole religion was the most explicit
sort of devil-worship, should not be acted by the devil to engage in some
early and bloody action, for the extinction of a plantation so contrary to
his interests, as that of New England was."

While New Englanders battled a constant Indian threat, they also
imported blacks, both from Africa and from the Caribbean, and
attempted to discern God's will for integrating enslaved people into the
Puritan experiment. One of those imports, ironically, was a girl from
Barbados probably of mixed Indian and African descent, named Tituba.
She served in the household of the Puritan minister Samuel Parris. In the
early 1690s, she confessed to teaching two other girls the arts of witchcraft, setting off what became the Salem witch trials.

Debating the place of race and slavery, New Englanders had to define
what constituted civilization and who could be rational versus who were
not capable of being so. New Englanders, however, also saw slavery as
a path to redemption, and their own soul-saving efforts as a way to save
themselves by saving others. They devised special catechisms, including
this one for enslaved New Englanders: "I must be Patient and Content
with such a Condition as God has ordered for me." They also instructed
black New Englanders to learn Ephesians 6:5–8 by heart, the passage
ordering servants to be obedient to their Masters.

Cotton Mather, the prolifically published Puritan minister of the late
seventeenth and early eighteenth centuries, argued for the humanity of
the slave and the Negro, in intensively biblical tracts such as *The Negro
Christianized*, while also justifying servitude through those biblical texts.
Christian slaves, he said, would know "that it is GOD who has caused
them to be Servants, and that they serve JESUS CHRIST, while they are
at work for their Masters." "Show yourselves Men," Mather wrote, "and
let Rational Arguments have their Force upon you, to make you treat,

not as Bruits, but as Men, those Rational Creatures whom God has made your Servants."

Mather's exhortations, part of a familiar litany of arguments in favor of Christianizing the slaves, met vigorous refutation among a number of northern ministerial writings in the eighteenth century. John Saffin, a Massachusetts jurist in the early eighteenth century and a slaveholder, enunciated an argument soon to be familiar in proslavery circles. The Bible sanctioned slavery, he insisted. The great patriarch Abraham owned slaves, so "our Imitation of him in this his Moral Action" was warranted. Captives from "Heathen Nations" could be enslaved, even if Christians could not buy and sell one another. Beyond that, God had "set different Orders and Degrees of Men in the World," including some the Divine had made "to be born Slaves, and so to remain during their lives." At the same time, and somewhat contradictorily, Saffin also articulated another point dear to the heart of proslavery theorists: that "it is no Evil thing to bring them [Africans] out of their own Heathenish Country, [to] where they may have the knowledge of the One True God, be Converted and Eternally saved." Saffin even composed his own doggerel on "the Negroes Character":

> Cowardly and Cruel are those Blacks Innate,
> Prone to Revenge, Imp of inveterate hate.
> He that exasperates them, soon espies
> Mischief and Murder in their very eyes.
> Libidinous, Deceitful, False and Rude,
> The Spume Issue of Ingratitude.

As the spread of Enlightenment ideas and evangelical Christianity began to impact the colonies in the mid-eighteenth century, proslavery ideology began to rise as well. Well before the full rise of proslavery thought in the mid-nineteenth-century South, proslavery ideologues in the North fleshed out many of the themes that would define the American defense of slavery. One popular argument was that God created people to exist in particular social stations, reflecting varying degrees of freedom or subjection. For some to enjoy full liberty, others would have to be servants; this best served the happiness of the whole. This traditional conservative stance was a defense of hierarchy, not overtly or especially related to racial considerations. But most expositions of this sort followed up with a defense of racial bondage in particular. They provided explications of why the enslavement of black people contributed to God's plan for the Americas. The African slave, wrote one Massachusetts conservative, was already enslaved to "the tyrannizing power of lust and passion" (the image of overpowering sexuality already being a standard image associated with blackness), and thus "his removal to America is to be esteemed a favor," for it brought Africans "from the state of brutality, wretchedness, and misery . . . to this land of light, humanity, and christian knowledge."

Christian colonizers assumed that acquiring religion meant also taking on the trappings of civilization. A Christian was, by definition, a civilized man. In English North America, to make a Christian was to make a white man, hence the need for devices of protection such as praying towns. When confronted with slavery, questions of Christianity and race arose in new and disturbing contexts. Christianity's central metaphors were those of freedom, which posed difficult questions of how to integrate such a faith with a social order dependent upon coerced labor and the ownership of humans. While Puritan thinkers devised some of the first extended proslavery arguments, the real issue of race, slavery, and Christianity was emerging rapidly in the colonies to the South—in particular, Virginia and South Carolina.

RELIGION, RACE, AND THE RISE OF SLAVERY

English colonizers in North America pondered whether Christianity would apply to black slaves at all. The answers they came up with depended in part on deciding whether Africans and African Americans were fully human. This debate raged for several centuries and indeed continued on into the post–Civil War era of scientific racism. English and Anglo-American theologians grappled with whether there was a separate category, apart from "man," into which blackness could be fit. For many, blackness conjured images of savagery even in the practice of religion itself. As one early commentator put it, Negroes were "a people of beastly living, without a God, lawe, religion, or commonwealth." The Reverend Morgan Godwyn, who ministered in seventeenth-century Virginia, charged that "nothing is more barbarous and contrary to Christianity, than their . . . Idolatrous Dances, and Revels."

As some slaves converted to Christianity, however, reality once again mugged ideology and theology. Anglo-Americans faced this question: Would baptism require freedom? That is, did baptism into the Christian religion make men white? Further, as the 1723 letter from the slaves to the bishop made clear, slaves recognized that conversion implied that they should have the rights of free men. The answers to these questions contained momentous implications for American ideas of freedom and the American practice of chattel slavery.

Colonial law attempted to resolve the ambiguous status of black slaves and the tradition that slavery was for heathen others, not fellow Christians. When some Africans converted to Christianity and as a result claimed their freedom, colonial assemblies in Maryland (1664) and Virginia (1667) responded by dissociating baptism from freedom. They defined "blackness" as a state of perpetual servitude continuing beyond one's potential baptism into the Christian faith. In 1664, the Maryland legislature worked out a law mandating that all slaves would serve for life. From that point on, Christianity and enslavement were theoretically compatible. Indeed, one of the main purposes of the law was to encourage conversion by disabusing anyone of the notion that it would lead to freedom from slavery. Instead, it was only about the freedom of the soul in Christ. Children born of slave women, even Christian slave women, would be bondspeople for life.

In the late seventeenth century, as slavery began to supplant indentured servanthood as the primary labor system in the Chesapeake, Virginians clarified further the meaning of race and Christian belief. The 1667 Virginia law read in full:

WHEREAS some doubts have risen whether children that are slaves by birth, and by the charity and piety of their owners made pertakers of the blessed sacrament of baptisme, should by virtue of their baptisme be made ffree; *It is enacted and declared by this grand assembly, and the authority thereof*, that the conferring of baptisme doth not alter the condition of the person as to his bondage or ffreedome; that diverse masters, ffreed from this doubt, may more carefully endeavor the propagation of Christianity by permitting children, though slaves, or those of greater growth if capable to be admitted to that sacrament.

The laws from the Chesapeake colonies provided a model for later legislation in other colonies. In 1705, Virginians further defined and enumerated the status of free and unfree people, detailing what had been more implicit in the initial legal forays of the 1660s. A law of that year added that servants who were "not Christians in their native country . . . before they were shipped" would be classified as slaves, "and as such be here bought and sold notwitstanding a conversion to Christianity afterwards." Baptism, the act stated, did not affect a person's status as slave or free.

The 1705 act protected indentured servants of Christian parentage but condemned non-Christians to slavery. The law gave new protections to English servants assuming they were white and Christian, including the prohibition of the whipping of a "Christian white servant naked." The act provided for the "Christian care and usage of all Christian servants" and forbade all "negros mulattos or Indians" from owning Christian servants. Further, Africans and Indians could not have the legal protections of marriage, and the legal rights of free people also were denied to those born of unions between Anglo-Virginians and enslaved Virginians. The 1705 laws defined white and Christian privilege by separating it from black (or Indian) and heathen submission. Thereby, as historian Rebecca Goetz explains, "Race trumped religion as the most important category in an ordered society."

White Virginians passed one law after another severing the legal connection of Christianity and freedom. The laws, however, reflected aspiration more than actuality. Regardless of what they said, slaves did not dissociate baptism from freedom. Anglican slaves understood themselves as free by the terms defined by the English. They continued to insist that Christianity should eventuate in freedom.

The laws also failed in one of their central tasks: to persuade planters that conversion was safe, as it would not lead to freedom. Despite the laws and reassurances, many Anglo-Virginians scorned the very notion of African conversion. Morgan Godwyn served a tour as an Anglican missionary in Virginia in the 1660s before going to Barbados in 1670. Even after the establishment of legal codes separating baptism from freedom, he encountered resistance to Christianization, with one planter telling him that baptism was *"to one of those [slaves] no more beneficial, than to her black Bitch."* Godwyn blamed this intransigence on "Hellish

Principles, viz. that *Negroes* are Creatures destitute of Souls, to be ranked among Brute Beasts." The Virginia law of 1667, while intending to aid conversion by reassuring slaveowners that Christians who became slaves could not claim freedom, clashed with the perception of one group of planters that the *"baptizing of their Negro's is the ready way to have all their Throats cut."*

Most white Christians could not feel secure in the extension of Christian freedom beyond the boundaries of Anglo-American society. This ambivalence, together with a cultural style of Anglican missionaries that appeared strange to African practices, hindered the work of groups such as the Society for the Propagation of the Gospel in Foreign Parts. Formed in 1701 in England by Thomas Bray and other devout Anglicans, the Society served as the primary missionary vehicle to spread the word sponsored by the Anglican Church and to combat false ideas propagated by Quakers, Catholics, and others. Over the course of the eighteenth century, the Society sent over four hundred missionaries to various parts of England's possessions in the New World, including several to the newly forming colony of South Carolina.

Francis Le Jau, an early missionary for the SPG, worked in South Carolina's Goose Creek Parish (near Charleston) in the early eighteenth century. Le Jau faced a challenging task in his program of preaching to and Christianizing black slaves and Indians. He rebutted the widespread view among his parishioners that religious instruction would make slaves "proud and Undutiful," with his contention that, in fact, Christianity would produce more obedient and diligent workers.

Moreover, many in the colony were skeptical of whether blacks and Indians could be said to possess souls. "Many Masters can't be persuaded that Negroes and Indians are otherwise than Beasts," he noted in 1709, "and use them like such. I endeavour to let them know better things." He could not "prevail upon some to make a difference between Slaves and free Indians, and Beasts." The Anglican missionary heard one well-off female colonist ask, "Is it Possible that any of my slaves could go to Heaven, & must I see them there?" Another young man swore he would not take communion while slaves were also invited to partake. In 1712, Le Jau recorded his desire to baptize some more slaves who had been "well Instructed" and had no complaints concerning their conduct but noted that "their Masters Seem very much Averse to my Design, Some of them will not give them Leave to come to Church to learn how to Pray to God and to Serve him, I cannot find any reason for this New Opposition but the Old pretext that Baptism makes the Slaves proud and Undutifull." He provided examples of "those who are Admitted to our holy Communion who behave themselves very well," to no avail. This was hardly surprising given the stories Le Jau also recounted of slaves beaten to death by Christian masters, who continued going to church after effectively murdering their slaves.

Le Jau was sensitive to the real possibility that slaves might feign conversion to achieve freedom. He sought to counteract that fear. He required the declaration that the slave did not "*ask for the holy baptism out of any design to free yourself from the Duty and Obedience you owe to your Master while you live, but merely for the good of your Soul and to partake of the Graces and Blessings promised to the Members of the Church of Jesus Christ.*"

But even the most careful and sensitive missionary, such as Le Jau, could not control the effect of the biblical message. His own converts did not always prove to be reliable at interpreting the meaning of Christianity correctly, in his estimation. One convert in particular, Le Jau recounted, although a "very sober and honest Liver," created confusion through his apocalyptic reading of biblical passages: "He had a Book wherein he read some description of the several judgmts. That Chastise Men because of their Sins in these latter days, that description made an Impression upon his Spirit, and he told his Master abruptly there wou'd be a dismal time and the Moon wou'd be turned into Blood, and there wou'd be dearth of darkness and went away." When he spoke of his vision to his master, "some Negroe overheard a part, and it was publickly blazed abroad that an Angel came and spake to the Man, he had seen a hand that gave him a Book, he had heard Voices, seen fires &c." That was not, to say the least, what Le Jau had in mind when he had taught him to read.

This early convert did not spell out in precise terms what his prophecy meant. Probably he did not have to. Planters could extrapolate from the imagery provided to the meaning intended. Drawing from this experience, Le Jau determined to exercise discretion in teaching select groups of slaves to read. He acknowledged that "it had been better if persons of a Melancholy Constitution or those that run into the Search after Curious matter had never seen a Book." Given how biblical stories could inspire ideas that ran contrary to what even the most careful missionaries (such as Le Jau) taught, it certainly made sense for whites to fear that apocalyptic ideas dangerous to the social order would be transmitted in Christian language.

Through the eighteenth century a variety of African American spiritual leaders sprang up and challenged the sole authority claimed by the whites over religious matters. In the Virginia Chesapeake, Anglican clergy explained to their head in London that slaves converted principally for two reasons: first, because they believed they would "meet with so much the more respect" among Christian masters once Christianized and secondly because some believed that "at some time or another Christianity will help them to their freedom." A rumored rebellion in 1730 suggested the ambiguities between religion and race even in what seemed to be a peaceable era of Anglican rule in the South. One Sunday, blacks assembled while locals were at church, supposedly choosing among themselves "Officers to command them in their intended Insurrection." Later, after their capture, Virginia officials hung twenty-four of the rebels, but many more escaped after committing "many outrages against the Christians." The revolt followed some meetings in which, one reported, there were "some Loose discourses that His Majesty had sent Orders for setting them free as soon as they were Christians, and that these Orders were Suppressed, a Notion generally Entertained amongst them."

Meanwhile, in South Carolina, religiously inspired revolt shook the foundation of a colony populated primarily by recently arrived Africans and blacks from the Caribbean. On the Sunday morning of September 9, 1739, an enslaved man named Jemmy, originally from the Kingdom of Kongo, gathered a group of slaves near the Stono River in South Carolina. An engagement ensued in which, according to South Carolina's quasi-official account, "one fought for Liberty and Life, the other for their Country and every Thing that was dear to them. But by the Blessing of God the Negroes were defeated." The group may have been inspired by recent runaways who had made it to Spanish Florida, where they had been promised freedom if they joined the Spanish military. The Kongolese South Carolinians understood the Spanish offers to join them in Florida as especially attractive. A previous group of slave escapees who had made it to St. Augustine were "received there with great

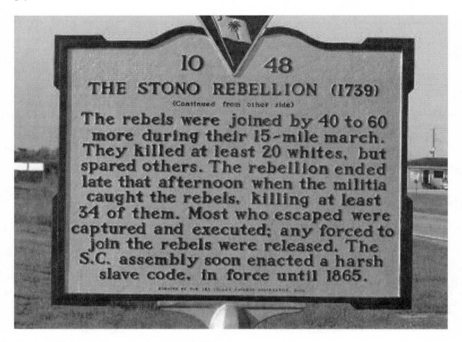

Historical Marker of the Stono Rebellion
Source: Copeland hdes.copeland/ Flickr CC.

honours, one of them had a Commission given to him, and a Coat faced with Velvet . . . the Jesuits have a Mission and School in that Kingdom and many Thousands of the Negroes there profess the Roman Catholic Religion. . . . The good reception of the Negroes at Augustine was spread about." The very date of the rebellion may have held a specific religious meaning for Kongolese Catholic rebels who believed September 8 to be the day of Nativity for the Virgin Mary. Kongolese Catholics believed that Mary held protective power for those who venerated her.

Led by Jemmy, the slaves gathered slaves near Charleston (then called Charles Town), broke into a store, secured firearms, and set about "burning and destroying all that came in their Way, so that the Messenger who came, told us the Country thereabout was full of Flames." Later, others joined them, "they calling out Liberty, marched on with Colours displayed, and two Drums beating, pursuing all the white people they met with." That afternoon, a posse of whites, many of whom had been worshipping (firearms by their side, as per colonial regulation) that morning at a nearby Presbyterian church, gathered and killed at least thirty of the rebels.

As with the case of the Anglican slaves who had petitioned for their freedom in 1723, the Stono rebels understood the connection between Christianity and freedom. Some of them may have known how to fight based on their military experience with militia orders in the Kongo kingdom, which had been Christianized in the sixteenth century following the conversion of its King. Like the English, they understood that violence sometimes was necessary for freedom and for faith. The Stono Rebellion shook the colony of South Carolina to its core. It would be the role of the leaders of the Great Awakening to preach to all without conveying messages too disturbing to the social order.

GREAT AWAKENING

These sorts of rumors and fears arose just as the Great Awakening swept down the colonies and produced a religious revolution. George Whitefield, the English Anglican who had perfected theatrical styles of expression in the pulpit, emerged as America's celebrity preacher of the mid-eighteenth century. He drew thousands wherever he went to preach and attracted admirers even among those, such as Benjamin Franklin, who viewed the evangelical with skepticism at best, contempt at worst. Most importantly for our story here, the Awakening drew in black and Indian converts and compelled evangelicals to consider anew the relationship of religion, slavery, and race. Most, like George Whitefield, settled on the conviction that while the slave trade engendered undeniable evils, slavery itself clearly was sanctioned in the Bible. Moreover, they perceived that God's plan for slavery was to take a potential evil and transform it into good by converting African peoples in preparation for the proselytization of the dark continent. A few religious idealists, such as the Quaker John Woolman, developed antislavery ideas, but they were in a distinct minority. Awakeners soon discovered that the Christian message attracted souls in subordination. It could also make them question that subordination.

Nowhere was this more evident than in the true origins of widespread Christianity among enslaved African Americans during the Great

Awakening and the rise of the Baptists and Methodists from the 1750s forward. During the Great Awakening and especially through the later eighteenth century, evangelical revivalists spread the word and welcomed black people into their midst. Slaves exposed to Christianity in this manner responded enthusiastically. The parallels between Baptist and Methodist preaching and practice (including, among the Separate Baptists, crying, falling down, and lying paralyzed on the floor) and African belief systems and religious rituals were apparent. White evangelists were both excited and troubled by this fact. The Presbyterian minister and evangelist in the Chesapeake region Samuel Davies preached to upward of one thousand slaves, converting about one hundred of them in his initial forays in the 1750s. Davies recognized the peculiar situation of preaching spiritual freedom to enslaved peoples: "Many of them," he wrote, "only seem to be, they know not what. They feel themselves uneasy in their *present* condition, and therefore desire *change*." Their "pious thirst for Christian knowledge" left him uneasy but exhilarated. Some slaves, he knew, recognized salvation as potential liberation; they desired baptism "that they may be upon an Equality with their Masters."

Just as significant is a lesser-known portion of this story, one only recently explored by scholars: the idea of an Indian Great Awakening. In assessing the impact of Protestant Christianity on native peoples in the mid-eighteenth century, scholars have examined both the conversion of Indians through the preaching of pietists such as the Moravians in Pennsylvania as well as New England New Divinity men such as David Brainerd and even Jonathan Edwards. The latter, most famous for his sermon "Sinners in the Hands of an Angry God" and an apostle of Calvinist doctrine, successfully ministered to natives on his mission tour of Stockbridge, Massachusetts, the most successful Christian-Indian settlement of the eighteenth century in the English-controlled part of the colonies. He was affected greatly by the Indians' response and contemplated deeply the theological mysteries of the movement of God's spirit in peoples from vastly divergent religious training. That is one significant part of the story. While the Great Awakening was certainly not aimed at Indian listeners, it nevertheless had a powerful effect among some who found meaning in its message within their own cultural contexts.

The Indian response to Christianity involved both acceptance and integration into tribal customs and in others resistance, both peaceful and forcible. The response had the common base of being a pan-Indian phenomenon in which natives found meaning in the revitalization of their own traditions combined with the invention of new ones. It was part of what one historian has called a "spirited resistance." In the multicultural world of mid-eighteenth-century America, a time in which Indian identities were being reformed all over the continent, Indian prophets and visionaries—some using Christianity, others profoundly opposed to the new ways and committed to recapturing the customs of the forefathers—found receptive audiences. In the imperial conflicts among Europeans and Indian groups in the mid-eighteenth century—culminating in the bloody and ever-shifting Great War for the Empire from 1754 to 1763—Indian groups allied themselves on all sides of a European struggle for dominance in the North American continent.

Through the national conflicts of the Europeans, Indians were in effect learning that they were *Indians*, as opposed to members of individual tribal groups. Just as white Americans had been in the process of developing ideas of whiteness and, later, of Americanness, Indians were learning that they were a "single people with common interests that transcended national rivalries."

The Presbyterian preacher David Brainerd, later the subject of a hagiography by Jonathan Edwards, learned of the Indians' racialized perceptions of the origins of the major racial groupings on the American continent. Speaking to a group in Pennsylvania in 1751, he heard an Indian version of the creation story that signified the solidification of racialist views. The story significantly paralleled the use of the Son of Ham story among white Christians to comprehend the origins of the alleged "curse" on Negroes:

> They told me that the great God first made three men and three women . . . the Indian, the Negro, and the White Man. That the White Man was the youngest brother, and therefore the white people ought not to think themselves better than the Indians. That God gave the white man a book, and told him that he must worship him by that; but gave none either to the Indian or Negro, and therefore it could not be right for them to have a book, or be any way concerned with that way or worship. And, furthermore, they understood that the White people were contriving a method to deprive them of their country in those

parts, as they had done by the sea-side, and to make slaves of them and their children as they did of the Negroes; that I was sent on purpose to accomplish that design, and, if I succeeded . . . I was to be chief ruler in those parts.

Although Brainerd attempted to assuage their fears, the Indians rejected his message and asked that he not return. Throughout Indian country, accounts of the separate creation of red, white, and black men would be retold in diverse tribes and inspire numerous prophets. Some had been influenced by Christianity, others spurned it as a dangerous potion of the white people. While European settlers on the frontier were making Indians into red men, Indians themselves were understanding "red men" as a category set up in opposition to Europeans, the white men. Religious conflict contributed to this racialization of peoples on the frontier.

Some European Christian sects, notably the Quakers and the Moravians, served as intermediaries on this volatile frontier. The Moravians in particular established a reputation for close connection with their Indian converts. They learned native languages and translated religious materials (including hymns) into them. As a Presbyterian minister noted of the Moravians' efforts, "They go among them without noise or parade, and by their friendly behaviour conciliate their good will. They join them in the chace, and freely distribute to the helpless and gradually instill into the minds of the individuals, the principles of religion." The Great Awakeners and the Moravians in Pennsylvania nevertheless recognized that preaching to the natives would be made easier when "the whites are so much increased that the Indians are Cooped up into a narrow Compass and Subdued."

Indian converts found the European pressure for land pushing them aside just as well as their non-Christian brethren. Even the Moravians, who established very close ties and alliances with tribes in their area of Pennsylvania and often served as the Indians' protectors and diplomats, needed to purchase land. In 1742, they received permission from the governor to "dispossess the Indians in Nazareth," land they had purchased from the Great Awakener George Whitefield, which had supported an Indian village. Delaware Indians resisted the loss of land, arguing in a petition to the governor of Pennsylvania that they practiced Christianity and had "attained some small Degree of Knowledge therein," and so were "desirous of living under the same Laws with the English, and praying that some place might be allotted to them where they may live in the Enjoyment of the same Religion and Laws with them." They had no more success than did the southeastern Indians of the nineteenth century, prior to their removal to Oklahoma.

John Heckewelder drawn by Henry Howe
Source: Howe, Henry (1907), *Historical Collections of Ohio*, The Ohio Centennial Edition, 3, invalid ID: The State of Ohio, p. 375.

The missionary John Heckewelder also observed the rise and eventually the explosion of ethnoreligious conflict between whites and natives. Competition for land and resources pitted white men against red men in bitter and violent struggles. A native of England, Heckewelder had come to Pennsylvania in 1754 and begun his missionary work among the Delawares in the early 1760s. He thereafter served as a Moravian missionary for several decades, as well as a careful chronicler and interpreter of Indians, especially of the Delawares.

Heckewelder's narrative of the Moravian mission, a sprawling canvass painting vivid scenes of white-Indian contact from the 1740s to the early nineteenth century, portrays backwoods white men as first thinking of the savages as "incapable of embracing the Christian religion." Whites in the backwoods classed missionaries and advocates of the Indian such as Heckewelder as part of the enemy. In his work, he frequently encountered many in the backwoods who held that "an Indian 'has no more soul than a buffalo'; and that to kill either, is the same thing." Once the embrace of Christianity by some natives undermined this view, white men in the backwoods demanded the removal of missionaries from the country because of "the loss the whites sustained in not having these Indians in their interest" and under the same control as before, "when they were accustomed to take unlawful liberties and advantages of them." Some compared the Brethren (the Moravians) as being "tinctured with Catholicism." Others censured them for "endeavouring to civilize the savages, a race of beings, which (in their opinion) had no claim to Christianity, and whom to destroy, both root and branch, would not only be doing God a service, but also be the means of averting his wrath which they otherwise might incur by suffering them to live, they being the same as the Canaanites of old, an accursed race, who by God's command were to be destroyed." To them, not destroying the present-day Canaanites could induce God to "bring about wars and chastisements" as punishment for their disobedience. Heckewelder perceived the aim of white settlers and aggressors to be "first, to cause a general consternation, thereby spreading devastation and misery over the country, and then to take the reins of government into their own hands."

The fears of Heckewelder and Indians in Pennsylvania and Ohio came to pass in the slaughter of dozens of Christian Indians at Gnaddenhutten (located in present-day Tuscarawas County, Ohio) in March of 1782.

While attempting to gather supplies from their old settlements to move away from conflict, a group of American frontiersmen accidentally stumbled on a group of Moravian Indians from Gnadenhutten. Insisting that the Indians were pro-British and in any case dangerous in spite of their demeanor, the American militiamen slaughtered ninety pacifist Indians, including twenty-seven women and thirty-four children. Even though the "Christian Indians were well known by their dress, which was plain and decent, no sign of paint to be seen on their skin or clothes" nor feathers on the head, white settlers still perceived them to be a threat. They had concluded that "when they killed the Indians, the country would be theirs; and the sooner this was done, the better!" The attacks also suggested that a Christian country could also be an aggressively expansionist one, and that notions of God's will easily incorporated paroxysms of violence.

CONCLUSION

The Great Awakenings of the eighteenth and nineteenth centuries effectively created popular evangelicalism as the dominant style of American religious expression. In doing so, the awakenings reinforced what was already evident to Indians and African Americans, namely, that spiritual freedom did not extend to temporal liberation and that religious expressiveness could be embraced but could also be repressed when it appeared threatening to the dominant Anglo-American community. Black and red Americans could be in, but not fully of, the world of evangelical America. They were to be permanent aliens in the new white Republic, subject to enslavement and colonial domination. Christianity itself, with its universal message, could invite all those in a community, but Christian institutions and the nation-state that emerged from the colonial era would draw sharp lines and divisions based on evolving but apparently solid notions of race.

In the early national era, repression and violence accompanied the expansion of the nation-state, one that countenanced a Christian America in formerly pagan or Catholic lands recently acquired from France and conquered from natives by force. The period from the American Revolution to the early Republic, from the 1770s to the 1820s, in fact, gave Americans both their greatest and most classic statements of liberty and freedom and also their most horrific instances of religiously sanctioned violence and repression. The dialectic of religious freedom and religious repression, one that roiled through the Puritan contests with natives in New England and the Spanish attempts to recover from the Pueblo Revolt, came into clearer focus in the first generation following the First Amendment. The religiously tolerant nation-state, and the racialized nation-state that increasingly defined itself as a white Protestant Republic, arose in tandem, defining the bounds of the habitation of American religion for much of the eighteenth and nineteenth centuries. The messianic and millennialist dreams that inspired the rise of a democratic culture as well as the aggressive expansionism that displaced and enslaved peoples all came together in the generation of the revolution and the young Republic.

2

Religious Freedom and Religious Repression in the Early United States

"We Love our country, but we love liberty more.*" (Black National Convention, 1843)

"Beware of the religion of the white man . . . every Indian who embraces it is obliged to take the road to the white man's heaven; and yet no red man is permitted to enter there, but will have to wander about forever without a resting place." (Gregory Dowd, 1745–1815)

In the first third of the nineteenth century, white Americans created a new republic that valorized democracy. Meanwhile, they seized vast tracts of lands from ancestral peoples and extended a plantation economic ecosystem that produced incredible wealth, in part because the collateralization of property in slave bodies fueled a credit boom. Millions of people moved into newly opening regions, including over nine hundred thousand slaves dragged there in the "internal middle passage" from the revolutionary era to the Civil War. During these same years, the "Second Great Awakening" implanted evangelical religion as a dominant force in American cultural life. By the Civil War, pietist Christianity and chattel slavery fundamentally shaped life in the United States. The two in tandem also led directly to the American Civil War.

African Americans and Native peoples attempted to make sense of the revolutionary transformations of the early antebellum era. From the mild *A Dialogue Between a Virginian and an African Minister* in the early nineteenth century and Richard Allen's work to create the nation's first black denomination in the early nineteenth century (the African Methodist Episcopal Church) to David Walker's 1829 *Appeal to the Coloured Citizens of the World* and the religiously inspired revolt of Nat Turner in 1831, they moved from dialogue with people perceived as fellow Christians, to confrontation with slaveholders perceived as demonic.

The religious ferment of the new Republic came to a head in the early nineteenth century. As Alexis de Tocqueville wrote in his epic study *Democracy in America*, there was "no country in the world where the Christian religion retains greater influence over the souls of men than in America." By the middle of the nineteenth century, some three-quarters of the American population of about twenty-three million regularly attended church. The Methodists, a small sect representing just two percent of American churchgoers at the time of the Revolution, comprised nearly twenty percent of the American population as a whole by 1820, and by mid-century numbered over one million, more than one-third of American churchgoers. By that time, there were about ten times more American Methodists than there were Congregationalists, the denomination that descended from the Puritans. With circuit-riding preachers combing the countryside on their horses, preaching to congregations throughout the newly settling areas, Methodists proved flexible enough to meet the need for religious organization on the frontier.

In the first years of the nineteenth century, the revivals in the newly settled region around Cane Ridge, Kentucky, kicked off decades of camp meetings. At these countryside fests, several ministers simultaneously preached in large communal services, while families (including slaves) camped out along the grounds. The day alternated between devotions and prayers, meals, and ecstatic religious experiences. Peter Cartwright, a tireless Methodist camp meeting exhorter through the early nineteenth century, recalled that, even though the preachers of the time "murdered the king's English almost every lick," nevertheless "Divine unction attended the word preached, and thousands fell under the power of God." Up to 10,000 people gathered from miles around and heard a dozen or more ministers of various denominations exhort. Converts at the early, most enthusiastic meetings from 1801 to 1805 recounted "trances and visions." In later decades, religious leaders enforced stricter codes of decorum, but the camp meeting remained a popular and effective tool of democratic Protestant proselytizers.

The democratic explosion of evangelical Christianity through the antebellum era accompanied a vast geographical expansion of slavery.

For African Americans in the southern states, the promise of the American Revolution collapsed under the weight of the expansion of short-staple cotton and chattel slavery into the newly opening states of the Deep South. The Revolution, the Louisiana Purchase, technological developments such as the cotton gin, military action, the subjugation of Indians in the Southeast, and the worldwide demand for cotton for textiles all fueled the rise of cotton-based economies in the Deep South. Eventually, they also spurred the rise of southern religious denominations and eventually a nascent albeit militarily conquered nation-state— the Confederate States of America.

For Native Americans, the era of democratic Christianity also represented the apogee of state-sanctioned ethnic cleansing. Most famous was the Trail of Tears episode, but that was only one of many such removals and land grabs. Democratic Christianity, the market revolution, the rapid expansion westward and southward, and a populist faith in self-determination joined together in upsetting fragile balances of power on the frontier and making the bounds of American habitations free and white. This chapter tracks particularly the varied responses from Native and African American leaders, writers, and religious prophets to the creation and rise of the white American republican experiment. The subjects include the Native prophets Tenskwatawa and Handsome Lake; the Moravian and Baptist missionaries among (and advocates for) Indians in the Southeast; and African American voices of protest from the African Methodist Episcopal Church organizer Richard Allen to Maria Stewart, Frederick Douglass, and Henry Highland Garnet.

NATIVES IN THE NEW REPUBLIC

Native Americans were compelled to respond to Anglo-American power in the new Republic. No longer able to play French territorial holdings and military threats against the British, and with the failure of some abortive attempts to ally with the British against their colonists in America during the Revolutionary War, Anglo-Americans reigned as the powers that be.

Native American leaders used religious awakenings to revitalize their beleaguered communities. From the visions of the Delaware Neolin in the mid-eighteenth century to the Shawnee prophet Tenskwatawa in the early nineteenth century, to Handsome Lake's teachings among the Iroquois, and to the Redsticks and militant nativists among the Creeks and Seminoles in the Southeast, religiously inspired prophetic resistance ran through Indian communities from the Great Awakening forward into the era of Anglo-American expansionism and ethnic cleansing through the remainder of the nineteenth century.

Although widely separated in time and geography, common visions and dreams unite the stories recounted by the Indian nativist prophets. Each of them took dream journeys and reached forks in the road along the way, with narrow roads leading to paradise and wide and more easily traversed paths taking the journeyer to some form of hell. Indeed, the concept of hell itself was probably the closest connection of these dreams to Christian theology; few Native American groups had any such definite idea of eternal torment prior to the introduction of Christianity. Those who took up the European vices, especially alcohol, found punishment. The Shawnee prophet Tenskwatawa's visions came in the early nineteenth century, following a feast in which Indians "danced and rejoiced before the Great Spirit and proposed to revive the religion of their ancestors." Americans were children of the Evil Spirit, he said, invoking Shawnee folklore of a serpent who had come from the sea, just as had white Americans. Observers among the tribes in the early nineteenth century noted the differing and contested theologies at play. Nativists and prophets insisted on the separate creation of peoples and the notion that the "Great Spirit did not mean that the white and red people should live near each other." After all, whites had "poison'd the land." Eventually, Tenskwatawa led a substantial force of Indians who had gathered at Tippecanoe (also known as Prophetstown), Indiana, where they were defeated by forces led by William Henry Harrison. Harrison's presidential campaign platform for his election in 1840 praised him as the hero of the Battle of Tippecanoe.

Another Indian seer of the revolutionary era, Handsome Lake (1735–1815), was born in upstate New York and lived through the severe decline of the Iroquois nation in the late eighteenth century. Following the American Revolution, which proved disastrous for the Senecas and other Iroquois people, Handsome Lake experienced visions and called for a renewal of rituals to restore spiritual power to natives who had been

Handsome Lake preaching his code at the Tonawanda longhouse
Source: Painting by Ernest Smith, Tonawanda Reservation. From the collections of
the Rochester Museum & Science Center, Rochester, NY.

corrupted by Anglo-American ways. Handsome Lake's original message
melded Iroquois lore and Christian beliefs learned from Quaker missionaries. "Our lands are decaying because we do not think on the Great
Spirit," Handsome Lake had written to President Thomas Jefferson, "but
we are now going to renew our Minds and think on the great Being who
made us all, that when we put our seeds in the Earth they may grow and
increase like the leaves on our Trees." Originally consumed with apocalyptic visions of Iroquois destiny, in later years Handsome Lake turned
to a gospel of sobriety and industry among Indians, peace with whites,
and preservation of Iroquois lands. In the religion of Handsome Lake,
salvation came through following the code of *Gaiwiio* ("Good Word"),
with a mixture of Iroquois practices (including a traditional ceremonial
calendar and a mythology consonant with older beliefs) and Christian
influences (temperance, confession, and a notion of conversion to a new
religion). Handsome Lake presented himself originally as a messenger of

the new code, a preacher, but later claimed special supernatural revelations and divine powers.

Native Americans faced an aggressively expansionist state intent on realizing Thomas Jefferson's vision of an empire for liberty. Some chose to Christianize and Anglicize. Others engaged in limited economic commerce with Europeans but otherwise maintained their own cultural practices. Still others resisted violently under the leadership of messianic individuals. For all, the outcome was more or less the same—forcible removal from their lands, repression of religious practices, and exile far westward out of the way of white settlers.

Along the way, Creeks, Cherokees, and others in Georgia and elsewhere picked up white allies, namely missionaries intent on using the force of the Americans' own legal codes to provide some degree of protection for besieged natives. Since the mid-eighteenth century, Moravians had established fruitful cooperative relationships with tribes in Pennsylvania, Ohio, North Carolina, and elsewhere. In the early nineteenth century, the Moravians established a mission at Springplace, Georgia, right on a main thoroughfare connecting the roads leading out of the northern part of the state toward Chattanooga, Nashville, and other important market destinations in the upper Southeast. The missionaries built a self-sufficient enterprise using land loaned them in part by the Cherokees. They played host to a constant stream of visitors, whites and Indians alike, in a place that became a central stopping and meeting point in the heart of Cherokee country.

At the Cherokees' demand, the Moravians quickly took in Indian students as pupils. For the Cherokees, the main point was practical education; few evidenced much interest in Moravian religious doctrines. From 1805 to 1821, the Moravian couple John and Anna Rosina Gambold took charge of the mission and the school, where Anna Rosina served as the primary teacher at the mission school. The daily diary entries and records they kept provide one of the most complete accounts of this portion of Indian country during the time of white expansion and settlement.

The Moravians were allowed to stay as long as they seemed to provide educational tools that might help lead to a defense of land sovereignty and to teach English needed to negotiate with powerful nation-states. Indians respected the Moravians. One Cherokee leader told the Gambolds, "We do not view you as *White people* at all, but rather as *Indians* . . . you are here only for our sake." They did not seem to possess the same rapacious desire for land they had encountered among other whites, a lust for expansion captured in the Creek Indians' slang term for white men—"those who grasp greedily after Indian lands." Thus, while other whites would have to leave the country, the Moravians could stay. They pointed out to the missionaries that "some Indians allow themselves to be taken in by the white people when they claimed that they were seeking their *true* interests, but actually only had *their own* in mind," leading to the sales of Indian lands for a pittance. He added that "it is basically not *our* earth, it is God's earth. He gave it to us to live on it. He makes grass and corn grow . . . One day, when we are all dead, God will burn this earth that He has given us, and that He has given the white people, and so on."

Evolving traditions, stories, and religious beliefs and customs suggested the struggles waged by Indians to comprehend the new world coming into being in the Southeast. The Moravians recorded the stories of a visiting group of Cherokees. While they were traveling, they went to an unoccupied house near a mountain. They heard a noise and looked out to see "a whole host of Indians arrive on the mountain from the sky. They rode on small black horses and their leader beat a drum and came very close to them. They were very afraid and wanted so to go back into the house." The leader urged them not to be afraid, for God had come to him and commanded him to let the Indians know that

> God is dissatisfied that you so indiscriminately lead the white people onto my land. You yourselves see that your game has gone. You plant the white people's corn. Go and buy it back from them and plant Indian corn and pound it according to your ancestors' ways. Make the people go away. The mother of the nation has left you, because all her bones are being broken through the milling. She will return, however, if you get the white people out of the country and return to your former way of life. You yourselves can see that the white people are completely different from us. We are made from red earth, but they are made from white sand. You may always be good neighbors with them but see to it that you get your old "beloved Towns" back from them.

Eventually the Moravian mission succumbed to the same pressures of land possession and Indian dispossession that dominated the story of southeastern Indians. Their presence there, however, suggests some of the complexity and nuance of a story that otherwise appears fated and inevitable.

Many native nations were riven between Christianized and "traditionalist" factions. And even those in the Christianized factions came to recognize that they were not going to be accepted in the white man's Christian Republic but instead usually simply forcibly removed from it. One of the climactic episodes of the encounter of the expansionist American state with its aboriginal peoples occurred in the early nineteenth century in the Southeast. The result was an expansion of Georgia and the creation of the state of Alabama in 1819. It involved the bloody crushing of a prophetic revolt, which drew from the native tradition of the "spirited resistance" dating from the mid-eighteenth century.

Internally riven by an incipient civil war between factions aligned economically and politically with Anglo-Americans and others who resisted all white influence, tormented by problems with alcohol, and economically devastated by a rapid decline of the economically essential trade in deer skins, the Muskogees cried out for a prophetic interpretation of contemporary catastrophes. As was the case with many prophets of the eighteenth century, Muskogees who sought renewal listened intently to natural signs. A series of earthquakes in 1811–1812 seemed to signify the displeasure of the Maker of Breath. Drawing from their own traditions of purging rituals and renewals, replayed yearly in the Busk, or Green Corn, ceremony, Muskogees sought to imbue their struggle for survival with sacred power.

By this time, however, the alliance between nativists and accommodationists which had formed in the revolutionary-era struggles had disintegrated, largely due to the growing power of the American presence. In the case of Alabama, Lower Muskogee chiefs, many of whom had economic ties with American agents, mostly refused to join the Redstick Revolt of the early 1810s. Their residence directly next to the state of Georgia instilled in them an awareness of their imminent peril. But some Muskogees had been listening to the Shawnee leader Tecumseh and his brother and prophet Tenskwatawa. They viewed themselves not as members of individual tribes but as red men militantly opposed to white men. To purge themselves of white influence was a necessary first step in a collective act of purging and a prelude to the renewal necessary for a recapturing of sacred power sufficient to resist the growing secular power of the Anglo-Americans. As historian Joel Martin writes, "By performing material acts of renunciation, they purified themselves of old identities and cleansed themselves of polluting symbols, spirits, and substances. . . . By renouncing their dependence on Anglo-American civilization, the people readied themselves for the assumption of a new collective identity." The targets of the Muskogee prophets were at first the chiefs friendly to the United States. Eventually, they fought against formidable forces of the United States, who squashed the Redsticks. U.S. Commander Thomas Pinckney declared that Almighty God had "blessed the arms of the United States" against the "insolent" and "perfidious" Muskogees.

American Protestant missionaries made inroads among the Cherokees in the 1820s and 1830s, especially through educating children in institutions such as the Brainerd School in Chattanooga, Tennessee. John Ridge, son of a Cherokee warrior who was educated in Moravian mission schools and later served as an assistant to Albert Gallatin in the federal government's dealings with the Creek Indians, noted the spread of Christianity among his people: "Portions of Scripture & sacred hymns are translated and I have frequently heard with astonishment a Cherokee, unacquainted with the English take his text & preach, read his hymn & sing it, Joined by his audience, and pray to his heavenly father with great propriety & devotion. The influence of Religion on the life of the Indians is powerful & lasting." One Indian schoolgirl noted that President Jackson's message about Indian removal had been read in school: "Miss Ames has been talking to the scholars and she felt bad and told them that they must get a good education soon as they can, so they can teach if they should be removed where they could not attend school and says that we must try to get religion for all the instructors ought to be christians. It seems that it will be a trying season to us and the missionaries if we should be separated from them, but she says if God suffers it to be, we ought not to complain." She recounted one child saying, "'if the white people want more land let them go back to the country they came from,'" and another adding, "'they have got more land than they use, what do they want to get ours for.'"

Regardless of the efforts of the Moravians and (beginning in the 1820s) northern Baptist missionaries, southeastern Indians found themselves

hemmed in. Economically, their sources of tribal sustenance were challenged. Politically, they were internally riven between factions advocating
opposing responses to white encroachment. In Georgia, state legislatures
employed every means necessary to clear out areas for land-hungry settlers and for the coffles of slaves being transported overland to the newly
opening regions. When missionaries among the Cherokees were ordered
to clear out as well, they refused to obey. State authorities arrested them.
Eventually, in *Worcester v. Georgia*, the famous case that arose from this
incident, Chief Justice John Marshall ruled in the Cherokees' favor. He
suggested in effect that as semi-sovereign and semi-wards of the federal
government, the state of Georgia did not have legal authority to dis-
perse them and enforce laws within the bounds of the Cherokee lands.
President Andrew Jackson was just as famously contemptuous of the
court's edicts. He knew that military force, not Supreme Court doctrine,
ultimately would triumph.

Jackson supported Georgia's position of maintaining sovereignty
within its own borders. In an address to Congress, he summarized the
advantages of Indian removal from the Southeast and the settlement of
those lands by whites:

> It will separate the Indians from immediate contact with settlements
> of whites; free them from the power of the States; enable them to pur-
> sue happiness in their own way and under their own rude institutions;
> will retard the progress of decay, which is lessening their numbers,
> and perhaps cause them gradually, under the protection of the Gov-
> ernment and through the influence of good counsels, to cast off their
> savage habits and become an interesting, civilized, and Christian com-
> munity.

Many religious Americans in the Northeast opposed Jackson's policies. The most prominent was Jeremiah Evarts, corresponding secretary of the American Board of Commissioners for Foreign Missions.
Jeremiah Evarts was a Whig Unionist who staunchly defended the role
of the federal government in dealing directly with Indian nations, without the intermediary of state governments. He argued vigorously against
removal, pointing out that "they will hardly get settled in their new location, before they will be urged to remove again." He concluded, "May a

gracious Providence avert from this country the awful calamity of exposing ourselves to the wrath of heaven, as a consequence of disregarding
the cries of the poor and defenseless, and perverting to purposes of cruelty and oppression, that power which was given us to promote the happiness of our fellow-men." Jackson was unmoved; he signed the act in
1830, which eventually displaced approximately 100,000 Indians. Whites
were soon streaming into Cherokee lands.

In response to missionaries and idealists such as Jeremiah Evarts and
Samuel Worcester, the well-known antebellum politician Lewis Cass
defended the necessity of removal. Matching Evarts' legal arguments,
Cass ultimately was more concerned with those who would mount
falsely philanthropic crusades and thus retard the progress of civilization.
The "rapid declension and ultimate extinction" of Indian nations had
long been foreseen, he suggested, and many were "carefully taught at our
seminaries of education, in the hope that principles of morality and habits
of industry would be acquired. . . . Missionary stations were established
among various tribes, where zealous and pious men devoted themselves
with generous ardor to the task of instruction, as well in agriculture and
the mechanic arts, as in the principles of morality and religion." All was
to no avail, Cass felt: "Unfortunately, they are monuments also of unsuc-
cessful and unproductive efforts. What tribe has been civilized by all this
expenditure of treasure, and labor, and care?" Cass insisted that there
was no doubt that the "Creator intended the earth should be reclaimed
from a state of nature and cultivated; that the human race should spread
over it, procuring from it the means of comfortable subsistence, and of
increase and improvement."

Cherokees split over the wisdom of removal. "The land was given to
us by the Great Spirit above as our common right, to raise our children
upon, & to make support for our rising generations," Cherokee women
petitioned in 1818 their leaders to resist the sale of tribal lands. Also, as
they pointed out, many had been Christianized, "civilized & enlightened, & are in hopes that in a few years our nation will be prepared for
instruction in other branches of sciences & arts." A number of Cherokees,
including the editor of the *Cherokee Phoenix*, Elias Boudinot, noted the
irony that Indian removal was occurring at precisely the same time that
the Cherokees were farming, creating an alphabet and spreading literacy among their people, expanding their slaveholding economy and

attending Christian churches: "That the Cherokees may be kept in igno-rance, teachers who had settled among them by the approbation of the Government, for the best of all purposes, have been compelled to leave them by reason of laws unbecoming any civilized nation—Ministers of the Gospel, who might have, at this day of trial, administered to them the consolations of Religion, have been arrested, chained, dragged away before their eyes, tried as felons, and finally immured in prison with thieves and robbers."

Eventually, the missionaries were forced to give way. In an 1840 let-ter, Samuel Worcester explained his position to a fellow clergyman who had urged him to withdraw his appeal before the Supreme Court. He had been condemned by Christians who had urged him to obey the pow-ers that be, a condemnation that was "a begging of the very question at force between us and the state of Georgia—the question of jurisdiction over us." Worcester pointed out his right to continue laboring among the Cherokees without having to ask permission of the state of Georgia or swearing allegiance to it. But after the Supreme Court's decision, he recognized that the edict could not be enforced without Civil War. "For what, then, should we run the hazard of bringing about a civil war? For our personal liberty? It was not worth the cost . . . For our honor? Honor, when it is contended for, ceases to be honor. And very little could we have honored *ourselves*, if we had been willing to purchase honor from others with the blood of our fellowmen." He would have continued on if there had been hope of advancing the cause of the Cherokees, but by the mid-1830s, there was no such hope.

For the New England Pequot Methodist convert William Apess, who preached for Methodist churches in the 1820s and 1830s while publishing prolifically, the melancholy results of white Christian ethnic cleansing appeared all too evident. His work *An Indian's Looking Glass on the White Man* and *Son of the Forest* reflected on the consequences of white colo-nization to native peoples since the time of the arrival of whites to New England. What was then in the process of being transformed, by Daniel Webster and other great orators and nationalists of the era, into the mythical story of heroic pilgrims and pioneers conquering the wilderness and spreading civilization westward through empty lands, appeared to Indians such as Apess as a history of conquest, violence, and repression.

Image from William Apess, *A Son of the Forest*
Source: Public domain.

William Apess's *Eulogy* in honor of King Philip (or Metacom, leader of the brutal conflict later known as King Philip's War of 1676) made clear this native author's understanding of American history:

Let the children of the pilgrims blush, while the son of the forest drops a tear, and groans over the fate of his murdered and departed fathers. He would say to the sons of the pilgrims (as Job said about his birthday), let the day be day, the 22nd day of December, 1620; let it be forgotten in your celebration, in your speeches, and by the burying of the Rock that your fathers first put their foot upon. For be it remembered, although the gospel is said to be glad tidings to all people, yet we poor Indians never have found those who brought it as messengers of mercy, but contrawise. We say, therefore, let every man of color wrap himself in mourning, for the 22nd of December and the 4th of July are days of mourning and not of joy.

What were the weapons of this vaunted Christian civilization, Apess asked? His answer: "rum and powder, and ball, together with all the diseases, such as the small pox and every other disease imaginable; and in this way sweep off thousands and tens of thousands." And what had become of Indians under this Christian civilization? "Had the inspiration of Isaiah been there," Apess averred, "he could not have been more correct. Our groves and hunting grounds are gone, our dead are dug up, our council-fires are put out, and a foundation was laid in the first Legislature to enslave our people, by taking from them all rights." The pilgrims had created a "fire, a canker" designed to "destroy my poor unfortunate brethren," and even up to the time of Apess himself the president "tells the Indians they cannot live among civilized people, and we want your lands and must have them and will have them." Indeed, it would be the policy of the government to "drive you out, to get you away out of the reach of our civilized people, who are cheating you, for we have no law to reach them, we cannot protect you although you be our children."

Apess's writings were mostly ignored at the time and forgotten afterward. His recently resurrected voice, however, suggests the constant counterpoint to white expansion, settlement, and Christianization among native peoples who had counted its cost. African American writers in the early national era were making the same points, for they too saw that liberty and equality were going to be racially proscribed by a white man's Republic.

AFRICAN AMERICAN VOICES IN A WHITE REPUBLIC

The documents of the founding of the United States enunciated universalist visions. Christianity and small "r" republicanism merged in antebellum America. In their conceptualizing of religion and the civil order, many were like the former Methodist turned Unitarian James Smith. He wrote to Thomas Jefferson that he had found "shelter under the mild and peaceable Gospel of Jesus Christ, the most perfect model of Republicanism in the Universe." The radical Christian Elias Smith exulted in "One God—one Mediator—one lawgiver—one perfect law of Liberty—one name for the children of God, to the exclusion of all sectarian names—A Republican government, free from religious establishments and state clergy—free enquiry—life and immortality brought to light through the Gospel."

But the early Republic was, in practice, racially exclusivist and white supremacist. The free white man was the basic unit of citizenship, and the first Naturalization Act of 1790 restricted citizenship to free white people. Just as the Declaration of Independence became a touchstone for African American thought, and as white idealists and missionaries took their Christianity to Indian tribes whom they defended against governmentally imposed removal and repression schemes, the universalist language of democratic Christianity provided a base for alternative visions. As James Forten, a free black man from Philadelphia who served in the colonial Navy during the American Revolution, expressed it, the truth that "GOD created all men equal" embraced the "Indian and the European, the Savage and the Saint, the Peruvian and the Laplander, the white Man and the African, and whatever measures are adopted subversive of the inestimable privilege, are in direct violation of the letter and spirit of our Constitution."

African Americans such as Forten seized on the universalist languages of Christianity and republicanism. Meanwhile, conservative ministers (mostly in eighteenth-century New England) articulated some of the first versions of the proslavery argument in America. Nineteenth-century southern divines picked up on its themes and added their own variations. Meanwhile, African Americans responded vigorously to the proslavery argument. They created an eloquent and voluminous protest literature that centrally engaged American ideas of freedom as expressed through Christian language.

Nowhere was this more evident than in the creation of the African Methodist Episcopal Church (AME) in Philadelphia and, a few years later, the African Methodist Episcopal Zion (AMEZ) denomination in New York City. The original African American denominations emerged from the labors of Richard Allen. Born a slave in Delaware, Allen purchased his freedom. He moved to Philadelphia, where he joined the St. George's Methodist Church. Through the 1780s and early 1790s, Philadelphia had become a haven for blacks seeking freedom in revolutionary-era America. Despite that reputation, former slaves and free people of color who migrated there often found themselves bound out to indentures, or at best placed in physically exhausting working-class positions. Allen found a receptive audience for his preaching among the struggling black population of the City of Brotherly Love. Together with his friend and comrade Absalom Jones, he formed the Free African Society, the first mutual aid group for African Americans in the United States. Allen believed blacks should have their own church, and he wanted it to be Methodist. Sometime in the early 1790s, while praying at the altar of St. George's Methodist Church, Allen and his colleagues were ordered to remove themselves to segregated seats at the back of a gallery set aside for them, until whites had finished their prayers. Jones, Allen, and the others in the black contingent removed themselves from the church, raised money for their own congregation, and opened Bethel Methodist Episcopal Church. "We all went out of the church in a body, and they were no longer plagued by us," Richard Allen tartly wrote later. They were still within the Methodist Episcopal order, but this was a church for African Americans.

In 1816, black churchmen from Pennsylvania and surrounding states convened to incorporate themselves as the AME Church. Six years later, African Americans in New York organized a rival federation, the AMEZ Church. James Varick, a black New Yorker resentful of Richard Allen's intrusions into his territory, insisted on the black Methodists there forming their own group. Both new black denominations, the AME and AMEZ Church, portrayed themselves as restoring the simplicity and purity of the old Methodist order. They adopted the *Doctrine and Discipline* of the American Methodist Church largely as their own.

Portrait of the Bishops of the AME Church from the nineteenth century
Source: Courtesy of the Library of Congress.

Unlike the white Methodists, however, the black Methodists followed Francis Asbury's rule prohibiting membership to slaveholders.

In 1817, one year after the formation of the AME Church, a group of elite southern and northern whites formed the American Colonization Society (ACS). Its purpose was to provide for the emigration of black Americans "back to Africa," thereby "solving" America's intractable problem of slavery and race. Soon thereafter, black proponents and opponents of colonization began debating the relationship of black Americans to their motherland, a philosophical and practical controversy that raged among black thinkers over the next century. Daniel Coker, ironically, most strongly urged mission work in and removal to the home shores of Africa. He and others held a providential view of history, by which God would use the evil of slavery to prepare a group of Christianized African Americans to bring the gospel message back to Africans who remained mired in heathen customs. Shortly after the formation of the AME Church, Coker became a missionary to Africa.

Richard Allen denounced colonization. While Allen and his AME comrades fought for the organization of a separate black denomination marked by the title "African," they also insisted on the rights of black people as Americans. Allen and his close comrade Absalom Jones put their philosophy into practice just as they originally formed their Bethel congregation in the 1790s. Absalom Jones authored one of the first African American petitions to Congress, on behalf of four men kidnapped back into slavery. Two years later, Jones authored an antislavery petition signed by some seventy others, including Allen. If the Bill of Rights and the Declaration of Independence meant anything, they said, blacks should enjoy the inalienable rights promised them in the founding documents.

Jones, Allen, and the early black Methodists fused Christian universalism, revolutionary liberalism, and black separatism. It was a delicate balancing act, one which thereafter defined the role of black Christian churches. They claimed an African heritage and understood black churches and societies to be necessary for the defense of African American rights. They also insisted on their status as free Americans, subject to every protection under the laws.

The church articulated African American interests through the antebellum era, most especially after the church was banned from the South in 1822. That year, Charlestonians had uncovered what they believed (with good reason, albeit derived from coerced testimony) to be an insurrectionary plot engineered by Denmark Vesey, a free black man known for broadcasting antislavery sentiments. Vesey was a member of the First African Church (later renamed Emanuel African Methodist Episcopal Church). Over 4,000 black Charlestonians formed the First African Methodist congregation. Its initial life was short. Local authorities shut it down several times and imprisoned its pastor for violating state laws against slave literacy. The Vesey Plot of 1822, whites believed, took shape in class meetings in the church, where "inflammatory and insurrectionary doctrines" fostered rebellious sentiments. After the discovery of the plot, thirty-five local blacks were executed, the church building was burned, and later the AME as an organization exiled from the state.

After the Civil War, Denmark Vesey's son helped to rebuild the church, which later came to be called Emmanuel AME in downtown Charleston. The church was rebuilt again following an 1886 earthquake, and in the 1960s it hosted a variety of civil rights leaders. In 2015, the church became famous due to the murder there of the pastor and eight parishioners during a Wednesday evening service, a shocking act of white supremacy that compelled the state finally to remove the Confederate battle flag from flying outside the State House in Columbia.

Although quasi-independent black churches in the South dated from the 1770s, it was primarily in northern black churches, most especially those affiliated with the AME and AMEZ, that provided African Americans with an independent voice, with publications, with educational institutions (including Wilberforce College, in Ohio), and with well-known ministers from Richard Allen to Daniel Payne. Beginning in the 1850s, the church's publication the *Christian Recorder* served as a central repository of African American thought. Later publications, including the *A.M.E. Church Review* and several others, gave African American ministers a forum for published theological discussion. The AME Church was, as the female church activist Mary Still put it, the first to "elevate and Christianize their outcast brothers and sisters by encircling them within the enclosure of the Church, and by faithfully administering and constantly instructing and encouraging them in the way to respectability to Heaven."

From the late eighteenth century, when Absalom Jones and Richard Allen prepared a pamphlet defending the conduct of African Americans during the yellow fever crisis in Philadelphia in 1793, to the famous (and infamous) *Appeal to the Colored Citizens of the World* of David Walker in 1829, to the published proceedings of the black convention movement later in the antebellum era, African Americans responded vigorously, passionately, and eloquently to the strengthening of slavery and the rapid spread of racist ideologies. They did so sometimes through carefully pitched dialogues and printed "conversations," and other times through angry pamphlets directed at white American hypocrisy.

In the few decades prior to David Walker's *Appeal* of 1829, black pamphleteers adopted a rhetoric of reasonable discourse with a (presumably) reasonable and largely white readership. For them, the clear relationship of American Protestantism and American freedom provided a clear means of dialogue with whites who could, and should, see the justice of ending slavery. Perhaps the best example of the point is Daniel Coker's "A Dialogue Between a Virginian and an African Minister."

Published in 1810, the fictional conversation features a Virginian speaking with a black minister and working through biblical passages on the Bible and slavery. For example, when Virginian brings up the standard litany of biblical passages about slavery from the Apostle Paul, the minister reminds him that Christians in Paul's time were under Roman yoke and had to take expedient stands accordingly. By contrast, "ours is not a heathen, but is called a Christian government, so that the Christians are not, by it, persecuted unto death. In such circumstances, therefore, had the apostle proclaimed liberty to the slaves, it would probably have exposed many of them to certain destruction, and injured the cause he loved so well," without freeing anyone. While Paul acted with "prudent reserve," it nevertheless could easily be inferred from the "righteous and benevolent doctrines and duties" of the New Testament that "slavery is contrary to the spirit and nature of the Christian religion." By the end of the polite dialogue, Virginian is convinced by the minister's proposal for a plan of abolition and education of black people toward their incorporation into American society as citizens.

Through the 1810s and 1820s, the assumptions of a universalist Christianity put in the context of a free and democratic Republic kept black Christian writers imbued with visions of the freedom that would soon come. "Wherever Christianity is considered as a religion of the affections," as one member of the Philadelphia black elite put it before a newly created black literary society, "every well instructed, practical Christian, habitually aspires . . . to yield a cheerful and unreserved obedience to the precepts and instructions of its heavenly founder." Christianity was peculiarly adapted to be a "universal religion," because "wherever its spirit enters into the councils of nations, we find it unbinding the chains of corporeal and mental captivity, and diffusing over the whole world, the maxims of impartial justice, and of enlightened benevolence." In another twist on this rhetoric, one mixed with a somewhat heterodox version of black messianism, a black New Yorker called on all "Ethiopians" to recognize "the power of Divinity within us, as man," which should implant "a sense of the due and prerogatives belonging to you, a people." The time was at hand, he proclaimed, "when, with but the power of words and the divine will of our God, the vile shackles of slavery shall be broken asunder from you, and no man known who shall dare to own or proclaim you as his bondsman. We say it, and assert it as though by an oracle given and delivered to you on high." Slaveholders would learn the bitter lesson that God's will rested not in their hands, but that, rather, "God decrees to thy slave his rights as man."

Written at a time after the Revolution when numerous manumissions created a substantial class of free people of color, and after the closing of the international slave trade to the United States in 1808, a dialogue toward resolving the issue of slavery still seemed possible. These kinds of polite dialogues, some of them not unlike John Eliot's ersatz "Indian Dialogues" put together for the aid of seventeenth-century proselytizers, gave way later in the nineteenth century to polemically powerful attacks on slavery and slaveholders. Twenty years later, at the time of Walker's *Appeal* and the appearance of William Lloyd Garrison's *Liberator*, the stakes appeared very different, and the rhetorical balance shifted dramatically.

The turning point was David Walker's *Appeal to the Colored Citizens of the World*. Born free in North Carolina, Walker was a used clothes merchant in Boston at the time of the publication of his jeremiad in 1829. It soon became nationally notorious and even blamed for Nat Turner's revolt in 1831. Copies were found sewn in the sleeves of black sailors aboard ships headed southward.

Walker's *cri de couer* was a jeremiad about America's sins, one that would have made any Puritan proud but for the subject. "Oh Americans! Let me tell you, in the name of the Lord, it will be good for you, if you listen to the voice of the Holy Ghost," Walker warned his readers, "but if you do not, you are ruined!!! Some of you are good men; but the will of my God must be done." The United States might have passed itself off as the "most enlightened, humane charitable, and merciful people upon earth." Yet its white citizens treated black people "secretly more cruel and unmerciful than any other nation upon earth." Walker mixed a rational appeal about the injustices of slavery with a kind of desperate jeremiad attuned to the hypocrisies of American as a Christian civilization. "*Christians!! Christians!!* I dare you to show me a parallel of cruelties in the annals of Heathens or of Devils, with those of Ohio, Virginia and of Georgia—know the world that these things were before done in the dark or in a corner under a garb of humanity and religion." Bitterly rejecting the nostrums of the ACS as well as those of his compatriots who had chosen repatriation to Africa, Walker insisted that "this country is as much ours as it is the whites, whether they admit it now or not, they will see and believe it by and by."

Rejecting biblical arguments from the Old Testament that identified blacks as the seed of Cain, murderer of his brother Abel, Walker could find no biblical warrant for such a genealogy. Instead, "I ask those avaricious and ignorant wretches, who act more like the seed of Cain, by murdering the whites or the blacks? How many vessel loads of human beings have the blacks thrown into the seas? How many thousand souls have the blacks murdered in cold blood, to make them work in wretchedness and ignorance, to support them and their families?" White people "know well, if we are *men*—and there is a secret monitor in their hearts which tells them we are," that the black man was made in the image of God, "though he may be subjected to the most wretched condition upon earth, yet the spirit and feeling which constitute the creature, man, can never be entirely erased from his breast, because the God who made him after his own image planted it in his heart, he cannot get rid of it." The fears of whites about black brutes attacking them had persuaded whites to "keep us in ignorance and wretchedness, as long as they possibly can." Americans might think that blacks were "so well secured in wretchedness" that catastrophic punishments would not wait. They were as deluded as those who doubted Noah, "until the day in which the flood came and swept them away. So did the Sodomites doubt until Lot had got out of the city, and God rained down fire and brimstone from Heaven upon them, and burnt them up. So did the king of Egypt doubt the very existence of God . . . Did he not find to his sorrow, who the Lord was, when he and all his mighty men of war, were smothered to death in the Red Sea? So did the Romans doubt, many of them were really so ignorant, that they thought the whole of mankind were made to be slaves to them; just as many of the Americans think now, of my colour."

Black thinkers and writers picked up on Walker's themes, if not his super-heated prose, and pressed their case for the Christian humanity of black people through the antebellum era. "These things have fired my soul with a holy indignation, and compelled me to come forward," wrote Maria W. Stewart, a schoolteacher and pamphleteer in Boston and New York. As was customary for preachers of the era, she pled her lack of education and her inability: "I possess nothing but moral capability— no teachings but the teachings of the Holy Spirit." With a prose smoother than Walker's exclamation-laden messianistic writing, but with a force of righteous anger equal to any, Stewart condemned those who held "religion in one hand, and prejudice, sin and pollution in the other." Drawing from an unusual Old Testament analogy, Stewart compared Americans to King Solomon, "who put neither nail nor hammer to the temple, yet received the praise." Likewise, the name of white Americans was great, but black workers had been "their principal foundation and support. We have pursued the shadow, they have obtained the substance; we have formed the labor, they have received the profits; we have planted the vines, they have eaten the fruits of them." America had become "like the great city of Babylon," thinking itself a queen while being "a seller of slaves and the souls of men . . . her right hand supports the reins of government, and her left hand the wheel of power."

Starting in 1830s and extending to the Civil War, free black northerners gathered in conventions. This black convention movement promoted ideas of moral reform, temperance, self-help among black Americans. Leaders also protested the rise of laws requiring separate and unequal lives for black northerners and fought back against the popular idea of colonizing black Americans abroad as a means of "solving" the race problem. The black convention movement debated the ideals of a color-blind society based on Enlightenment and universalist ideals versus the clear necessity of separate organizations for African Americans. The project of black freedom always had been premised on the universalist language dating from the Enlightenment, documents such as the Declaration of Independence, and the ideals of the American Revolution. Northern black thinkers in particular enthusiastically joined in the rhetoric of America's mission in the world and God's plan for the nation. At the same time, nationalism fused with religiomessianic ideals increasingly informed black thought as the antebellum era progressed. Enlightenment universalism and black nationalism often merged, for both spoke to profound and deep aspirations of African Americans as a people. Also, both came out of Afro-American religious traditions. Christianity was a universal message of the gospel, and yet particular forms of it thrived in ethnonational and racial groups, as everyone recognized. Black clergyman J. W. C. Pennington suggested that the "highest obligation of an oppressed people, is fidelity to god and firm trust in Him as the God of the oppressed." God himself demanded people who showed themselves worthy of the full rights of citizenship. This was a variation of the politics of respectability that would be a staple of black sermons.

African American writers and orators repeated many of the same phrases about the divinely appointed destiny of America as did their white contemporaries. This did not mean they spared America of biting critiques for its racist oppression, but that they saw the true American ideals as within the "ultimate design of God." As black writer William J. Wilson put it, "On this continent, which for so many centuries lay buried from sight of civilization, God intends in his providence, ultimately to bring men of every clime, and hue, and tongue, in one great harmony, to perfect the greater system of man's highest earthly government." In this scheme, black Americans were the agents of national redemption and salvation, for, as one Pennsylvanian expressed it, "God may use them to save this nation from that abyss of ruin towards which its brutal pride and folly are driving it headlong." And, if America was to be God's instrument, then it would be necessary first to "purify her own domains," such that the "laws of our country may cease to conflict with the spirit of that sacred instrument, the Declaration of Independence."

Blacks capitalized on the rhetoric of republicanism, for it provided a powerful intellectual basis for an antislavery argument. Antislavery advocates found their most powerful voice in Frederick Douglass. After escaping from his Maryland plantation in the 1830s, Douglass then embarked on a remarkable career as an internationally known evangelist for human freedom. A brilliant writer and polemicist, Douglass was probably the single most effective proselytizer for the antislavery cause. In the 1840s and 1850s, while residing in Rochester and publishing the black abolitionist organ the *North Star*, he rhetorically devastated the slave system and the so-called revivalism that accompanied the spread of the iniquitous institution. As Douglass told one gathering, "Revivals in religion, and revivals in the slave trade, go hand in hand together. The church and the slave prison stand next to each other, the groans and cries of the heartbroken slave are often drowned in the pious devotions of his religious master . . . while the blood-stained gold goes to support the pulpit, the pulpit covers the infernal business with the garb of Christianity." Douglass highlighted the hypocritical pieties of white southern slaveholding religion, in part through his famous mocking imitations of white southern preachers, as recounted in this episode from a meeting he addressed:

> They would take a text—say this: "Do unto others as you would have others do unto you." And this is the way they would apply it. They would explain it to mean, "slaveholders, do unto *slaveholders* what you would have them do unto you:"—and then looking impudently up to the slaves' gallery, (for they have a place set apart for us, though it is said they have no prejudice, just as is done here in the northern churches;) looking high up to the poor colored drivers, and the rest, and spreading his hands gracefully abroad, he says, (mimicking,) "And you too, my friends, have souls of infinite value—souls that will live through endless happiness or misery in eternity. Oh, *labor diligently* to make your calling and election sure. Oh, receive into your souls these words of the hold apostle—'Servants, be obedient unto your masters.' (Shouts of laughter and applause.) Oh, consider the wonderful goodness of God! Look at your hard, horny hands, your strong muscular frames, and see how mercifully he has adapted you to the duties you are to fulfill! (continued laughter and applause) while to your masters, who have slender frames and long delicate fingers, he has given brilliant intellects, that they may do the *thinking*, while you do the *working*." (Shouts of applause.)

Douglass memorably extended his withering satire in his famous speech "The Meaning of July Fourth to the Negro," delivered in Rochester in 1852. The first half of the lengthy address praises the founding fathers for what they accomplished in standing up to the British. Indeed, Douglass suggests that July 4 for Americans was akin to the Passover celebration for Jews, a sign of great deliverance from an evil tyranny. Midway through, though, Douglass pivots to an analysis of the meaning of July 4 for the more than three million slaves who remained in bondage. "What, to the American slave, is your 4th of July?" he asks rhetorically, and then answers that the day simply reveals the "injustice and cruelty" of the United States for black Americans:

> To him, your celebration is a sham; your boasted liberty, an unholy license; your national greatness, swelling vanity; your sounds of

rejoicing are empty and heartless; your denunciation of tyrants, brass fronted impudence; your shouts of liberty and equality, hollow mockery; your prayers and hymns, your sermons and thanksgivings, with all your religious parade and solemnity, are, to Him, mere bombast, fraud, deception, impiety, and hypocrisy—a thin veil to cover up crimes which would disgrace a nation of savages. There is not a nation on the earth guilty of practices more shocking and bloody than are the people of the United States, at this very hour. Go where you may, search where you will, roam through all the monarchies and despotisms of the Old World, travel through South America, search out every abuse, and when you have found the last, lay your facts by the side of the everyday practices of this nation, and you will say with me, that, for revolting barbarity and shameless hypocrisy, America reigns without a rival.

Douglass concluded that slavery demonstrated that American republicanism was a "sham" and its much-vaunted Christianity a "lie." Slavery, he said, "saps the foundation of religion; it makes your name a hissing and a bye-word to a mocking earth." It blocked progress, endangered the Union, stanched education, fostered boastful pride and vice, and yet Americans clung to it "as if it were the sheet anchor of all your hopes. Oh! be warned! be warned! a horrible reptile is coiled up in your nation's bosom."

Unlike some radical abolitionists, white and black, Douglass maintained a strong faith in the Constitution. Even his famous speech on the meaning of the Fourth of July to the slave ends with a paean to the constitutional wisdom of the founders and a plea to work within the American constitutional system. Douglass's faith in American Christianity, however, was not so strong. And over the antebellum years, romantic nationalism and American messianism gave way increasingly to a language of racial separatism. Black religious thought entertained the notion that black Americans were to take the initiative in pressing forward God's will. Black minister Henry Highland Garnet most clearly articulated black nationalist ideas. Garnet delivered his famous "Address to the Slaves of the United States" to a national convention in 1843. Considered too inflammatory to publish then—Frederick Douglass judged "that there was too much physical force, both in the address and the remarks of the speaker last up"—it appeared in print five years later along with David Walker's *Appeal*. They were probably the two most widely read and discussed classics of antebellum black nationalism. Recounting the history of the forced migration of African Americans to the land of slavery, Garnet determined that God had "frowned upon the nefarious institution, and thunderbolts, red with vengeance, struggled to leap forth to blast the guilty wretches who maintained it." It was too late, for slavery already had "stretched its dark wings of death over the land" even as the Church stood by silently—"the priests prophesied falsely, and the people loved to have it so. Its throne is established, and now it reigns triumphant." Garnet made his view as directly as he could, with language resonant from Walker's *Appeal*: "TO SUCH DEGRADATION IT IS SINFUL IN THE EXTREME FOR YOU TO MAKE VOLUNTARY SUBMISSION." Garnet recognized the "forlorn condition" of slaves, but insisted this did not "destroy your moral obligation to God," for it was the slaves' "SOLEMN AND IMPERATIVE DUTY TO USE EVERY MEANS, BOTH MORAL, INTELLECTUAL, AND PHYSICAL THAT PROMISES SUCCESS . . . The humblest peasant is as free in the sight of God as the proudest monarch that ever swayed a scepter. Liberty is a spirit sent out from God, and like its great Author, is no respecter of persons." The motto of black Americans should be "resistance! *Resistance!* RESISTANCE! No oppressed people have ever secured their liberty without resistance."

The 1843 convention in Buffalo narrowly voted down Garnet's call for physical resistance. They recognized that any direct call for bloodshed was suicidal and a result either of "an unpardonable impatience or an atheistic want of faith in the power of truth as a means of regenerating and reforming the world." Instead, figures such as Frederick Douglass and Alexander Crummell insisted that the "voice of God and of common sense, equally point out a more excellent way, and that way is a faithful, earnest, and persevering enforcement of the great principles of justice and morality, religion and humanity. . . . Let us invoke the Press and appeal to the pulpit to deal out the righteous denunciations of heaven against oppression, fraud and wrong, and the desire of our hearts will soon be given us in the triumph of Liberty throughout all the land." But black conventions continued the struggle, insisting, as did the 1847 National Convention of Colored People in Troy, New York, that "there shall be no peace to the wicked, and that this guilty nation shall have no peace, and that we will do all that we can to *agitate!* AGITATE!! AGITATE!!"

While the monumental figure of Frederick Douglass consistently articulated universalist ideals of black integration into the American Republic and resistance to all forms of separatism or colonization, black nationalists such as Garnet and Martin Delany pressed the case for resistance and separate black institutions. As Delany put it:

> Our friends in this and other countries, anxious for our elevation, have for years been erroneously urging us to lose our identity as a distinct race, declaring that we were the same as other people; while at the very same time their own representative was traversing the world and propagating the doctrine in favor of *a universal AngloSaxon predominance*. The "Universal Brotherhood," so ably and eloquently advocated by that Polyglot Christian Apostle of this doctrine had established as its basis, a universal acknowledgement of the Anglo-Saxon rule.
>
> The truth is, we are not identical with the Anglo-Saxon or any other race of the Caucasian or pure white type of the human family, and the sooner we know and acknowledge this truth, the better for ourselves and posterity.

The "determined aim of the whites," Delany said, was to "crush the colored races wherever found," with the Anglo-Saxon taking the lead in "this work of universal subjugation."

CONCLUSION

Free northern black thinkers, ministers, and educators debated the merits of universalist aspiration within a white Republic that defined African Americans as dishonored aliens. Meanwhile, southern slaves created powerful forms of cultural expression that suggested the depth of theological ideas held by the most oppressed in American society. In both cases, black Americans let it be known that the bounds of their habitation set by white Americans were not those of their own making or of God's plan. As slavery exploded through the Southeast, ranging from the

Chesapeake to the Brazos by the end of the antebellum era, and as free blacks faced narrowed options and heightened restrictions in the northern states, black Christians turned to the language of the Bible to envision freedom and justice. The Civil War seemed, for a time, to vindicate that hope.

3

Religious Ways of Knowing Race in Antebellum America

THROUGH THE ANTEBELLUM YEARS, evangelicalism and slavery exploded across the American landscape nearly simultaneously. The movement of peoples into new states and territories fueled the growth of an evangelical and benevolent empire. A myth of innocence wrapped together benevolent and violent expansion into a single ideological and material force that subsumed other peoples, propelled the massive internal slave trade from the Upper South to the Lower South, and began to create the evangelical South of the antebellum era. At the same time, the combination of forces arising from the antislavery movement in antebellum America and then the force of the war itself radically challenged how Americans conceived of the bounds of habitation in race and religion. So did early encounters with "other" religions, particularly Hinduism and Buddhism, first seriously discussed by the same intellectuals of the era who were involved in antislavery thought and politics. The boundaries of race, religion, and Christianity were in flux and highly contested in the antebellum era, even as evangelicalism established itself as the dominant force in American religious life for a good many ordinary people.

This chapter explores these themes through the persons of the slave rebel Nat Turner and the anonymous collective authors of the slave spirituals which came to be the defining cultural expression of the Christianity of enslaved people, through the writings of proslavery thinkers such as Richard Furman and Stephen Elliott and through a variety of intellectuals who experimented in early versions of what would later come to be called "comparative religion," including Hannah Adams, Ralph Waldo Emerson, and Henry David Thoreau. The story focuses on the dual forces of expansion and contraction. White Americans tried to define themselves in relationship to "others" around them. Meanwhile, those others made their voices known even when enslaved and oppressed.

NAT TURNER AND THE DANGERS OF SLAVE CHRISTIANITY

In August 1831, whites in Southampton County, Virginia, discovered in Nat Turner their worst nightmare of what evangelical notions of equality and liberty might produce. Instigator of the bloody uprising that month that took the lives of nearly sixty whites and, in the aftermath, a number of blacks executed in revenge, Turner was a Baptist messianist who sensed a divine mission to purge the guilty land with blood. From his younger years, he felt he had been set aside for some special purpose. He confirmed his mission while reflecting on biblical verses which convinced him that the same "Spirit that spoke to the prophets in former days" now had come to him, and that he had been "ordained for some great purpose in the hands of the Almighty." Visions from the skies told him that the "Serpent was loosened, and Christ had laid down the yoke he had borne for the sins of men, and that I should take it on and fight against the Serpent." Later, visions of blood in the morning dew foretold his targeted campaign of violence directed against local slaveholding families in his immediate vicinity. After being captured and tried a few months later, when asked if he still felt justified given his impending execution, Turner replied simply, "Was not Christ crucified?"

Turner's revolt shocked and unsettled Virginians in a way comparable to how the violence of September 11 upended the national psyche. Contemporary commentators in Virginia pinned the blame for Turner's rampage on an egalitarian religious fanaticism. Evangelicals, many believed, were to blame. Their message effectively incited insurrection. A report from a Richmond newspaper blasted evangelical preachers who were full of a "*ranting cant* about equality." After the Southampton County bloodbath, Virginia Baptists gathered numerous reports that since Turner's revolt, black members had "constantly exhibited a most rebellious and ungovernable disposition." John Floyd, the governor of a state whose white citizens now felt themselves under siege, interpreted Turner's revolt as the culmination of a chilling logic coming from those who had sown the "spirit of insubordination" in the South by "telling the blacks, God was no respecter of persons—the black man was as good as the white—that all men were born free and equal—that they cannot serve two masters—that the white people rebelled against England to obtain freedom, so have the blacks a right to do." The governor was convinced that "every black preacher in the whole country east of the Blue Ridge was in the secret." Allegedly, they had been egged on by northern abolitionist presses and by those who had made them "aspire to an equal station" in life. By 1832, Baptist churches began examining black members for signs of incipient insurrection, refusing to ordain black men to preach, and authorizing white members to serve as patrollers. The bounds of the habitation of southern slaves, even Christianized ones, were straitening.

Discussions of the Nat Turner revolt in the Virginia legislature in 1832 considered the future of slavery in the state. The final votes, however, closed down any remaining hopes for emancipation, whether gradual or immediate. The revolt instead helped to spur the "mission to the slaves," a concerted effort to propagate Christian doctrine in slave communities. In addition, it led to a significant strengthening of proslavery thought. Christianity wove its way into the ideology of the master class. At the same time, subversive readings of the Bible and of Christianity spread through slave communities. It periodically frightened white authorities enough to monitor or prohibit black religious meetings.

By the 1830s, southern clerics and intellectuals had elaborated a vigorous theological defense of the peculiar institution. Some of them argued that slavery was a necessary evil, a living emblem of man's sinful and fallen state. For them, slavery was the lesser of evils. It could not be abolished without bringing even greater evils (anarchy, sedition, or even race mixing) in its wake. Others interpreted slavery as a kind of Christian way station, educating black converts in Christianity so that in God's due time they could carry the message back to their home continent.

Some took up more folkloric or mythic explanations justifying the peculiar institution. Passages from the Old Testament, especially Genesis 9:18–27 (which outlined the curse on Canaan, son of Ham, who had originally espied Noah's naked drunkenness), provided at least a start at a religiomythical grounding for modern racial meanings. The "curse" on Canaan, son of Ham, originated in the medieval era, with deep roots

in antisemitism. It was revived as a mode of biblical interpretation during the modern age of exploration. As Americans came to understand
it, Ham as a figure represented black people. Shem stood in variously
sometimes for Indians, other times for Jews. Japheth supposedly was the
progenitor of white people. God had doomed Ham's offspring to lives
of servitude to the superior racial descendants of Shem and Japheth and
commanded those blessed with a white heritage to avoid contaminating
themselves through intermixing. Allusions to the passage appeared frequently in antebellum biblical discussions, sermons, Sunday School lessons, and sectional polemics. The Ham fable deeply, but incompletely,
penetrated the consciousness of ordinary white southern Christians. The
story seemed to justify racial separation, but the reference to slavery had
to be inferred. Moreover, the story's meanings were unstable and subject to dubious speculative interpretations that disturbed orthodox white
churchgoers. While many of the best-educated theologians had little
patience with it, the story persisted, haunting southern (and American)
thought for centuries. It was, according to the historian Winthrop
Jordan, "probably sustained by a feeling that blackness could scarcely be
anything but a curse and by the common need to confirm the facts of
nature by specific reference to Scripture."

More broadly, the biblical proslavery argument spoke to the biblical commonsense literalism of many evangelicals. For them, the Bible
clearly meant to justify, not to abolish, slavery. What else could explain
the frequent references to biblical patriarchs of the Old Testament owning slaves and New Testament passages in which the sainted apostles
instructed slaves to obey their masters. "Can'[t] tell you how many times
I done heard that text preached on," one enslaved Christian scoffed.

The top ranks of southern theologians outlined a powerful proslavery
argument. Good order pleased God; anarchy and theological infidelity
did not. Conservative theologians of both regions developed and presented a coherent proslavery argument that could not be rebutted successfully with the commonsense biblical principles of the day. If the Bible
meant what it said, and readers could discern its plain meaning from the
text, then it was virtually impossible to refute the argument that biblical passages supported the obedience of slaves to masters. The proslavery
argument relied on the evangelical synthesis to make its points. As one
religious southern proslavery writer put it for *DeBow's Review* in 1850,
"What we have written is founded solely upon the Bible, and can have no

force, unless it is taken for truth. If that book is of divine origin, the holding of slaves is right; as that which God permitted, recognized and commanded, cannot be inconsistent with his will." If Jesus and the Apostle Paul had considered slavery wrong, then why didn't they say so? And why did Paul clearly command obedience to masters?

This proslavery sermonic literature began to appear in the eighteenth century and over time developed into a formidable intellectual edifice. Richard Furman of the South Carolina Baptist Convention contributed one of the earliest expressions of the genre with his address in 1823, just following the abortive Denmark Vesey Rebellion in Charleston. He sought to allay fears among some masters that acquainting slaves with scriptures would disturb domestic peace, only because opposition to slavery has been attributed by abolitionists to the "genius of Christianity." If holding slaves was a moral evil, he asserted, then it "cannot be supposed, that the inspired Apostles . . . would have tolerated it, for a moment, in the Christian Church." The idea that the Golden Rule condemned slavery was absurd. For example, if a son wished that his father would follow his commands, did that mean that fathers were obligated to obey orders from their sons? Furman acknowledged the evils and cruelties that had been attendant upon slavery. But such abuses also had been true of other primary social institutions, such as marriage, and that hardly proved that "the husband's right to govern, and parental authority, are unlawful and wicked." When tempered with "humanity and justice," slavery might provide a state of "tolerable happiness" for those in the lower orders of society. And in doing so, masters had a right to "demand and receive from them a reasonable service, and to correct them for the neglect of duty, for their vices and transgressions." Governments, he continued, were justly concerned "not only to provide laws to prevent or punish insurrections, and other violent and villainous conduct among them (which are indeed necessary)" but also to prevent unreasonable acts of cruel masters.

Furman's views seeded the growth of the religious paternalist proslavery theology that spread through the antebellum South. Typically, these defenses rejected any hint of the scientific racism that was just then being invented by phrenologists and early anthropologists such as Josiah Nott of Mobile. Instead, they were founded on a conservative vision of a godly social order and warnings of the potential dire implications of violating that order. In this, southern Protestants joined with Catholics, for while Catholic social philosophy excoriated the slave *trade*, it classed abolitionism as a worse social evil than the institution of slavery. New York Archbishop John Hughes of New York articulated that philosophy. The "fathers on the frontier" in the South, concentrated particularly in Louisiana and around Louisville, defended the peculiar institution. The white southern religious community closed ranks and produced reams of literature combating abolitionist propaganda.

Just at the beginning of the Civil War, the well-known Episcopalian divine Stephen Elliott reinforced God's plan for slavery and the war to a population just then engaged in a death struggle for their existence and way of life. He found the meaning of the war in God's plan for the "poor despised slave as the source of our security." He proclaimed that God had "caused the African Race to be planted here under our political protection and under our Christian nurture, for his own ultimate designs"— that being their preparation to return the Christian word to their home continent of Africa. How else, Elliott asked, could one explain the providential history of slavery itself and its perpetuation in spite of so many obstacles against it:

> God protected it at every point, made all assaults upon it to turn to its more permanent establishment, caused the laws of nature to work in its behalf, furnished new products to ensure its continuance and, at the same time, ameliorate its circumstances, made its bitterest antagonists to furnish arguments against its destruction, and raised up advocates who placed it, through reasoning drawn directly from the Bible, upon an impregnable basis of truth and necessity, connecting it, as we have shewn you, with sublime spiritual purposes in the future. And, finally, when the deeply-laid conspiracy of Black Republicanism threatened to undermine this divinely-guarded institution, God produced for its defence within the more Southern States an unanimity of sentiment, and a devoted spirit of self-sacrifice almost unexampled in the world and has so directed affairs as to discipline into a like sympathy those border States which were not at first prepared to risk a revolution in its defence.

If God kept his own chosen people in the Old Testament enslaved for four hundred years, as part of their preparation to "go forth as a nation among nations," then surely history would teach that American slavery was the yoke Africans would be under until God "saw fit to break it and to carry them, a humbled and prepared people, into the land which had been marked out for them as the scene of their future glory." In this sense, the very presence of slaves in the Confederacy was its greatest security and the protector of the proper bounds of habitation. Enslaved people articulated a very different vision.

CHRISTIANITY AMONG THE ENSLAVED

The dual revolutions of the antebellum South—the expansion of the empires of evangelicalism and slavery—generated a passionate response among black Americans forced to confront the reality that Christianity underlay the ideology of the master class. At the same time, subversive readings of the Bible and of Christianity spread through slave communities. As the former slave Charles Ball noted, it was not possible to reconcile the slave to the idea of "living in a state of perfect equality, and boundless affection, with the white people. Heaven will be no heaven to him, if he is not to be avenged of his enemies. I know from experience, that these are the fundamental rules of his religious creed; because I learned them, in the religious meetings of the slaves themselves." The "cornerstone" of slave religion, he thought, was "the idea of a revolution, in the condition of the whites and the blacks."

Enslaved Christians might have attended white-sanctioned and supervised services, sung the hymns of whites, and listened to white ministers enjoin them to obedience and patience with their lot in life. But they also created their own covert religious culture. Enslaved African Americans developed a religious culture that brought together elements of their African past and their American evangelical training. After the Civil War, the invisible church would become visible, as African Americans after the Civil War formed thousands of their own churches and denominational institutions. Before the war, however, when such independent institutions were impossible, black religious life emerged most clearly in the religious rituals of their own services. These included including ring shouts, spirituals, and chanted sermons.

Many spirituals have some base in the white popular evangelical tunes that were making their way (in the form of shape-note hymn books) to churches through the newly settling and developing areas. Whites also employed a variety of lyric books from the eighteenth century, including the hymns of Isaac Watts, and set those to familiar tunes. Many originated as songs compiled by Richard Allen, the Philadelphia Methodist who had created the African Methodist Episcopal Church. His widely reprinted songbook circulated quickly through the South. So did shape-note hymnals (named for the fact that the "shape" of the notes, rather than their position on the staff, signified their pitch for those singing) which started to emerge from southern publishers with the publication of *Southern Harmony* in 1835.

Enslaved Christians also brought their own images, literary devices, and musical stylings to the songs circulating through evangelical America. The spirituals, as poetry and literature set in musical form, took on many meanings, depending on the time and circumstance and individual. For generations of slaves, there was simply no viable hope that freedom would come in this life. "Trials on my way, Pray, sister pray/Heaven is my home, Pray, brother, pray," slaves sang in southern Georgia. "'Tis hard to serve the Lord," they added. In times of turmoil and war, when the very future of slavery was in question, songs about freedom took on more obvious meanings. Confederate authorities jailed some Charleston slaves for publicly singing what were now obviously subversive lines, such as "We'll soon be free." Recording these lines, Thomas Wentworth Higginson, a member of the Boston literati and white army officer who commanded a black regiment during the Civil War, wrote that the chant was "no doubt sung with redoubled emphasis during the new events." As one of his soldiers told him, "'De tink *de Lord* mean for say *de Yankees.*'"

The spirituals exalted Old Testament heroes such as Moses as well as more obscure figures. They often turned New Testament figures such as Jesus into Old Testament avenging heroes. These biblical heroes, moreover, were available now, for the slaves' sacred world invoked a kind of constant present. Slaves quickly adopted the story of the enslaved Israelites in Egypt as their own. "Go down Moses," with its exhortation to tell Pharaoh to release the captives in Egypt, is a well-known example. Thomas Wentworth Higginson provided even more powerful evidence as he recorded the praying and singing of former slaves, now Union soldiers, laying to rest one of their own. As they reflected on their lives, their army service (with its obvious perils, including reenslavement or a quick death if captured by Confederates), and their faith, one soldier publicly prayed his hopes to serve as a Christian soldier for freedom: "Let me lib wid de musket in one hand an' de Bible in de oder,—dat if I die at de muzzle ob de musket, die in de water, die on de land, I may know I hab de bressed Jesus in my hand, an' hab no fear."

Slaves placed the crucifixion, resurrection, and triumph of Jesus in the present tense. One song announced that "Mass Jesus is my bosom friend." The son of God was also a friend, comforter, and deliverer. In a song recorded by the white Georgia Presbyterian missionary Charles Colcock Jones in 1834, lowcountry slaves sang out, "Jesus sends the comfort down/In my soul, in my soul/Go reign, go reign, kind Saviour reign." Jesus walked on earth like a man, a suffering servant who chan-neled God's power. Peter Randolph, an ex-slave memoirist, described how slaves linked their suffering savior with their own hardships: "The slaves talk much of the sufferings of Christ; and oftentimes, when they are called to suffer at the hands of their cruel overseers, they think of what he endured." Enslaved Christians understood human suffering profoundly, as seen in lines such as "Sometimes I feel like a mother-less child," or "this world is not my home," or "I've been in the storm so long." They also longed for the peace coming after the turmoil of this life. Thomas Wentworth Higginson recorded the lyrics to "I Know Moon-Rise." On its surface, this spiritual is about the peace that death will bring: "I'll lie in de grave and stretch out my arms; Lay dis body down." But the lyrics attest to the conquering of death. The spirituals recognized the evanescence of human power: "Did not old Pharaoh get lost, get lost, get lost . . . . get lost in the Red Sea."

The ever-changing roster of lyric motifs for the spirituals came alongside a repertoire of group performance strategies that were key in bonding slave communities. They also evidenced that the bounds of the habitation of African religious practices found new homes. This was most evident in the ritual that accompanied the singing: the moans, shuffles, and ring shouts central to African American religious expres-sion. In slave cabins (oftentimes with great secrecy, including a tradition of turning a pot upside down at the door to "catch" the sound, a tradi-tion probably derived from African folklore), or in other secluded set-tings, slaves would form a circle and begin singing. A leader would sit in the middle and become the caller, often chanting lines followed by the rest of the group responding. Gradually, the group would begin a slow shuffle, clapping their hands and moving rhythmically counterclock-wise, circling the leader. Sometimes after hours of the singing, the ring shout leader picked up the tempo, with successive verses and refrains of familiar tunes. Participants called out new verses to the spirituals, includ-ing local names and locations. By such means, stock phrases came out as new material, some of which found their way into the versions of the spirituals. Finally, the intensity of the ring shout waned, and the informal services finished off with slower and more solemn spiritual tunes. White observers of the ring shout, dating from the early nineteenth century, were fascinated with the ritual, as in this account: "The fascination of the music and the swaying motion of the dance is so great that one can hardly refrain from joining the magic circle in response to the invitation of the enthusiastic clappers, 'No brudder!' 'Shout, sister!' 'Come, belieber!'"

The Christian culture developed by a significant minority of enslaved people reassured whites, on the one hand, because it proved the success of their missions to a people they considered as formerly heathen. Biracial churches in southern cities, with whites sitting in the main auditorium and blacks often seated in a balcony, side wing, or outside, seemed to represent an ideal of southern Christianity: two peoples worshipping and praying together, but doing so in ways that reflected and reinforced social hierarchies. But those who oversaw the system should have been disturbed rather than comforted. Within the Christianity of enslaved Americans lay a deep culture of aspiration for freedom in both body and soul. Those aspirations took flight when the Union Army provided the opportunity for escape from slavery and service to the cause of freedom.

RELIGION, RACE, AND ABOLITIONISM

The antislavery movement in the United States is most often associ-ated with the famous nineteenth-century figures who propelled it for-ward from the early 1830s to the Civil War, including William Lloyd Garrison (1805–1879), Lucretia Mott (1793–1880), and an entire network of female antislavery activists who bombarded Congress with petitions in the 1830s. Their relationship to the conventional evangelical religion of the era was troubled. Faced with a rising proslavery argument that drew deeply from biblical verses and theology, abolitionists most often found themselves appealing to the *spirit* of religious texts, particularly the Golden Rule. Abolitionists demanded that antislavery principles be put into action in America's denominations—by, for example, not appointing slaveholders as missionaries. Abolitionists successfully convinced many northern Protestants that association with slaveholders in denominations was, in effect, complicity with sin, and that they should separate themselves from that sin. The result of this was a splintering of many of the major American denominations by section, resulting in the Northern and Southern Methodist Church. Baptists similarly divided, resulting in the formation of the Southern Baptist Convention in 1845 by southerners angered by the rise of abolitionist sentiment among northern Baptists. In the twentieth century, it would grow into the nation's largest denomination.

To the degree that abolitionists were successful, it was through invoking a sentimental religious rhetoric about what Jesus would think about slavery, and what slavery did to families. Slavery was wrong, they said in effect, because it robbed human souls of their God-given dignity. It also interfered with God's plan for how humans should flourish within families. Harriet Beecher Stowe's novel *Uncle Tom's Cabin* catalyzed antislavery sentiment more than all other antislavery pamphlets combined. Stowe capitalized on the most effective religious antislavery arguments. Her hero Uncle Tom, a far cry from the "Uncle Tom" slogan that later became an epithet for cringing weakness, was powerful precisely because of his Christian faith. Stowe's other black heroes, including the famous runaway fugitive slave mother Eliza, were as well. Stowe softened the strident abolitionism of the pamphleteers and propagandists with a compelling and sentimental story and deeply Christian plot line that attracted millions of readers worldwide. Meanwhile, antislavery Christians flooded the nation with pamphlets, appeals, ghostwritten slave memoirs, and imagery that forced Americans to ask the question posed by the famous slave print from eighteenth-century England that became a symbol of the worldwide abolitionist movement. On it, a chained and kneeling slave asks, "Am I not a man and a brother?" Female abolitionists created a corresponding print of a female slave asking, "Am I not a woman and a sister?"

By nineteenth-century standards, many abolitionists held remarkably egalitarian ideals of human unity across racial lines. They tested the bounds of America religious and racial habitations. Black abolitionists, as discussed in the previous chapter, did so more vigorously, and without the overlay of racial paternalism that appeared strongly in some of the white abolitionist literature. They understood that the crusade against slavery, although indispensable, was not enough. The true realization of God's will for America would only come with the application of the ideals of the divinely inspired Declaration of Independence and other founding documents. Black abolitionists pushed their white colleagues throughout the antebellum era, but the rise of the kind of abolitionist vision embraced in mainstream political movements (such as the Free Soil Party) and in literature such as *Uncle Tom's Cabin* separated abolition and racial equality, and tended to encourage the ideas of colonization that Douglass and others found so contemptible.

Abolitionists came out of the world of Protestant liberalism and Unitarianism that reshaped religious thought in antebellum America. Antislavery moderates found American slavery morally repugnant but also disdained abolitionist zealots and extremists. The antislavery moderates—men such as William Ellery Channing, Horace Bushnell, Calvin Stowe (Harriet's husband), and Francis Wayland—joined with abolitionists in condemning slavery's relationship to unbiblical notions of racism. But because proslavery thinkers were so successful in using the Bible to defend slavery *in the abstract*, apart from any *particular* form of slavery in concrete historical instances, antislavery thinkers who still wished to cling to biblical arguments eventually arrived at a progressive notion of biblical truth. Unlike the proslavery side, which could rely on commonsense thinking, and the abolitionists, who were essentially forced to reject the Bible (precisely because many of them shared the presuppositions governing biblical reading with the proslavery thinkers), antislavery moderates effectively invented liberal Protestantism by providing an account of progressive revelation and the historicization of morality. Further, they developed the idea of "organic sin," a sin so interwoven with a society's institutions that individuals themselves were not morally culpable. Salvation then could come through a slow ascent to a higher plane of social morality—thought that developed much further in the social gospel movement of the early twentieth century.

Beyond the middle position staked by the antislavery moderates, Protestant liberals, radicals, abolitionists, and early advocates of modernism searched outside the Christian tradition for versions of the truth. In combination with the emerging missionary movement to India, they looked especially to Asian thought. So did the first generation of foreign missionaries. In their case, it was not because they thought they would find truth, but because they needed to know what ideas they would be up against as they tried to implant truth in South Asia.

RELIGION, RACE, AND THE ORIENT

Americans in the first half of the nineteenth century were the first generation to dabble in the contemplation of Asian religious traditions. Thomas Jefferson and John Adams carried on a correspondence speculating on the relationship of Buddhism and Hinduism to Christianity; the remarkable independent scholar Hannah Adams published her *An Alphabetical Compendium of the Various Sects Which Have Appeared from the Beginning of the Christian Era to the Present Day* and other works investigating, from a Unitarian Christian point of view, the origins of non-Judeo-Christian traditions; Ralph Waldo Emerson and Henry David Thoreau picked and chose what they wanted out of Hinduism and Buddhism to fashion their own critique of Protestantism in America and introduce Americans to terms such as "Oversoul."

Much as colonial Americans had done with African and Native religious practices, white American Protestants of the nineteenth century experimented with a succession of terms and concepts—heathen, Hindoo, Oriental religions, mystery religions, and others—as they tried to explain Eastern religions to American readers. In the process, they effectively invented religious traditions, such as "Hinduism," out of what had been a menagerie of loosely related practices emanating from a multitude of regions in India.

The pioneers—Hannah Adams, Joseph Priestly, John Adams, and the Transcendentalist writers—compared religions across the world. They wrote at the origins of what we would now call religious studies or comparative religions. They did so within a world of debates within American Protestantism about theological boundaries and racial definitions. The early writers, including Hannah Adams and Priestly, intended to demonstrate the superiority of a true Protestant faith, defined liberally.

Cover of *A Memoir of Miss Hannah Adams* Boston: Gray and Bowen, 1832
Source: Public domain.

Adams in particular showed how humans had evolved out of heathenism to the capacious Protestantism of nineteenth-century Unitarianism.
She and others told a story of religious development through the ages
in which a once honorable religious sentiment had devolved into

heathenism and polytheism. Yet within the original system could be found evidences of God's truth. Religious leaders in India, the brahmans, had corrupted the originally reasonable system. The ancient religion of the Hindus, while not on a par with Christianity, still had parts of the truth, as evidenced by their alignment with some of the truths of Christianity. Missionaries arriving in India would bring the message of the Bible and Christian progress and uncover the ancient truths that had been there all along but had gotten smothered. Joseph Priestly argued, similarly, that in early Hinduism "there is one God, the original author of all things," but added to this truth "many inferior deities presiding over different parts of the system."

Ultimately, as Adams and Priestly saw it, Hinduism was not a full-fledged religion but a subset of a larger category of heathism. Even so, it had recognizable elements of religion, including texts, beliefs, and rituals. As scholar Mike Altman puts it, while Adams "sought to make sense of religious diversity throughout the world and found a place for Hindus in the narrative of human progress toward Protestant truth," Joseph Priestly "defended Christian revelation, against unbelieving intellectuals and Orientalists, who sought to prove the Bible derived from ancient Indian texts, by denying that any truth could be found in Hindu religious thought." This difference would continue to divide representations of Asian religions.

Much of this played into Protestant arguments with each other over the definition of true Christianity. It stemmed as well from the Protestant critique of the idolatry and superstition characterizing not just heathen religions, but also Catholicism. Congregationalist James Goodrich, for example, in his work *Religious Ceremonies and Customs*, saw in Tibetan Buddhism "the counterpart of the Romish. They believe in one God, and a trinity, but full of errors, a paradise, hell, and purgatory, but full of errors also. They make suffrages, alms, prayers, and sacrifices for the dead; they have a vast number of convents filled with monks and friars. . . . They have their confessors who are chosen by their superiors, and receive their licenses from the Lama, as a bishop, without which they cannot hear confessions, or impose penances." Tibetan and Romish hierarchy were parallel, he concluded, as was the approach to the Dalai Lama and the Holy Father—"In approaching him, his votaries fall prostrate with their heads to the ground, and kiss him with incredible veneration."

During the same time, Protestants began organizing the first over-
seas missionary effort, under the auspices of the American Board of
Commissioners for Foreign Missions. The early mission advocates placed
non-Christian worlds in "hierarchies of heathenism," implicitly judging
their readiness to receive missionary efforts. Native American civilizations ranked low; Asian civilizations, with their long histories of religious development and cultural products that Christian Americans could
appreciate as substantial, merited a higher score. They thus attracted the
interest and attention of early missionary efforts, which were designed to
bring them the fruits of civilization and extend the American empire of
civilization abroad.

Andover Seminary, founded by Jedidah Morse in 1807, trained an early
generation of missionaries to Asia and helped lead to the formation of
the American Board of Commissioners for Foreign Missions (ABFCM).
Founded in 1810, the ABFCM sent out missionaries soon to be legendary
in American Protestant lore: Adoniram and Nancy Judson, Samuel and
Harriet Newell, Roxanna and Samuel Nott, and Luther Rice. Their missionary writings, published in *The Panoplist* and *The Missionary Herald*,
gave American Protestant readers many of their first chances to "see"
heathen religions. What they described was raw heathenism—blood
and sacrifice (again akin to Catholicism), noise, and a disturbing eroti-
cism. All of this spoke to Protestants of the New Divinity School, who
preached that disinterested benevolence should govern the Christian's
life. Evangelicals saw authentic, true religion, as leading humans toward
the rational and the ordered; Hinduism was precisely the opposite.

Meanwhile, mariners sailing to and from India, operating from the
major seaport of Salem, Massachusetts, interested themselves not at all in
the abstractions of doctrine but instead in Oriental material culture. This
included icons and deities and all manner of items to stow away in cabi-
nets of curiosities. These objects represented lands of ancient mysteries.
They were alluring, exotic, but dangerous in comparison to the progressive development of modern human civilizations, culminating in the best
that the Anglo-American world had to offer. "The Orient" was all that
New England was not. That was precisely what made it fascinating and
for a few intellectuals alluring in its more sensuous approach to truth. It
was also why it could not be a foundation for a true modern civilization.
Transcendentalists, however, were interested in finding religious truths

that would satisfy a deeper longing unfulfilled by Protestant Christianity. As a result, they could accept Oriental religions, including Hinduism, as something other than pure heathenism. And when they began to envision the religions of the "contemplative and spiritual East," some challenged the traditional conception of heathenism.

Later in the nineteenth century, Protestant liberals, Unitarians, and those who rejected Protestantism as an exclusive source of truth envisioned the role of religions in world civilizations differently. They contextualized Hinduism within a larger model of comparative religions meant to find universal truth across all the great religions. Hinduism was part of "The Orient," opposed to but complementary also to the West. The Transcendentalists imagined and created Oriental religions. They imagined an Orient, and a Hinduism, in a manner that fit what they needed and wanted in their ongoing dialogue with other New England Protestants. It allowed them to exalt contemplation, oneness, and unity, and pair that with Western action and practice. Asia, Ralph Waldo Emerson said, believed in "the idea of a deaf, unimplorable, immense Fate," while "the genius of Europe is active and creative." Emerson sought to bring together the two and found that his reflections on Plato gave him the opportunity to do so. Emerson essentialized West and East, made their differences eternal, but also wanted a fusion of qualities that incorporated Eastern concepts as an implicit critique of Western Protestantism. Emerson mused that "the unity of Asia and the detail of Europe, the infinitude of the Asiatic soul and the defining, result-loving, machine-seeking, surface-seeking operagoing Europe, Plato came to join, and, by contact, to enhance the energy of each."

The division between contemplation and action, moreover, was universal. Emerson sought unity between the two streams of human civilization, between Oneness as conceived in the East and the many truths of the practical West. In Transcendentalist publications, they printed excerpts from Hindu religious texts in the "Ethnical Scriptures," which they saw as pointing to universal truth. Religious difference, formerly signifying cultural gulfs, now pointed to universal truth.

Later in the nineteenth century, Lydia Maria Child's *The Progress of Religious Ideas Through Successive Ages* (1855) and James Freeman Clarke's *Ten Great Religions* each argued that all religions contained at least partial truths. When compared and fused, they could point the way

James Freeman Clarke (1810–1888)
Source: Public domain.

to transcendent truth. Clarke believed Christianity to be the summa of religions. "Every ethnic religion has its positive and negative side," Clarke wrote, containing some "vital truth" but missing some other "essential truth," meaning ethnic religions were true but "limited and imperfect."

Christianity, by contrast, alone was a "fullness of truth, not coming to destroy but to fulfil the previous religions; but being capable of replacing them by teaching all the truth they have taught, and supplying that which they have omitted." Christianity was not a system, creed, or form, "but a spirit," and thus "able to meet all the changing wants of an advancing civilization by new developments and adaptations, constantly feeding the life of man at its roots by fresh supplies of faith in God and faith in man." Thus, Christianity alone ("including Mohammedanism and Judaism, which are its temporary and local forms") was the "religion of all races." The Transcendentalists invented a religion called Brahmanism in trying to understand India and envisioned it as governed by "veneration and mysticism," or, as Clarke called it, "pure Spiritualism." As he saw it, God was "an intelligence, absorbed in the rest of profound contemplation." He also saw declension leading to the degradation of modern India.

And a few, such as Frederick Douglass, proposed ideas such as Douglass's "composite nationality." In an 1869 speech defending Chinese immigration, he noted with approval the theory that "each race of men has some special faculty, some peculiar gift or quality of mind," and that each race "has a definite mission in the world." The role of America in this was to "make us the most perfect national illustration of the unity and dignity of the human family that the world has ever seen." Much as W. E. B. Du Bois proposed in his "Conservation of Races" in the early twentieth century, Douglass listed qualities that individual races either had in abundance or lacked: "In one race we perceive the predominance of imagination; in other, like the Chinese, we remark its total absence. In one people, we have the reasoning faculty, in another, for music; in another exists courage; in another, great physical vigor. . . . All are needed to temper, modify, round and complete the whole man and the whole nation." And, he added, religious liberty itself would benefit from the "clash and competition of rival religious creeds." In the twentieth century, others would take up Douglass's notion; it was a nascent cultural plural-ism, still full of the language of the nineteenth century, but pointing to an ideal of nationalism in which diverse peoples would, as Douglass put it, "vibrate with the same national enthusiasm, and seek the same national ends."

Transcendentalists helped to invent comparative religion. They used it to find religious truth, whether in Clarke's liberal Protestantism, Child's religious liberalism, or elsewhere. Hinduism, or Brahmanism, imparted to religion contemplation and mysticism rather than action, and in doing so provided exactly what Western religions had lost. Transcendentalists saw Americans as lacking in the contemplation of a more ethereal, pantheistic spirituality. Herman Melville parodied their view in *Moby-Dick*, in a famous passage about the watchman on the boat becoming so immersed and "at-one" with the sea that he fell right into it. But for the Transcendentalists, India could provide Americans with access to the mystical and spiritual, the very qualities that hard-driving and hard-bargaining Yankee Protestants were too busy to contemplate. This tradition of seeing in India the spiritual, and in America the practical, obviously had a long life, continuing into the 1960s and "seekers" who traveled to India in search of spiritual truth.

Schoolbooks from the era also relied on systems of comparative religion. But while built on past representations, they envisioned Hindus and Buddhists as Oriental others, different not just in terms of religion but also differential racially from Caucasian Christians. Thus, while missionaries imagined Hindus as religious others, Americans more generally categorized them as racial others and thus as doubly threatening. Eventually, this conception would play crucially into Supreme Court cases which racialized Hindus (and Sikhs) precisely because of their religious practices. And all this intellectual seeking of truths from this era did not prevent a great upsurge of violence directed against Asian immigrants in the years after the Civil War, nor the passage of the Chinese Exclusion Act of 1882 and its subsequent reratification for decades afterward. Thus, the nineteenth-century paradox—intellectual longing for grasping the mysteries of Asian religions, together with the contempt for and eventual exclusion of actual Asian people—carried forward into the twentieth century. Intellectual hunger, Orientalist writing, and nativism together made up a package that essentialized Asian religions and racialized Asian peoples.

LATINO CATHOLICS IN A PROTESTANT REPUBLIC

In the Southwest, those egalitarian ideas faced a different challenge in dealing with Latino Catholics in a Protestant Republic. In the antebellum era, as the cotton and slave economy expanded rapidly into the newly opening states of the Deep South, Americans also looked southward and westward, into Texas and California and the Southwest. The rhetoric of Protestant triumphalism, Anglo-Saxon supremacy, and Manifest Destiny crested. Populist and antiformalist religious groups, especially the Baptists and Methodists, expanded rapidly, and visions for the future of the Protestant republic resounded in the literature of the period.

Protestant thoughts excluded Catholics generally from the category of Christian, especially when it involved brown Catholics in lands desired or already conquered by white settlers. Writing of the missions around San Antonio, one author in 1851 noted how, after the removal of the Franciscans, "everything went to decay. Agriculture, learning, the mechanic arts, shared the common fate; and when the banners of the United States were unfurled in these distant and desolate places, the descendants of the noble and chivalric Castilians had sunk to the level, perhaps beneath it, of the aboriginal savages." Of Catholic priests in California, Hubert Howe Bancroft wrote that they "possessed little learning or intelligence, and this little they devoted to the crushing and plundering of their people," while the parishioners were "supercilious, yet ignorant and superstitious, and full of beastly habits."

Following the glory period of the missions in the eighteenth century, the areas under Mexican dominance had declined and could only be redeemed by the force of U.S. westward expansion and civilization. Ignoring the presence of some missions and the vital tradition of Hispanic Catholic worship that continued in the area, Anglo-American propagandists and settlers assumed that these lands lay in spiritual isolation and desolation, awaiting the coming of Christian (Protestant) civilization. As one Protestant leader expressed it, the Anglo-American expansion into Texas indicated the will of Providence to spread Christian truth into Mexican lands and suggested as well "the beginning of the downfall of [the] Antichrist, and the spread of the Savior's power of the gospel."

Anglo-American colonists to Texas would have seen their situation as just the reverse of that of the pilgrims. Rather than fleeing religious persecution and finding religious freedom in America, they saw themselves as leaving religious freedom to go to a land dominated by the church most closely associated with religious intolerance. "Rome! Rome!" Stephen F. Austin exclaimed. "Until the Mexican people shake off their superstitions & wicked sects, they can neither be a republican, nor a moral people." Protestant churches were officially prohibited until the independence of Texas, although Protestant ministers were active in the state. Tejanos in San Antonio faced the dilemma of tolerating or ignoring the Protestant presence and thus violating the official Mexican law or actively prohibiting Protestant preaching and thus offending the very Anglo-American settlers that they had sought to come to their land in the first place. The result was a sort of modus vivendi in which Protestants could work as long as they were not too open and obvious about it. Nonetheless, Protestants had to adapt to the Mexican and Tejano Catholic presence, as there appeared to be no imminent signs of any complete conversion of the Catholic population to American ideas of Protestant freedom. The continuance of festivities such as Our Lady of Guadalupe processions, with participation by Anglo-Americans who had intermixed with the Tejano Catholic elite, and the popularity of fandangos and other Tejano Catholic social customs, made it clear that Tejanos would retain a Catholic identity even as they incorporated Anglo Protestants into the texture of life and government in San Antonio itself.

Tejanos, then, adapted to the Anglo-American presence, bringing them into their public celebrations and processions and creating in the process a Tejano identity that had roots in, but was increasingly distinct from, the Mexican homeland. By that time, Hispanic Texas identity was established as Tejano, and a distinct form of Catholicism, with particular public celebrations and practices, was a part of that. Tejanos did not see themselves as a Catholic immigrant group, but as long-standing settlers who had created the major institutions of the region and had welcomed in outsiders and brought them into their social customs and public life. Historian Timothy Matovina explains,

> As Tejanos were separated from Mexican political jurisdiction and incorporated into the United States, they responded by claiming their own history, origin legends, and Texan birthright as the basis for a renewed group identity. This renewed identity fostered religious and ethnic pluralism at San Antonio, as it distinguished native-born Tejanos from recently arrived immigrants and formed the basis of Tejano defense against Anglo-American aspirations for cultural dominance.

Catholic and Protestant leaders alike condemned the religious celebrations of ordinary Latino Catholics. As a Baptist minister sarcastically wrote of one ritual in Santa Fe in 1853, the celebrations accompanying Good Friday involved "the farce of crucifying the Savior." Protestant visitors to the Southwest especially condemned the brotherhood of *Los Hermanos de Nuestro Padre Jesus Nazareno,* popularly (and notoriously) known as the *Penitentes.* By 1833, when the bishop of Durango visited, the *Penitentes* were well established, enough so that the bishop warned against them: "I prohibit those Brotherhoods of Penance—or more accurately or Butchery," he decreed. Pastors and church administrators, he ordered, should ensure that "not a single one of these Brotherhoods remains and that there is no storeroom or other place to keep those huge crosses or other instruments of mortification which some men half kill their bodies, which at the same time they take no care of their souls, leaving themselves in sin for years on end." Moderate penance was good and healthy, he suggested, but illegal Brotherhoods which encouraged bodily excess were sinful: "Let every man whom the Good Spirit calls to do so take up the usual instruments, which bespeak mortification rather than self-destruction; but let them wield them in privacy."

Similar criticisms and attempts to ban the *Penitentes* came from future archbishops as well as from other Catholic officials as well as Presbyterian missionaries—to no avail. In many isolated rural communities, the Brothers of Blood (younger penitente members primarily responsible for carrying out the excruciating physical actions involved in the central ceremonies of the group) and Brothers of Light (older and revered Brothers no longer required to do their penances) effectively *were* the church. With no priest or perhaps only one visiting occasionally, and with many of the other institutions of civil society relatively inaccessible to relatively poor and isolated New Mexicans, the Brotherhoods provided communal bonds that were essential. They provided informal courts for law and order, took care of burials and looked after the sick, and negotiated with outside authorities when necessary. They also controlled politics in parts of northern New Mexico and southern Colorado, despite criticisms by church authorities and attempts to stop them.

As Protestant Americans came into control of lands taken from Mexico, they contemplated how to bring Spanish-speaking residents into the light of American ideas of freedom. Some emphasized parades and public celebrations as a means of cultural assimilation. As one white San Antonio resident put it in 1851, "We have many foreigners among us who know nothing of our government, who have no national feeling in common with us. . . . Let us induce them to partake with us in our festivities, they will soon partake our feelings, and when so, they will be citizens indeed." Despite the persistent drumbeat of complaint and the frequent attempts by church authorities to repress Hispanic Catholic practices, the relative isolation of many Latino communities in places such as northern New Mexico and southern Colorado allowed for the maintenance of cultural customs. At a celebration for Our Lady of Guadalupe in the San Luis Valley of Colorado in 1874, for example, a Jesuit priest in attendance described how the "enthusiasm and devotion of the faithful were great throughout the day," powerfully suggestive of the "religious spirit of the people of this locale."

In other cases, conflicts developed between local Hispanic Catholic priests and higher authorities (usually bishops or archbishops), usually French or Irish, who were their overseers. In one particularly well-known episode, Padre Antonio Jose Martinez, a native of Taos who pursued a distinguished career in the law, the church, and politics, fought bitterly with Archbishop Jean-Baptiste Lamy, who arrived in 1851 to preside over the parishes centered around Santa Fe. Lamy immediately reinstituted mandatory tithing as part of Catholic Church membership and threatened to excommunicate heads of family who would not comply. Martinez took his objections public, making known his displeasure in the *Santa Fe Gazette* and also in correspondence with Lamy himself. "Your excellency is well aware that in our republican form of government citizens have the freedom to express their opinions and even to publish them in the newspaper, especially when it involves issues that threaten the common good," Martinez wrote to Lamy in 1857, one of a series of public letters that followed Lamy's suspension of Martinez. Eventually, Lamy excommunicated Martinez for disobedience and insubordination, worsening the schism between Martinez's supporters and the leaders of the Santa Fe diocese. Martinez was then 64, and Lamy excommunicated him "for grave and scandalous faults, his writings against due order and discipline in the Church." Martinez had started a coeducational school to train seminarians, served in the New Mexico legislature during the Mexican period, and generally refused to obey orders from European and North American bishops that he saw as inimical to the interests of Latinos in New Mexico. Martinez later became the basis for a character in Willa

Cather's *Death Comes to the Archbishop*. His bitter feud and struggle with Lamy, a French Ultramontane Catholic who perceived Latinos in the Southwest as lacking in vitality and spirituality, presaged generations of conflict in the American Catholic Church. Those conflicts often took the form of Euro-American Catholic leaders berating the local practices and customs of Latino, black, Italian, and Eastern European adherents.

CONCLUSION: RACE, RELIGION, AND THE CIVIL WAR

On November 29, 1860, some 2,000 parishioners gathered at the First Presbyterian Church of New Orleans to hear the leading Southern Presbyterian (and founder of what became Rhodes College) Benjamin Morgan Palmer defend secession and more generally explain the role of the South in God's plan for the world. Southerners, he said, had a "providential trust to conserve and to perpetuate the institution of slavery as now existing . . . a trust to preserve and transmit our existing system of domestic servitude, with the right, unchallenged by man, to go and root itself wherever Providence and nature may carry it." Through the war, Palmer repeated his theological view that God had assigned special missions to nations. The Confederacy's role was to persevere through trials and conflicts to carry out God's will.

These theological pronouncements fit with millennialist views common in the era in both North and South. Divines sanctioned the war in speeches and sermons, forecast the blessings to come out of it, and led fast days and other public ceremonial civil religious events for their sections. Prominent ministers of the Confederacy sanctified the creation of their new nation. They interpreted victories and losses as part of God's plan to bless as well as to chastise the new nation. White southern Christians praised the religiosity of their new government and its leaders. All the white southern denominations endorsed the formation of the Confederacy as a political entity.

The outcome of the Civil War and the advent of Reconstruction raised difficult theological questions. Southern Christians hoped they might come out of the trial purified for God's work, but the questions proved more difficult than those kinds of pat answers. If God had sanctioned white caretaking of Negroes in bondage as the divine plan for southern

Christian civilization, then what was God's will in a world without slavery? What might be salvaged out of a cause that was lost?

For black southerners, who had awaited the coming of this moment for generations, the meaning of freedom would be linked to the spread of Christianity, civil rights, and civilization, each complementing the other. Where whites sought redemption, a cleansing of the regional soul from the taint of the rule of Reconstruction, black southern Christians embraced a new version of both revivalism and revolution. Ultimately, no matter what whites early in the conflict said, this was a war about the meaning of freedom, and African Americans understood that to be a spiritual and moral as well as an economic and political question. They understood that black freedom and black Christianity were just at the moment of their true rebirth. They perceived that the constricted bounds of habitation for black Americans was about to expand, and they trusted that God was the author of that revolution.

The coming decades, from the end of the war to the early twentieth century, would see a massive contest to reorient conceptions of religion, race, and citizenship. The end result was a re-creation of white American nationalism. But that form of racial nationalism took form within the context of a massive immigration of European Catholics and Jews and the domination of the last groups of Native peoples who fought to preserve their lands and liberties in the West. These racialized conceptions of nationalism in the post–Civil War era arose alongside the rapid pluralization of the American populace. That basic paradox set the terms for the discussion of religion, race, and citizenship from the end of the Civil War to the twentieth century. And it framed a discussion which, to this day, has never fully disappeared.

4

Religion, Race, and the Reconstruction of Citizenship

IN THE IMMEDIATE POSTWAR YEARS in New Orleans, a handful of local black men met to summon the spirits of the ancestors. Those spirits, when they came, delivered messages addressing the volatile political situation of African Americans after the Civil War. Afro-Creole members of the Spiritualist group *Cercle Harmonique* furiously transcribed messages emanating from spirits of historical personages ranging from Confucius and Montezuma to Thomas Jefferson, Abraham Lincoln, a litany of Catholic saints, Union heroes from the Civil War, and even Robert E. Lee. The spirits also commented on the long history of abuses to which African Americans had been subjected, including those perpetrated by the Catholic Church. The spirit voices rejoiced in the fact that "the chains of slavery are falling under the voice of Reason and Logic." Another voice recorded by the *Cercle* praised Jesus and Lincoln: "one will regenerate humanity, the other the U.S. Republic." Jesus died to save humanity, while Lincoln "was sacrificed for wishing to liberate the black race, subdued under a degrading yoke by brute force; and to elevate the white citizens of the south, subdued under a moral yoke more powerful than a physical one." They also condemned the institutional Catholic Church for sanctioning slavery, and for "blessing banners of the battalions which were forging new and stronger chains for their brothers, black as well as white." An egalitarian society clearly was heavenly writ. "God demands liberty," the spirit of slain black war hero Andre Cailloux called out.

The transcriptions left by members of *Cercle Harmonique* suggest much about the hopes and aspirations, as well as struggles and difficulties, facing black Americans during Reconstruction. From the 1860s to the 1890s, Americans fought over the rapidly altering definitions of race, religion, and citizenship. It involved political wrangling and normally messy democratic processes. It also incited violent acts of terrorism and a wrenching reshaping of the terms of race, religion, and citizenship. Race, reunion, and rights formed the central core of the story of religion and citizenship after the war and going forward into the decades leading to the twentieth century.

Because of its connection to the Civil War, Reconstruction historically has been placed within the framework of the struggle for freedom and citizenship among African Americans in the post–Civil War South. More recently, historians have broadened this to include discussions of Native peoples, Asian Americans, and Latinos in a Southwest that had recently been forcibly incorporated into the United States. As a topic of historical study, Reconstruction has gone national, incorporating stories not just from the North/South and white/black conflict but also the West, and incorporating other racialized groups.

Following that historiographical move, this chapter follows the life stories of the Georgia legislator black religious leaders William Jefferson White and Henry McNeal Turner, the Paiute Prophet Wovoka (Jack Wilson), and the Chinese American Congregationalist minister Jee Gam. It also discusses the struggle between the Catholic establishment and Latino parishioners over proper Catholic practice and who should be in positions of church leadership. In an era redefining whiteness as a standard of American citizenship, Jim-Crowing blacks, excluding Chinese immigrants, and attempting to assimilate (or eliminate) Indians, each sought a path to navigate an America after the reforging of the white Republic following the Civil War.

These seemingly disparate stories of race, religion, and Reconstruction are linked. Defining citizenship for black Americans in the Fourteenth Amendment, for example, involved a deliberate discussion of whether race or religion was the fundamental constituting element of American citizenship. If black Christians could be included in the Republic, what about heathen others? And what about Christian others, including Christianized Indians, Chinese Protestants in California, and Latinos who had been assimilated into the United States after 1848? Looking at these questions through short biographical sketches here provides some insight into how Americans thought about how race, nation, and religion came together in the context of a pluralizing society in the late nineteenth century.

RECONSTRUCTION

On the evening of January 12, 1865, following the Union Army's successful capture of Savannah, the Baptist minister Garrison Frazier led a delegation of black Georgians in a meeting with conquering General William Tecumseh Sherman, Secretary of War Edwin Stanton, and Oliver O. Howard, soon to be head of the Freedmen's Bureau. The African American ministers from the Georgia lowcountry advised Union war officers on the strong desire of freedpeople to till their own land with their own labor. By doing so, "we can soon maintain ourselves and have something to spare," they assured the Union officials. Following the meeting, as a temporary measure Sherman set aside for black war refugees lands in the lowcountry on a coastal strip from northern Florida to the region just south of Charleston. Some freedpeople took this as a governmental promise to provide land and hoped for a more egalitarian society.

For black Americans, Reconstruction presented the prospect of triumph over oppression and the ability to win rights to land and to the ballot box. Knowing that, southern white Redemptionists—those who sought to "redeem" the South from "Black Republican" rule—targeted ministers and religious institutions as part of their campaign to restore white supremacist rule in the region. The freedpeople had significant white allies in the North, but even more menacing opposition from whites who lived all around them.

After the Civil War, newly independent churches and black religious organizations sprang up. A black "exodus" from white-run churches transformed the nature of southern religious life. This process occurred over a number of years. Individual ex-slaves weighed competing principles and desires in deciding on church attendance. Still, by the end of Reconstruction, racial separation in Protestant religious organizations was nearly complete, and segregation of Catholic parishes and services was the norm as well.

Reconstruction transformed struggles over political power in the postwar South into religiously latent symbols. For white southern Christians,

the term "Redemption" infused sacred meanings into often deadly political struggles. Redemption was simultaneously a bloody cleansing for
the body's soul and for the body politic. For black Americans, churches
served as central points of social formation and political organizing. One
ex-slave most succinctly expressed his view of what the violence endemic
in the postwar South really meant: "That was about equalization after
freedom. That was the cause of that," he said, indicating his acute understanding of the contest over the changing terms of religion, race, and
citizenship, and over the bounds of American religious habitations of
citizenship.

Black clergymen after the Civil War insisted that freedpeople were
equal citizens who deserved just treatment under the law. This was
subversive preaching, especially given the connection of black church
leaders to the Republican Party. The political activism of many clergymen matched the religious rhetoric. Well over two hundred black clergymen held local, state, or national office during Reconstruction. The
first African American to win a seat in the U.S. Senate, Hiram Revels of
Mississippi, was an African Methodist cleric and had once served as pastor of a large free black congregation in Louisville, Kentucky. Ministers
organized and led Union Leagues, working men's associations, civic
organizations, and temperance and masonic societies.

The central role of black churches during Reconstruction showed
how the power of African American religious practices developed
under slavery and in free black communities could become visible,
public, and political. Major urban congregations, such as First African
Baptist in Richmond, articulated the grievances of the freedpeople to
governing authorities. After the war, the church quickly became a focal
point to draw up memorials of protest against continued mistreatment
of people who were now free, including the arrest of several hundred
blacks in Richmond in the summer of 1865 for violating curfew or not
holding passes. In June, 3,000 black Richmonders met to file protests
to the governor and send a delegation to confront President Andrew
Johnson directly.

When Congress held hearings in the early 1870s to document the
results of Klan activity in the South, the extent of violence perpetrated against freedpeople became clearer. So did the extent to which
whites concentrated attacks on black ministers and churches involved

in Republican politics. One testimony among hundreds told the story of Lewis Thompson, murdered in June 1871 by Klansmen. Lewis had gone to preach in Union County, South Carolina. While there, he had been handed a paper with a coffin drawn on it and the notation "Here is the coffin that they have marked out for me if I preach in Goshen Hill township." Thompson, a Methodist minister, defied the threat and preached that night, but then fled the area. Later, in June, he returned to preach again. Klansmen (according to the testimony of other family members) then dragged him from his house, stabbed and castrated him, and dumped his body in the river. Locals feared giving him a burial, as Klansmen threatened anyone who helped his family.

Black and white missionaries in the post–Civil War South, including the black Methodist stalwart Henry McNeal Turner, pursued the work of "political evangelization." They fought to secure religious and political rights for the former bondspeople. He was central to the reemergence in South Carolina of the African Methodist Episcopal Church—the same denomination associated with the Denmark Vesey Revolt in 1822 and exiled from the state as a result.

Born free in 1834 in South Carolina, and by 1848 an avid Methodist, Henry McNeal Turner learned early on the importance of black self-reliance and respectability. In the 1850s, Turner moved to Georgia, the state where he would make his name and career. There, biracial crowds eagerly gathered to hear his powerful preaching. Turner's message was evangelical, and his politics fairly conservative in the context of his day. He would move a long way over the next several decades.

Following service as a Union Army chaplain, Henry McNeal Turner established himself as a prominent AME churchman, missionary, legislator, newspaper editor, and rhetorical firebrand. Remembered later for his caustic editorials advocating black American emigration to Africa and denouncing the American flag, Henry McNeal Turner's major life work was helping to establish the African Methodist Episcopal Church in the South. Turner and his fellows envisioned their religious work as essential to securing full citizenship rights for the freedpeople. Civil rights, church organization, and racial uplift would go hand in hand. By "uplift," they meant imparting education and the norms of proper public behavior to freedpeople left illiterate and untrained by the oppression they lived through in the antebellum South.

REV. H. M. TURNER, CHAPLAIN FIRST UNITED STATES COLORED REGIMENT.

Rev. H. M. Turner, chaplain of the First United States Colored Regiment, 1863
Source: Courtesy of the Library of Congress, Prints and Photographs Division.

Turner also served as a delegate to the postwar constitutional convention in Georgia. In his brief term in the reconstructed state legislature, Turner preached a conciliatory gospel, tried to work together with white preachers and leaders, and urged everyone to consider their common interests together. That message extended into the Civil War and after.

"The interests of white and black are one and the same," Turner proclaimed, for all were citizens in common who should cooperate to reach the same goal of advancing America socially, economically, and morally. Turner pointed out the importance of combining religious and political work. "I have put more men in the field, made more speeches, organized more Union Leagues, political associations, clubs, and have written more campaign documents that received large recirculation than any other man in the State," he said. Meanwhile, white Democratic opponents targeted him, and white Republicans grew jealous of his prominence. He soon lost his political position, a result of an effective coup staged by white Democrats in the Georgia legislature.

After being tossed out of the legislature in 1868, he pointed out his constant efforts at conciliation, including supporting a pardon for Jefferson Davis and approving of literacy restrictions on suffrage and protection for white property owners unable to pay new taxes imposed by the state legislature. Despite all those efforts, he and his black colleagues found themselves removed. Turner thundered, "Because God saw fit to make some red, and some white, and some black, and some brown, are we to sit here in judgment upon what God has seen fit to do. As well might one play with the thunderbolts of heaven as with that creature that bears God's image." Whites attacked defenseless blacks, even though "you know we have no money, no railroads, no telegraphs, no advantages of any sort, and yet all manner of injustice is placed upon us." The "manner of injustice" Turner himself experienced included receiving threatening notes from the Klan. Whites in Macon, Georgia, attacked him after his patronage appointment to be postmaster of the city.

Following Reconstruction, Turner threw himself into church and missions work for the rest of his life. He traveled constantly, edited the official denominational hymnal, and eventually rose to the position of bishop of the AME Church. As early as the 1870s, he began to preach that black Americans should prepare themselves to "assume control of our vast ancestral domain," meaning Africa. Critics blasted him for cooperating with the remnants of the American Colonization Society, a remarkable transformation given that he long been a protégé of the late Senator Charles Sumner of Massachusetts. The overturning of Sumner's Civil Rights Act of 1875 by an 1883 Supreme Court decision seemed to ratify Turner's growing disillusionment. The decision, he said, had made the American flag into "a rag of contempt instead of a symbol of liberty." The court, he said, "wickedly, cruelly and infernally turned us over to the merciless vengeance of the white rabble of the country." He began to articulate the ideas that would later become crucial to the rise of what would come to be called black theology. Turner expressed this sentiment when defending the continued use of the word "African" in the AME denominational title. "The curse of the colored race in this country, where white is God and black is the devil," he insisted, was in "the disposition to run away" from blackness. Turner advocated a different course. "Nothing will remedy the evils of the Negro but a great Christian nation upon the continent of Africa," he said, for in America "White is God . . . and black is the devil. White is perfection, greatness, wisdom, industry, and all that is high and holy. Black is ignorance, degradation, indolence, and all that is low and vile."

When southern-style racism swept the country in the 1890s, Turner blasted American hypocrisy. As editor of the *Voice of Missions* in the last two decades of his life, Turner articulated what later would be called black theology. In the 1890s, as he began missionary work in parts of Africa and read challenges to biblical literalism from the likes of Elizabeth Cady Stanton, Turner left behind his formerly more straightforwardly evangelical readings of the Bible. Just as Stanton critiqued the Bible's use in gendered hierarchies, Turner saw that "the white man's digest of Christianity or Bible doctrines are not suited to the wants, manhood growth, and progress of the Negro. Indeed, he has colored the Bible in his translation to suit the white man." Speaking to the newly organized National Baptist Convention in 1895, Turner first announced that "God Is a Negro," compelling white Baptist home missions organizer Henry Lyman Morehouse to rebuke him: "Talk of this sort is the race spirit gone mad."

But Turner was not finished. In 1898, he published one of his most famous pieces about God and race. In it, he insisted that since everyone else projected a "race" onto God, black Americans had every right to do the same. "For the bulk of you, and all the fool Negroes of this country, believe that God is a white-skinned, blue-eyed, straight-haired, projecting nosed, compressed-lipped and finely robed *white* gentleman, sitting upon a throne somewhere in the heavens." Turner said that he would rather be an atheist or a pantheist than "to believe in the personality of a God and not to believe that He is a Negro." It was "contemptuous and degrading" for blacks to accept the white God handed to them by the theology of American society. Turner died in 1906, memorably eulogized by the great black intellectual W. E. B. Du Bois as "a man of tremendous force and indomitable courage. . . . In a sense Turner was the last of his clan: mighty men, physically and mentally, men who started at the bottom and hammered their way to the top by sheer brute strength."

Throughout the South, black ministers and missionaries forged equally significant lives in political evangelization. Serving the Baptist church and black residents of Georgia at the same time as Turner included William Jefferson White. The son of a white planter and a mother who was probably of mixed Native American and African American ancestry, the ambitious young Georgian could pass as white but self-identified as black. In the 1850s, he worked as a carpenter and cabinet maker. Like Turner, his artisanal skills complemented his preaching abilities, giving him a secure economic base that underwrote his independence into the era of black freedom. As a stalwart of Augusta's free black community, an educational leader, newspaper editor, and political spokesman, White labored for freed African Americans. At the first meeting of the Georgia Equal Rights and Education Association (held at Augusta's historic black Springfield Baptist Church in early 1866), William Jefferson White's eloquent address drew the attention of General Oliver O. Howard, director of the federal Freedmen's Bureau. White also helped to found schools for freedpeople in the growing southeastern Georgia town, including Augusta Baptist Institute, the school that eventually, after its move to Atlanta, became Morehouse College, a critical center for the education of black men (including Martin Luther King, Jr.,) since the late nineteenth century.

In 1880, White began publishing the *Georgia Baptist*. With its masthead reading "Great Elevator, Educator, and Defender of the People," the *Georgia Baptist* was one of the most widely distributed black newspapers in the late nineteenth-century South. The Republican Party activist and pastor of Harmony Baptist Church in Augusta aggressively defended black rights amidst the growing racial turmoil. "The dark clouds of internal discord have gathered in some localities," he wrote after witnessing the racial pogrom in Wilmington (North Carolina) in 1898. He warned that the "irresponsible and irrepressible mobs" were not be satisfied but with the taking of innocent black lives. His hopes later in the nineteenth century that the tides of racial hatred were turning were not realized. After publicly denouncing a local lynching and defending its victim, White's life was threatened. Privately, he was profoundly disturbed by the turn of events. "We seem to be standing on a volcano," he wrote to his son.

White lent vocal support to streetcar boycotts that sprang up in a number of southern cities in the early twentieth century in response to the newly enacted segregation laws on public transportation systems. "The colored people of Augusta are keeping off the street cars because of the revival of Jim Crowism on them, and some of the white papers of the city are howling about it," he exclaimed. "They howl if colored people ride on the cars and howl if they stay off of them. What in the name of high heaven do the white people want the colored people to do?" In 1906, White joined W. E. B. Du Bois, John Hope, and other race leaders to establish the Georgia Equal Rights League. The brutal Atlanta riot of that year again mocked their hopes for a racial truce. Leaders such as White should be exiled from the South, a local white newspaper opined. "The place for them is, either where there are no Jim Crow laws or where it is too hot for street cars. Augusta has no room for such incendiary negroes, and we should waste no time letting them know it." By the time of his death in 1913, White's Reconstruction-era hopes of equal rights for all were a distant memory. Unlike Turner, he never abandoned hope in the United States as a potential land of equality and opportunity for African Americans. Yet the fellow Georgia Reconstruction-era comrades ended their lives at a relative low point for black hopes. They had lived through what historians later called the "nadir" of black life in post–Civil War America.

Both Turner and Jefferson witnessed the rise of the phenomenon of lynching and, more generally, legal and extra-legal violence committed against black southerners in the late nineteenth century. It crested in the tumultuous years of the 1890s. A vividly public and ritualized version of lynching emerged. Participants documented the events. They posed for photographs, sent postcards relating details, and purchased body parts as souvenirs. Upward of 4,000 acts of lynching occurred in the United States from the 1880s to World War II. By the late nineteenth century, roads, railroads, the press, cameras, and other modern forms of transportation and communication aided the communal nature of the spectacles. Crowds gathered for acts of purification. Clergymen pronounced benedictions as men crucified and set afire black bodies. Present at the horrific and well-documented lynching of Jesse Washington in 1916, Baptist pastor Joseph Martin Dawson felt "entirely helpless because five thousand monsters participated and who was I, a lone individual, to do anything about it." The lynching victim in this case was innocent of the crime; the guilty party was soon thereafter found. When Dawson introduced a resolution at a pastor's association denouncing the act of lynching Washington, he later recalled, "to my utter surprise, when they discovered they had burned an innocent man, they found the guilty, the only comment I heard around town . . . was 'Well, it's fine. At last, they got the right Nigger.'"

By the 1890s, many black churchpeople responded to the rise of legalized racial proscription by arguing for a slow rise of African Americans at first through their own institutions. Segregation as social policy could not be defeated, they said, so blacks should promote their own churches, businesses, clubs, masonic and fraternal orders, and social institutions. For religious idealists who had lived through the revolutionary promise of the Civil War and Reconstruction, however, the disillusionment was intense. Henry McNeal Turner articulated the level of despair he heard in rural black communities, where he had spent so much time as a church organizer after the war. In 1890, he explained that black elites in southern cities failed to grasp the degree of oppression in the rural South. While the black establishment would deny the impulse to emigrate, Turner knew the sentiments of the people, including their desire to leave the South, or even the United States, in search of "freedom, manhood, liberty, protection or the right to protect themselves." A few decades later, rural southern followers of Marcus Garvey articulated much the same sentiment. Meanwhile, as will be traced in the next chapter, a black version of the social gospel movement was taking root. It would soon find its institutional expressions in the social outlets created by large urban churches. It also shaped the founding of such political protest organizations such as the NAACP and influenced black churchwomen such as Ida B. Wells-Barnett, Nannie Burroughs, and Lugenia Burns Hope. They pinned their hopes on progressive reform as a way to improve the living conditions of black neighborhoods, reform the behavior of black individuals in and out of church, and protest the new and constricted bounds of habitation set for black Americans in the era of Jim Crow.

RELIGIOUS FREEDOM AFTER THE CIVIL WAR

As the struggle to redefine religion, race, and citizenship became a dominant theme of national politics during Reconstruction, similar issues affected other ethnoracial communities. In each case, as well, the de facto nationally recognized religion of white Protestantism defined what was and was not acceptable religious behavior. If the "bounds of their habitation" were no longer those of slavery, the boundaries would include those recognized by white Christians *as* Christian.

The post–Civil War years saw one of the most significant cases in American history for the history of church-state relations—the *Reynolds* case of 1878. The issue arose over whether the Utah territory had the right to ban polygamy, which was still then part of the official theology and practice of the Church of Jesus Christ of Latter-day Saints (the Mormons). The plaintiff in the case argued that the First Amendment protection of religious freedom extended to a social practice such as plural marriage that was enjoined on members of the Mormon Church. The government of Utah territory arrested and convicted George Reynolds of taking a second wife. He pled not guilty and was tried. Appealing his case, the Supreme Court issued what became a landmark decision in church-state relations. Perhaps most significantly, the Court revisited the debates over religious freedom at the time of the Constitution, attempting to ascertain the original intent of Madison and Jefferson in crafting the classic documents of religious freedom (such as the Virginia Statute of Religious Freedom). The court concluded that "Congress was deprived of all legislative power over mere opinion, but was left free to reach actions which were in violation of social duties or subversive of good order."

Applying that doctrine to the case at hand, they found that, since "the word 'religion' is not defined in the Constitution," searchers must look elsewhere for its meaning, and particularly to the meaning the founders intended to convey. In doing so, the court noted the government position that laws were meant to govern actions and practices, "while they cannot interfere with mere religious belief and opinions, they may with practices." Suppose, for example, that an American religion called for human sacrifice. Obviously, the government would have the right to interfere and prevent such a practice, regardless of the private beliefs of those involved. The same for a woman who desired to practice *sati* and throw herself on the funeral pyre of her deceased husband. Here, the court's chosen examples, drawn from Mormonism and Hinduism, indicated how the justices conceived of religious practices outside the norm. Permitting plural marriage, they concluded, would be equivalent to making the "professed doctrines of religious belief superior to the law of the land, and in effect to permit every citizen to become a law unto himself. Government could exist only in name under such circumstances."

In short, the government had no business prescribing or proscribing belief, but it could regulate conduct provided that the laws were applied to all citizens equally. Much later, in the 1980s, Supreme Court Justice Antonin Scalia employed similar reasoning in a case regarding peyote use by members of the Native American Church who were also employed by the State of Oregon (discussed further in chapter 7). The state, he said, had the right to prohibit peyote use even by card-carrying members of a church for whom that was their central sacrament, because the law was generally applicable to all and neutral in intent.

In making its decision, the court certainly was not thinking about ring shouts among ex-slaves, or the ghost dances among Lakotas, or Mexican American Catholic festivals in the Southwest. Yet the principle it articulated defined dominant American thinking about what the boundaries of religion were. Religious belief per se could not be regulated, but social behavior and legal norms arising from those could. Religious customs were the best barometer of religious freedom. The construction of an urban bourgeois order entailed the creation and enforcement of norms of public respectability, the ways people should act in the public sphere, in ways which discouraged practices that invoked spirits. While a ritual such as the African American ring shout was not specifically forbidden by law, religious norms and denominational leaders pushed it to the outskirts of acceptable religious behavior.

The same was the case for many customs of Latino Catholics (and, to a lesser degree, Italian Catholics), although, in their case, the home or domus-centered nature of their religions provided a natural place of refuge. In other cases, religious customs deemed threatening, particularly those of Native peoples, led to direct conflict, most famously in the Ghost Dance Tragedy at Wounded Knee in 1890 but repeated in a large number of lesser-known cases as well. In many ways, the late nineteenth century saw the apogee of the de facto Protestant establishment. Its cresting paralleled the coming of freedom for African Americans after the Civil War and the influx of Catholic and Jewish immigrants from lands both familiar and strange. The result was a period of a nascent and embattled pluralism emerging through the cracks of the de facto establishment.

ASIAN RELIGIONS IN POST–CIVIL WAR AMERICA

As congressional leaders debated various wordings of what became the Fourteenth Amendment, they began to grapple with what was becoming a more multicultural America. Race issues had been dominated by the struggle over slavery and the place of black people. Later in the nineteenth century, they more centrally involved Indians, Asians, and Latinos. Only admitted as a state in the Union in 1850 and before that property of Mexico and before that the Spanish Empire, Californians first defined discussions of what the place would be for nonwhite peoples in a multiracial America. In drafting the Fourteenth Amendment, Republican congressional leaders faced objections from Californians that, in trying to make citizenship more universal, they might inadvertently enfranchise or otherwise provide the benefits of being citizens to "heathen" Chinese, just then starting to arrive in sizable numbers as laborers in the West. Historically, citizenship had been restricted by race; the nation's first citizenship law in 1790 ensured that the "free white person" was the fundamental unit defining full citizenship rights in the young Republic. Republican leaders sought to extend those benefits, and access to the franchise, to black men as well. They saw this as a fulfillment of Lincoln's call for a "new birth of freedom." Should the new constitutional amendments be written, or construed, too broadly, however, to *all* men for example, then a whole new class never envisioned by many Republicans as citizens would be empowered.

   Democratic opponents of racial equality pointed out the discrepancy in California. Republicans desired to extend suffrage to African American men but deny it to Chinese and others. John S. Hager, a future senator from the state, expressed the common view that "I believe this country of ours was destined for the Caucasian—our own white race." He asked, "Must we not concede there are distinctions which we can neither conceal or deny?" Just as there were many houses in the Father's mansion, so "it might also be said in our Father's family there are many races or species of mankind. We cannot change it by legislation. . . . For man cannot cover what God has revealed." The California legislature subsequently roundly rejected approving the Fifteenth Amendment, which prohibited restricting voting rights according to race, color, or previous condition of servitude. The Republican view, as expressed by a senator from New Jersey, was "not that a man must be a Christian to be a voter, but that it was not our duty to extend the rights of naturalization and citizenship to a pagan and heathenish class."

Several redrafts of the amendment later, the national Fourteenth Amendment extended citizenship rights to "all persons born or naturalized" in the United States, providing just the leeway needed to deny citizenship to those neither born here nor eligible for naturalization. Only fourteen years after the Fourteenth Amendment, Congress subsequently passed the first of several Chinese Exclusion Acts, making it more clear than ever who enjoyed the protections of U.S. citizenship. Writing for the American Home Missionary Society in 1885, the well-known minister and pioneer social gospeler Josiah Strong expressed the common view that Anglo-Saxon control of the United States was God's will. The role of American Christians was to assimilate the feeble races of the world. This meant Christianizing immigrants in order to Americanize them and prepare Americans for the work of saving the world.

Missionaries responded to the scientific racism of the late nineteenth century with their own language that blended and conflated conversion and assimilation. They insisted, for example, that the Chinese, with the aid of missionaries, would be assimilable. William Speer, a Presbyterian minister in San Francisco, was an early defender of the rights of Chinese immigrants, underneath the broader argument that Chinese, like all humans, could be Christianized, Americanized, and assimilated. This was a common stance of mid-nineteenth-century missionaries.

His argument came to some grief when, in 1876, Chinese American businessmen brought to the city Fung Chee Pang, who drew crowds to his lecture on Confucianism. The *San Francisco Chronicle* warned the missionaries and defenders of immigrants against turning over the West Coast to the "dominion of the worst form of paganism in the attempt to convert an inconsiderable few of the benighted heathen to the gospel of Christ." An account of the conversation with Pang parodied the Emerson and Thoreau school of interpretation: "Talk no more of 'feasts of reason' and a corresponding 'flow of soul,' but wrestle with the history, the doctrines, the sayings of the grim old Confucius," the paper wrote, introducing an extended discussion of the "beatitude of Mongolian classics, ethics, morality, and religion." By the late 1870s, the formerly strong mainstream Protestant position in favor of immigration came under sustained and successful attack. Pro-immigration ministers came to be seen as those who would "Mongolize the land in a vain missionary effort to bring the Chinaman to a knowledge of the true God." Disputing the part of the verse of Acts 17:26 which said that God had made of one blood all nations, critics suggested that "it is the economy of Providence that man shall exist in nationalities, and that they shall be divided by the antipathies of race."

By the 1870s, ministers increasingly swam with the growing tide of anti-Chinese sentiment. Some argued that God had protected America for its experiment in liberty. That opportunity was not to be wasted by old evils, idolatry, immorality, and clannishness that came with equal immigration. Chinese immigration was "exposing our whole country and its policy to volcanic eruptions of heathen hosts and abominations." Already "reeling under the burden and force of European debasement," would America now fall under that from Asia? By protecting California, those espousing immigration restriction were also protecting America from an unassimilable heathenism.

Chinese Americans converted by missionaries and Protestants working on the West Coast continued to offer arguments based on the possibilities for Christianization, Americanization, and assimilation. Born in 1849, Jee Gam made his way to the West Coast in 1863, where he settled in the Bay Area. As a young man, he began working as a house servant to a Congregationalist minister in Oakland; Jee Gam himself converted and by 1870 began working to distribute Bibles to the Chinese settled in the Bay Area. He became a member of the First Congregationalist Church of Oakland. He later was ordained as a Congregationalist minister himself,

Portrait of Congregationalist Jee Gam
Source: N. R. Johnston's *Looking Back from the Sunset Land*, 1898.

and he used his position to advance his concepts of Christianity, civilization, and Chinese American political and social rights.

Given the emphasis of white Americans on denying citizenship and basic rights (including voting and testifying in court against whites) to

Chinese Americans based on racial and religious arguments, Jee Gam countered with his own life and message as an example of the universalism of Christianity. Speaking out against the Geary Act of 1892, which extended the Chinese Exclusion Act of 1882 for another decade and required all Chinese to register or be deported after one year, Jee Gam proclaimed that "I am not any less Chinese for being a follower of Christ," for "my love to Jesus has intensified rather than belittled my love for my native country." But by the 1890s, having spent thirty years in the United States, he felt himself an American first. He called Chinese exclusion "un-American, barbarous and inhuman. It is unchristian, for it is contrary to the teaching of Christ." Gam was proud of his sons and daughters; he taught them American patriotism. Thus, it was all the more painful to see unjust and discriminatory laws such as the Geary Act, one which "dishonors America as well as injures my countrymen and native land." The Act withdrew "sacred rights" such as those found in the Declaration of Independence, by specifically requiring of the Chinese measures required of no other nationality in the United States. For Jee Gam, Christianity was inclusive of all: "The beggar can have it as well as the king. The poor can have it as well as the rich; and the negro, the Indian and the Chinaman."

Others joined Jee Gam in joining their Christianity to political activism, particularly in condemning anti-Chinese sentiment and legislation. Chan Hon Fan, head of a Methodist mission to the Chinese in Portland, attacked local white clergyman for their racist sentiments, saying that they had "become great stumbling blocks before a race of benighted souls whom Jesus came to save." Others reminded white Protestants of a basic rationale: converting Chinese in the United States would build up a ready-made mission force to return to China with the word. Ultimately, the arguments failed to persuade a broader public fearful of the consequences of Asian immigration, intent on protecting labor rights for white men, and concerned for the Christian future of America's soul.

INDIAN RACE AND CITIZENSHIP IN THE ERA OF THE DAWES ACT

The same impulse that drove abolitionism and egalitarian ideals of citizenship after the war fed directly into Indian policy. The result, however, was social policy with catastrophic consequences, intended and unintended.

With the end of the Civil War, northerners grew fascinated by the drama of cowboys, Indians, and expansion into lands controlled by "wild" Indian tribes. Missionaries, philanthropists, and legislators bought into the motto: "kill the Indian, save the man." Jesus in this environment became an agent of imperialism. Soldiers, missionaries, and politicians teamed up to take land, but give Native Americans in return the white Jesus. They were to lose their old souls and replace them with those of the Christian citizen. As the American Missionary Association's Charles W. Shelton put it, "The Indian *must go down*. Extermination or annihilation is the only possible solution of the question. . . . You can send to the Indian the rifle and exterminate him in this way . . . or we can send to the Indian the gospel of Christ, this great power of civilization, and through its influence exterminate the *savage*, but *save the man*."

Members of the Indian Rights Association, founded in 1882 by white proponents of civilizing "the Indian," thought it impossible for the Indian as a tribal member to survive the "aggressions of civilization." But, they suggested, his "individual redemption from heathenism and ignorance, his transformation from the condition of a savage nomad to that of an industrious American citizen, is abundantly possible." Since Christ touched the individual, he could refashion souls and citizenship at once. As one leader claimed in 1893, Indians could only be "redeemed from evil" by breaking up the "mass" and as "we get at them one by one, as we break up these iniquitous masses of savagery, as we draw them out from their old associations and immerse them in the strong currents of Christian life and Christian citizenship, and as we send the sanctifying stream of Christian life and Christian work among them, they feed the pulsing life-tide of Christ's life."

The Dawes Act of 1887 was the critical instrument of breaking up tribal lands and ways and replacing them with an American Christian individualism. Written by Massachusetts Senator Henry Dawes, the act divided tribal lands into individual "allotments." Male heads of families received 120 acres and sales of leftover "surplus" lands funded Indian boarding schools. The best known of these schools, such as Carlisle and Pratt, uprooted Native children from widely scattered locales. Often wrested forcibly from their families, the children were punished in the schools for "talking Indian," dressing in traditional clothes, or engaging in "heathenish" practices. The Dawes Act was the legislative culmination of a lengthy discussion about how to implement the philosophy of kill the Indian, save the man. And notably, the act emerged from the same kind of idealistic impulses that had shaped policies of education and citizenship during the Reconstruction. Like the freedman, the Indian could become a citizen; both were members of child races who could be instructed to grow into full adulthood, so the reasoning went.

In the final decades of the nineteenth century, a new messianic challenge emerged to the implementation of such measures of assimilation and Christianization: the ghost dance. It promised salvation for Indian peoples stripped of lands and traditional practices. Its visionaries prophesied the return of the buffalo and the punishment of whites for their sins. The modern dances originated among the Bannock and Shoshones in southern Idaho, found their way to Nevada by the 1870s, and became a deep part of Indian life among a variety of groups in the Rocky Mountains and upper plains.

The Paiute Prophet Wovoka became its most spectacular representative, and his religious innovations reflected his mixed cultural and racial heritage. Wovoka's Paiute father died when he was a teenager. He then was raised by David Wilson, a white farmer, in Nevada. He took the name Jack Wilson. In the late 1880s, suffering from illness and despair, he experienced a series of transformative visions. He took from his native background ideas about controlling the weather, beliefs in dreams and visions, and practices of ritualistic dances. From his white father's Presbyterianism, Wovoka drew resurrection images of the dead in heaven and the leading role of a charismatic preacher figure.

In January 1889, near to the time of a solar eclipse, Jack Wilson/ Wovoka had a near-death experience and a new revelation. Soon, Wovoka came to be seen as, one white testified, "a Simon pure, yard wide, all wool Christ . . . who advised peace and performed miracles which made all people feel good." Ethnologists of the age saw him as fitting the Plains Indians idea of waneika, a Christ "returned to Earth to benefit Native Americans and to punish whites on a second sacrificial go-around." Wovoka rejected direct connections of himself to "the Messiah." Yet on a photograph of himself taken in 1917, he wrote, "I am the only living Jesus there is. Signed, Jack Wilson." Wovoka claimed the mantle

Wovoka, Paiute Shaman
Source: National Archives and Record Administration.

of a prophet preaching the rituals necessary for pan-Indian renewal. One Western agent explained, "He tells them he has been to heaven and that the Messiah is coming to earth again and will put the Indians in possession of the country."

More than a prophet, many envisioned Wovoka as their new Christ. In his study for the Bureau of Ethnology, the pioneering anthropologist James Mooney recorded one curious Indian observer noting that that those living in Paiute land were "anxious to see Christ. Just before sundown I saw a great many people, mostly Indians coming dressed in white men's clothes. The Christ was with them. They all formed in this ring around it . . . I had always thought the Great Father was a white man, but this man looked like an Indian." He instructed everybody to join "the Christ singing while we danced." One Indian, according to Mooney, thought he was beholding the risen Jesus: "I had heard that Christ had been crucified, and I looked to see, and I saw a scar on his wrist and one on his face, and he seemed to be the man."

Jesus as a figure increasingly stood in for the symbolic Indian, standing in judgment of whites. In his rendering of a letter from the Indian Messiah, Mooney said that Wovoka claimed to be revealing and concealing Christ's return and that righteous judgment was about to come: "Do not tell the white people about this. Jesus is now upon the earth. He appears like a cloud. The dead are all alive again."

At Wounded Knee in South Dakota shortly before the end of 1880s, soldiers from the U.S. Army warily eyed Indians who danced continuously for days, fell into trances, and foresaw the deaths of their enemies and the re-creation of an Indian world. Forces both within the military, and from Republican politicians eager to secure new states for their political column, pressured for a public response to the apparent uprising. In late December, the ghost dance turned into a bloodbath. When federal troops led by Colonel James Forsyth attempted to disarm Sioux warriors in South Dakota—warriors who claimed to have no arms—U.S. forces opened fire on women, men, and children. Four days after Christmas in 1890, almost two hundred natives died for living their faith.

Memories of Custer and the epic defeat of American troops at Little Bighorn played directly into the massacre at Wounded Knee. Veterans of Little Bighorn felt they could get their revenge fourteen years later. The political and spiritual leader of the Indian alliance in Montana, Sitting Bull, was killed at Wounded Knee by Indian agency police in a tragic prelude to the larger massacre to come at the hands of frightened and ill-led members of the 7th Calvary. This was the same 7th which had been surrounded, harassed, and killed in substantial numbers by the Lakota/ Cheyenne alliance in Montana which possessed superior numbers, firepower, and tactical savvy. It was the same 7th led into battle by Custer's favorite Irish jig of a battle tune, "Garry Owen," played later to honor the brave soldiers at Wounded Knee who had withstood the treacherous savages (including at least seven infants and a number of boys between five and eight years of age) and received their Medals of Honor.

Perhaps most importantly of all, in both cases (Little Bighorn and Wounded Knee), the political spin machines and telegraph-driven need to feed the sleepless beast of the national news cycle went into overdrive as soon as the events were over. In the case of Wounded Knee, Americans at the time did not really come to know truth; the story of heroic soldiers defending innocent whites held the day. In both cases, when compelled to choose between printing the fact or the legend, the legend, as usual, won. And Wounded Knee ushered in a period that constituted the "nadir" of Native American existence (in terms of population numbers and spiritual despair), much as the advent of Jim Crow and racial violence in the 1890s forced black Americans to confront what seemed to be an endless night of Jim Crow. The hopes of many for remaking American citizenship in the age of Reconstruction met the powerful forces of a rising tide of sentiments of racial supremacy and the "reforging of the white Republic" in the late nineteenth century.

LATINO CATHOLIC ENDURANCE

Jean-Baptiste Lamy, the first Archbishop of Santa Fe, New Mexico, entered New Mexico territory in 1851. Lamy joined a group of European-born priests who sought to rationalize and systematize a Catholicism in the Southwest that they saw beholden to superstitious traditions. One Protestant home missionary late in the nineteenth century summarized the views of Lamy and his fellows in the priesthood as well. As he saw it,

> The people in this place are industrious but they are living in darkness and superstition. They believe in witches. They believe that people turn into cats, and may become men and women again at pleasure. The paganism in this land of Christian liberty would astonish Eastern people. We call it home missionary work. It is as foreign as though the Pacific Ocean separated us from the United States.

The Southwest had become part of the United States through the Treaty of Guadalupe-Hidalgo in 1848, but its people were far from assimilated. Latino Catholicism did not fit within the bounds of habitation white Americans had constructed for what would be recognized as respectable religion.

By 1865, Lamy had recruited thirty-seven priests, erected forty-five churches, and enlisted the Sisters of Loretto to look after schools. Lamy ordered the *retablos* taken down from church walls and replaced with images more akin to French Catholic iconography, in a move strikingly reminiscent of the priests' policy toward Indian religious objects in the seventeenth century prior to the Pueblo Revolt of 1680. In the late nineteenth century, in the period following Mexican independence and into the era of American expansion, bishops derided the perceived decline of religion in the Southwest, comparing it to an alleged golden era arising from early missionary work. In this view, American clergy would now have to fill the vacuum left by the decline of the local church in the Mexican era. The continuance of faith traditions among Latino communities was ignored, for this would call into question their need to be rescued. He also worked to discipline the *Pentitente* brotherhoods and put them under church authority. Some scholars argue that Lamy tried to eliminate the *Penitentes* entirely. The evidence for this is not clear. Certainly, however, Lamy sought to strengthen and centralize church authority over the disparate practices of the region. In doing so, he fought with local Latino leaders such as Padre Antonio Martinez, as detailed in chapter 3.

In Arizona and elsewhere, Euro-American Catholic leaders banned Mexican fiestas and other celebrations. Bishop Thaddeus Amat y Brusi (usually shortened as Bishop Amat), the first Bishop of Los Angeles, feared that public expressions of Latino devotion would simply play into rampant anti-Catholicism. Likewise, in New Mexico, Archbishop Lamy felt that the practices of the *Penitentes* and other groups were "contrary to modern ecclesiastical order and harmful to the image of Catholicism in the eyes of newcomers from the East." The bitter anti-Catholicism of some civil leaders persuaded Lamy even further in his effort to ban practices out of line with what he saw as Church teaching. For example, in administering the sacraments, Lamy queried recipients as to whether they were *Penitentes*, since members were denied the sacrament. Into the early twentieth century, the position of the bishops was represented by Charles Buddy, first bishop of San Diego, who condemned some practices as a "source of scandal" that could "easily weaken the faith of the people," notably public dances during the feast of Our Lady of Guadalupe.

Local Latino Catholics responded simply by resisting efforts to eliminate tradition. At a confirmation in Las Cruces, New Mexico, in the late nineteenth century, the presiding minister, Bishop Henry Granjon, noted the enduring tradition of confirmation and the practice of *compadrazgo* (co-parentage), the extending of family ties to a child's godparents. "You can ask any service whatsoever of your *compadre*," he wrote. The ties that were created made for attachments between families and maintained the "unity of the Mexican population," allowing them to "resist, to a certain extent, the invasions of the Anglo-Saxon race." Mexicans would not learn English but instead "observe their own traditions and customs as they did before the annexation of their lands by the American Union."

The spread of national parishes in the post–Civil War era fostered this observance of "their own traditions and customs" among a multitude of Catholic immigrant groups, including Latino Catholics from Mexico, Puerto Rico, and elsewhere. National parishes posed something of a dilemma for church leaders. On the one hand, the church sought to be more assimilated into American society, to seem less foreign and un-American. On the other hand, the huge waves of Catholic immigrants from diverse lands that came to American shores necessitated separate language parishes. This came in part because of the swelling demand among parishioners for priests who spoke their home languages, respected their saints, and ate their foods. In this sense, Latino Catholics were part of a broader trend. In another sense, they remained separate and unequal, because of discrimination within the church as a body and the difficulty Latinos had in promoting their own to the priesthood. To a large extent, the Irish and German (and, later, Polish) traditions defined mainstream American Catholicism; Latino Catholicism still seemed tainted by its connection to "pagan" Indian ways. Most especially, this included the devotion to *La Morenita*, the Virgin of Guadalupe, the apparition who mythically appeared to the Indian neophyte convert Juan Diego outside Mexico City in 1531.

Mexican American Catholics found some success in the postwar years in achieving national parishes. Latino Catholics in San Francisco in 1871, for example, convinced Archbishop Joseph Alemany to establish Our Lady of Guadalupe. "We believe," they wrote to "Spanish and Latino Americans of San Francisco," that the "happy idea of building a parish church exclusively for the Latino American residents and visitors to this

ever growing city is not only consistent with evangelical doctrine, which
commands us to propagate the faith by means of persuasion and the practice of virtue, but also reestablishes, in this great city, the splendor, bril-
liance, and influence of our race. Even if at present it finds itself in the
backwaters of society, our culture's greatness, dignity, and humanism are
not diminished." Answering fears that Latino Catholics were too poor
and "invisible" to support such a project, the authors insisted that "our
race is invisible because it is the precious stone buried in the soil of this
populous city. . . . Our energy, virtues, and perseverance will make up
for our relatively limited numbers; our self-sacrifice and endurance will
overcome our lack of money and material goods." San Francisco was to
be the "place of encounter between North Americans and the peoples of
our race." A national parish would preserve the language in which Latino
Catholics could best "express their affection, open their conscience, and
lift their prayers to the Lord of mercy—their hearts would never feel ful-
filled or unburdened unless they pray in the sublime language and in the
same prayers their tender mother taught them." Churches with Spanish-
language teaching were "as essential to many members of our race as
faith itself is as essential for salvation." This emphasis on the spiritual
nourishment of the Spanish language in the church setting continued
strongly through the twentieth century, as Latino Catholic leaders fought
the influx of Protestantism in the Latino community as well as the strong
anticlericalism of radicals.

   In Texas, the Mexican Catholic population, numbering about 9,000 at
the time of the Texas Republic, grew to 30,000 Latino Catholics in the
diocese of Brownsville alone by the time of the Civil War, and Latinos
were a large percentage of the 40,000 Catholics in San Antonio in 1870.
At the turn of the twentieth century, Latinos made up close to half of
all Catholics in Texas. The Mexican Catholic population in Texas sky-
rocketed through the early twentieth century, as the demand for migrant
labor pulled working-class Mexicans northward. In Texas, many maintained close ties to Mexican culture and popular Catholicism. Again,
Euro-American priests encountered the opportunities as well as the challenges involved with ministering to their flock. One father in San Benito,
Texas noted that the Mexican Catholics possessed a "great religious mind
in their own way": they were respectful of the religion and of the fathers
and constructed home altars including religious pictures and paintings

that inspired faith. Mexican American Catholics were also solicitous of holy days, leading this priest to conclude that "certainly our Lord will deal leniently with many of these poor people['s] defects and faults when he sees them keeping holy the day of his suffering." In Texas as in New Mexico, images of the suffering Christ moved the people. They reenacted the Passion in dramas, *penitente* rituals, and myriad other forms.

In Los Angeles, from the 1850s to the 1870s, a smaller population, the need for law and order, and the lack of priests and pastors in the area in the 1850s and 1860s effectively required religious cooperation. The arrival in 1856 of Bishop Thaddeus Amat, by birth a Neapolitan, brought a directed effort to guide the Los Angeles Catholic Church into line with Catholic norms, very much as Archbishop Lamy was doing in New Mexico at the same time. The clerics, explains historian Michael Engh, wanted to "segregate Catholics culturally and socially from the mainstream of an antagonistic Protestant American society." Following the rules set down by the Second Plenary Council in Baltimore in 1866, which attempted to regulate the spiritual expressions of the laity and enforce a "uniform adherence to ritual practices, patterns of religious behavior, and forms of prayer," Bishop Amat worked to ensure that "one and the same discipline is everywhere observed." Amat replaced the historic Mexican Madonna as patroness of the diocese with a Roman saint that he remembered from his own childhood. He was also intent on building an impressive cathedral, dramatizing the stability of Roman Catholicism and piety in the new land and magnifying the importance of the offices held by church officials. Amat also sought to limit the influence of secret societies such as the Fenians and Odd Fellows, and in general to separate his people from the growing power of Protestantism in Los Angeles and California.

In the process, he effectively segregated and repressed Latino Catholics, most of whose practices were deemed "superstitious" or otherwise insufficiently spiritual and orderly. Amat and other bishops such as Lamy were in effect responding to the nativist sentiment expressed politically in Know-Nothing groups and political parties. In the process of enforcing national norms of what it would mean to be an American Catholic, though, they relegated Latino Catholicism itself to a secondary status.

By the 1880s, though, the situation changed dramatically, as Protestant populations increased dramatically and Latino Catholics were in relative social decline. Still, even an increasingly Protestant Los Angeles looked like a pluralistic mosaic, with Latino Catholics, a substantial Jewish population, and a growing variety of Protestants (with Episcopalians, ironically, experiencing the most success at first, followed by the Methodists, who established the University of Southern California) creating a diverse local religious picture.

Latino Catholic influence in southern California declined in the early twentieth century. This was because of the "Americanization" of Catholicism as well as the Protestantization of Los Angeles. The relative degree of tolerance in the smaller and pluralistic Los Angeles of the 1850s through the 1880s increasingly gave way to a thriving Protestant majority. A variety of nativist and Protestant supremacist groups such as the American Protective Association grew in influence. The centrally controlled Catholic clergy hunkered down in the struggle against Protestant and modernism. They refashioned a separate Catholic culture, which was responsive to central norms of Catholic doctrine and culture.

As the city and county grew faster than the Catholic Church could attend to their needs, the historic role of the home in Mexican American religion became more important than ever. As one migrant laborer from Mexico put it, "I never go to church, nor do I pray. I have with me an amulet which my mother gave to me before dying. This amulet has the Virgin of Guadalupe on it and it is she who always protects me." Another interviewee said that her grandmother had delineated the three pillars of religion: "Our Lord, Our Lady of Guadalupe, and the Church. You can trust in the first two, but not in the third." Many churches were named in honor of the Virgin, and often the churches were built with funds and labor from the people, with priests only following later. Informal associations and mutual aid societies, such as the *Santo Nombre* for men and the *Asociacion Guadalupana* for women, kept alive Latino traditions, particularly in areas where Mexican priests were unavailable.

CONCLUSION

Latino Catholicism within a pluralist but predominantly Protestant Los Angeles represented a small part of what was becoming the larger American story of race and religion. By the early twentieth century, the realities of pluralism, largely a function of massive immigration, clashed with a revival of Nativism and Anglo-Saxonism, nineteenth-century holdovers given a patina of scientific respectability by thinkers ironically dubbed as progressive. As cities grew more diverse, Protestant activists and anti-immigrant crusaders sought to shape American society in their own image. But the image of American society itself was in the process of transforming what constituted the bounds of American religious and social habitations.

5

Race, Religion, and Immigration

Photograph from the World's Parliament of Religions, 1893
Source: Public domain.

THE CHICAGO WORLD'S FAIR was the place to be in 1893. The gleaming "White City" advertised technological and social utopias to come, while popular cultural attractions out on the Midway stretching outside the fair offered more physical thrills as well as curiosities and exotica (including human beings) on display. The fair brought together large audiences for intellectual fare, as well. The young historian Frederick Jackson Turner, fresh from his PhD from the pioneering American history program at Johns Hopkins University, gave his talk "The Frontier in American History," the American historical equivalent of the Big Bang. In it, he enunciated how movement westward explained American development and implicitly warned of challenges to the American character to come now that the age of the frontier was over. Meanwhile, spiritual leaders from around the world gathered at the World's Parliament of Religions. In many ways, the gathering there proved to be as significant for American religious evolution as Turner's address was for American historical thought.

John Henry Barrows, pastor of the First Presbyterian Church of Chicago and organizer of the late nineteenth-century religious assembly, offered these words of welcome to the representatives of the "great world religions" gathered at the Parliament: "We are met in a school of comparative theology, which I hope will prove more spiritual and ethical than theological," with men "determined to bury . . . our sharp hostilities." No sectarian flag of any religion would fly over the Parliament. Instead, the goal would be to "broaden and purify the mental and spiritual vision of men." Barrows envisioned the Parliament as part of a culminating vision of teaching the great truths of liberal Protestantism, the summa of all religions: "Christendom may proudly hold up this Congress of the Faiths as a torch of truth and love which may prove the morning star of the twentieth century."

The event veered from the path Barrows planned for it. In particular, representatives of Hinduism and Buddhism stole the show. One of them, Swami Vivekananda, vaulted from the Parliament into celebrity status. As, in effect, the first Hindu missionary to America, he explained how Hinduism consisted not in a struggle to believe in dogma, but "in realizing; not in believing, but in being and becoming." Protestants hypocritically lambasted Asian religions, but, he rhetorically asked, when a Christian goes to church, "why is the cross holy, why is the face turned toward the sky in prayer? Why are there so many images in the Catholic Church, why are there so many images in the minds of Protestants, when they pray? My brethren, we can no more think about anything without a material image than it is profitable for us to live without breathing." For Hindus, "all the religions from the lowest fetichism to the highest absolutism mean so many attempts of the human soul to grasp and realize the Infinite, determined by the conditions of its birth and association, and each of these mark a stage of progress, and every soul is a child eagle soaring higher and higher." And ultimately, "in the heart of everything the same truth reigns." The true religion would be the same for all. With no location in place or time, it would be infinite like God, with no place for intolerance. It would "recognize a divinity in every man or woman, and whose whole scope, whose whole force would be centered in aiding humanity to realize its Divine nature." It would constitute the sum total of the world's religions but still have "infinite space for development; which in its catholicity would embrace in its infinite arms and formulate a place for every human being."

Vivekananda's fame attracted followers, imitators, and proselytizers. One of the most prominent, Swami Paramananda, established Vedanta societies in East Coast cities and a retreat in southern California. Famously, he argued that Jesus had instructed followers to love their neighbor, while Hindu sages explained *why* you were to love your neighbor. "Until we have this realization of oneness with the Supreme, it is not possible to rise above all our differences and feel true love for our fellow-man. We too often forget that Christ Himself was an Oriental." The Aryans of India, he added, never condemned any faith because "universal tolerance is the dominant note of their teaching . . . and those who follow sincerely any one of these manifestations will surely reach the final goal of Truth." Men had within themselves the "germ of perfection," so "why then talk of sin?"

The visions propagated by the engineers of the White City and the universalist religious message promoted by the Parliament came at a transformative moment in post–Civil War American history. From the 1870s to the mid-1920s, approximately 24 million immigrants entered the United States. Some came from traditional sending destinations, including the British Isles, Germany, and Northwestern Europe. Many more came from Italy, southern and eastern Europe, Russia, and Mexico. Just to take one decade as an example, from 1900–1910 about 1,800,000 people arrived from northern Europe. By contrast, over, 3,800,000 came from eastern Europe (including Russia) and another 2,400,000 from southern Europe, particularly Italy. The bulks of those immigrants were Jews and Catholics and were numerous enough over a several decade period to make America's status as an evidently Protestant and Christian nation seem far less secure then it was before. In the 1920s, Congress attempted to wrest the flow of immigrants back to traditional sending countries. The National Origins Act of 1924 limited quotas of immigrants from any country to two percent of the number from that country who were residing in the United States in 1890. Over the next generation and a half, until the Hart-Celler Act of 1965 radically altered immigration patterns again, the American population settled, religiously, into a Protestant-Jewish-Catholic triad. That was reinforced by the national unity and rhetoric of Judeo-Christian civilization that came out of the World War II era.

This chapter examines the evolving notions of religion and race from the tumultuous years of the late nineteenth century to the World War II era. While the 1924 Immigration law seemed to seal a revitalized definition of whiteness now defined as Anglo-Saxon heritage, intellectual currents of cultural pluralism arose in the era which would soon fundamentally reshape America's heritage of race and racism. Concepts of race, religion, and citizenship were contested, reformulated, and shaken up. Through the period, powerful nativist sentiments, expressed in law, contended with rising pluralist ideas, expressed mostly in the reality created by immigrants and by intellectuals responding to a different vision of America. Contending forces shaped the American bounds of religious habitation during this era. Abstract intellectual ideas, messy social realities, and religious thinkers and activists intent on promoting pluralism all played a part.

Here, we follow the complicated tangle of race, religion, nativism, and pluralism in this era through a comparative examination of Jews and Asians in early twentieth-century America; the rise of the social gospel movement, including religious liberals and radicals who helped to form the NAACP; the advent of William Seymour and the Holiness-Pentecostal tradition in American religion, which brought with it an emphasis on interracial worship, faith healing, premillennialist thought; the racism and nativism of novelists such as Thomas Dixon, films such as *Birth of a Nation,* and pseudo-intellectual writers on the character of immigrants such as Madison Grant; and the responses of Indian leaders in the Progressive Era to the effects of the Dawes Act and the complicated tangle of Indian nations and citizenship. At the intellectual and abstract level, ideas of racial purity remained powerful, but contended with younger notions of a pluralist vision for America. At the grassroots level, popular cultural forms of religion reshaped racial interactions at everyday levels; the full significance of that development would be seen in decades to come. All these clashing forces fundamentally reshaped ideas and practices by which Americans governed the bounds of habitation of race and religion.

RACE, RELIGION, AND IMMIGRATION

The immigration of a new generation of Jews from Eastern Europe and Russia offered a serious challenge to America's vaunted claim to tolerance. Jews had a long history of relative acceptance in American life. Jews had been accepted in colonial America, so much so that George Washington famously wrote to a Jewish congregation in Rhode Island that "happily, the Government of the United States, which gives no bigotry no sanction, to persecution no assistance, requires only that they who live under its protection should demean themselves as good citizens . . . . May the children of the stock of Abraham who dwell in this land continue to merit and enjoy the good will of the other inhabitants while every one shall sit in safety under his own vine and fig tree and there shall be none to make him afraid." A relatively small number of Jews, largely of German origin and highly assimilated into Western culture, arrived through the first two-thirds of the nineteenth century.

But the latter decades of the nineteenth century, and going forward to World War I, witnessed a far more massive migration, fueled by pogroms and economic decline in Eastern Europe and Russia. In Cincinnati, Rabbi Isaac Mayer Wise invented Reform Judaism as a religious mechanism by which Jewish people could maintain some traditions while participating fully in the modern world and in American democracy. Late nineteenth-century Jewish immigration challenged this pact, for Russian and Eastern European Jews brought with them an Orthodoxy and a "foreignness" that concerned the same kinds of nativists and Protestant thinkers who decried the transformative immigration patterns of that era. The relationship of Jews to whiteness seemed more in question, as the predominance of German Jews from an earlier era gave way to immigrants from stranger lands further east in Europe.

Nativist Protestants responded partly by attempting to reclaim Jesus in the defense of Protestant whiteness. They distanced Jesus from his Semitic heritage. Madison Grant served as a key propagandist. A New York attorney and self-styled public intellectual, he warned of imminent threats to America's racial stock and heritage. In his influential *The Passing of the Great Race: The Racial Basis of European History* (1916), he raised the specter of the millions of "new immigrants" flooding into the United States during the previous thirty years. He worried

Madison Grant
Source: Image from *Our Vanishing Wild Life* (1913).

that nonwhites—Italians, assorted Eastern Europeans, Russians, Jews, Asians—would spell doom for America. It would kill America's heritage in being settled by the Nordic race. To avoid "race suicide," as Grant called it, white Americans must realize who was truly white.

"Nordic" whites, of course, stood atop the racial hierarchy. Since, as he argued, "[m]ental, spiritual and moral traits are closely associated with the physical distinctions among the different European races," the greatest moral teacher in world history—Jesus—must have been white and not Jewish. Grant grounded his proof in how biblical Jews responded to Jesus: They "*apparently* regarded Christ as, in some *indefinite* way, non-Jewish." Grant pointed to the history of European art for painting Jesus as Nordic. "In depicting the crucifixion no artist hesitates to make the two thieves brunet in contrast to the blond Savior . . . Such quasi-authentic traditions as we have of our Lord strongly suggest his Nordic, possibly Greek, physical and moral attributes."

Yet Judaism was a religion, one respected by Christians who understood themselves to be in the same religious universe as Jews—as opposed, for example, to Asian Buddhists. Thus, while Judaism as practiced might pose some challenges to a Protestant or Christian Republic, it could be incorporated, for Jews were not racialized in the way other groups were. As an ethnoreligion that provided the historic basis for the Christian story, Judaism gradually found its way into the American language of religious tolerance and pluralism—the so-called Judeo-Christian tradition, a term that took hold in the 1950s but can be traced back conceptually to earlier decades.

This immigrant story also compelled a reexamination of the meanings of race, ethnicity, and religion. If Jews could be understood as at least partially white, and with a religious narrative that spoke to deep American understandings, such as the Exodus story, the same could not hold true for Asians and Pacific Islanders. They were never eligible for assimilation into whiteness. Asian immigrants practiced diverse varieties of religious traditions but none that counted as deserving full respect. And yet, the Asian religious presence was ambiguous in one sense: "Oriental" religious thought had long since drawn the intense interest of American intellectuals and seekers, most especially the Transcendentalists who translated "Eastern" religious texts into English. Moreover, spectacular religious events, such as the World's Parliament of Religions of 1893, introduced certain strands of Eastern Indian thought. Many Americans already were participating in alternative, metaphysical, "New Thought," and other movements that self-consciously drew from their invented versions of "Eastern traditions." Thus, while Asian immigrants and their everyday religious practices met discrimination, harassment, and out-right exclusion, "Eastern" religious thought drew respect. Americans from Ralph Waldo Emerson and Henry Steel Olcott, called America's first "white Buddhist," to the followers of New Thought and "Unity" all found themselves drawn to their own versions of what constituted Asian religious thought. They prepared the way for the later Beat writers and poets such as Allen Ginsberg and Gary Snyder.

Below the level of the intellectual or the exotic, however, Asians and their religions were racialized in a way that made it impossible to claim the privileges of whiteness. Starting with anti-Chinese riots through the late nineteenth century, and with legislation such as the Chinese Exclusion Act of 1882 which remained in force until the 1940s, white Americans could not conceive a place for Asians in the republic. They signified their disdain in the 1917 immigration law creating an "Asiatic Barred Zone," prohibiting immigration from most of Asia and the Pacific Islands. Part of this resistance and hostility derived from economic factors, such as working-class men's attacks on Chinese railroad workers and Japanese farmers in some of the richest regions of California. A considerable part, too, came from the sense of religious unassimilability. Aside from those who might have been Christian converts, Asian immigrants simply had no historic fit in dominant notions of American religiocultural nationalism.

The presumed whiteness of Jesus even shaped legal arguments about citizenship for immigrants. When Syrian immigrant George Dow faced a challenge to his eligibility for American citizenship in the 1910s, the Syrian American Association rallied to his defense. Syrians were not "Asiatic," they protested, unless one counted Jesus, "the most popular man in history," as "Asiatic." Syrian Americans reasoned that "if Syrians were Chinese then Jesus who was born in Syria was Chinese." They played on some lower court decisions about Dow, some of which had suggested that the Semitic heritage of Syrians meant they could be classed as white. Jesus's Jewishness helped to save Dow. He won the case and remained in America, white and free.

The case of Bhagat Singh Thind in 1923 made the contrasting point. In 1920, Thind, a Sikh from northern India, sued for citizenship under the claim that he was scientifically classified as a Caucasian and was therefore white. A unanimous Supreme Court decision, however, ruled against him on the grounds that whiteness was equivalent to assimilability, and that therefore a "Hindoo" (never mind that he was a Sikh) was not in anyone's actual working definition of whiteness.

Thind's lawyers had argued he was Caucasian in the scientific sense. The court replied that the founders and those who wrote the Naturalization Act of 1790 were not familiar with the term "Caucasian." They instead were thinking of "free white persons," and it would be "illogical to construct words of common speech used in a statute into words of scientific terminology" when the science of the early twentieth century would not have been known to the framers. This was in fact the opposite of the premise of Dow, which had relied on an analysis of "scientific" terminology regarding race. The court argued that the language of the Naturalization Act of 1790, and the reigning concept of whiteness then, had to be respected. The justices wrote, "It may be true that the blond Scandinavian and the brown Hindu have a common ancestor in the dim reaches of antiquity, but the average man knows perfectly well that there are unmistakable and profound differences between them today." The mere possibility of some sort of common Aryan language in common proved nothing. After all, the justices reasoned, millions of Negroes spoke English, and no one presupposed they had any common ancestors with people from England. The framers, therefore, really only intended to "include only the type of man whom they knew as white" within the common understandings of the day, when immigration was almost exclusively from northern Europe. People from various parts of Northwestern Europe—English, Irish, French, German, Italian, Scandinavian, and so on—quickly melded into American life and culture, whereas those from the Punjab "would retain indefinitely the clear evidence of their ancestry," and Americans "instinctively recognize it and reject the thought of assimilation." The 1917 Act of Congress prohibiting all Asian immigration, including of people from India, clearly expressed the general "attitude of opposition to Asiatic immigration generally" and of a similar attitude toward "Asiatic naturalization as well, since it is not likely that Congress would be willing to accept as citizens a class of persons whom it rejects as immigrants."

Like obscenity, apparently, the justices could not define whiteness, but they knew it when they saw it—and it did not include anyone wearing a mysterious headdress. Not a citizen but a legal resident, Thind married a white woman and later became well known as a sort of proto–New Age author of books about the ancient wisdom of the East, playing off the very stereotypes that had defeated him in court.

RACE AND THE RISE OF THE KLAN

If the immigration of millions of people from around the world to the United States and spectacular events such as the World's Parliament of Religions represented the social and intellectual turn to a kind of Protestant-directed pluralism, the intensely nativist and racist responses from the era signified the continued power of the religion of whiteness. The turn to the social gospel in the early twentieth century, usually seen as part of an era of progressive reform, also could spur racially illiberal sentiments. In the South, in particular, progressives supported segregation and prohibition together. They sought to reform politics and clean up cities, but also (in some cases) to promote eugenics as a scientific program to improve the human race. They demanded child labor laws and educational reforms for the benefit of whites. And some sensational pastors of the era capitalized on the national move toward racism. One particularly important exponent of white southern racialism was the North Carolina minister, novelist, and stage actor Thomas Dixon. Perhaps more than any other single figure from the era, he turned history into lightning.

A former Southern Baptist minister turned popular novelist, Dixon helped transform the suffering savior of the Lost Cause into a herald of American power. Dixon's most famous works, *The Leopard's Spots* and *The Clansman*, sanctified white supremacy. He set out to convince the nation that Klan members were the real protectors of God's racial plan for the United States and world. "We believe," one of his fictional white characters explained, "that God has raised up our race, as he ordained Israel of old, in this world-crisis to establish and maintain for weaker races, as a trust for civilisation, the principles of civil and religious Liberty and the forms of Constitutional Government." Dixon determined that the Anglo-Saxon family was the core of the American nation and God's plan to redeem the world. In Dixon's historical imagination, the KKK was a new church, formed "for their God, their native land, and the womanhood of the South."

"'Do you not fear my betrayal of your secret?'"

Image from Thomas Dixon's *The Clansman* (1905)
Source: Reproduced at *Documenting the American South*, http://docsouth.unc.edu/
southlit/dixonclan/dixon.html.

Through Dixon, the cross became the ultimate symbol of the Klan. Indeed, the popular association of burning crosses and white robes with the Klan stems not from their origins in the Reconstruction era but from Dixon's fictions and their popularization in the epic film *Birth of a Nation*. Not for the first, or last, time in American history, a piece of racialized popular culture "created" reality and history for a viewing public. Duly outfitted, Klansmen of the 1910s and 1920s became champions of Christ. Scene descriptions and illustrations accompanying the story in *The Clansman* showed Klan members and their horses with large crosses emblazoned on their robes. Then, at secret ceremonies, Klan members raised flaming crosses to proclaim their allegiance to Christ and white supremacy. The pioneering film director D. W. Griffith picked up on these images and placed them directly into *Birth of a Nation*. In one of the film's promotional posters, atop a rearing and powerful horse, a Klansman thrust the "fiery cross of the Ku Klux Klan" into the air.

When the new Klan formed after *Birth of a Nation*, members placed Jesus and the cross squarely at the center of their white supremacist culture. They did so effectively, influencing local and state politics through considerable swaths of the country. The opening prayer of the officially prescribed Klan ritual of the 1920s called members to adopt "the living Christ" as the "Klansman's criterion of character." One Texan put it simply: Jesus "was a Klansman." Christ's act upon the cross perfectly symbolized the Klan's turn to Jesus as the emblem of suffering, pain, service, and sacrifice. "Since Jesus's wounded body bore the sins of the world," a Klan historian explained, "a member should follow Jesus's example. . . . It was not necessary to sacrifice one's life, but to sacrifice one's selfhood for the greater body of Klan membership."

The white robe, its symbols, and burning crosses became emblems of the Klan's claim to Christ. As one minister in the movement surmised, "I think Jesus would have worn a robe." A Klan newspaper explained, "Pure Americanism can only be secured by confidence in the fact that the Cross of Jesus Christ is the wisest and strongest force in existence." The Klan's cross, uniting faith and nation in one symbol, had been "sanctified and made holy nearly nineteen hundred years ago by the suffering and blood of the crucified Christ, bathed in the blood of fifty million martyrs who died in the most holy faith, it stands in every Klavern of the Knights of the Ku Klux Klan as a constant reminder that Christ is our criterion of character." Illustrations from Klan histories of the age had Klansmen in the place of Christ's disciples. They helped him pass out bread and fish to the multitudes without food. On another occasion, Jesus distributed the "Tenets of the K.K.K." as spiritual and civic nourishment for "100% Americans."

The white, militant Christ of the suffering South had become an American emblem of segregation and white supremacy. When *Birth of a Nation* appeared, it was a national, not just a regional, hit. Klansmen now marched in public and exercised significant influence in local and state governments. From the end of the Civil War to the early 1920s, Jesus in the United States became a symbol of white supremacy. For many, and certainly for those with white nationalist sympathies, Jesus's whiteness defined his essence.

RACE AND THE SOCIAL GOSPEL

Figures such as Madison Grant and Thomas Dixon and his ilk represented the nativist side of Progressive-Era thought. Ultimately, however, the most powerful movement (over the long term) to emerge from this time came from those who interpreted the social gospel as a call to swim against the deeply held currents of American racism.

In the mid- to late nineteenth century, pastors, writers, working-class union organizers, and women involved in missions work developed a broad-based "social gospel" movement. It may also be called social Christianity. The one unifying element in the diverse coalition emphasized applying the lessons of Christianity to social life, and in doing so to make the social order more in keeping with God's plan for human life. Social gospelers came in all varieties, and enunciated a multitude of ideas and programs, but that one general concept united them.

Historians once criticized the leaders of the social gospel movement of ignoring issues of racial justice. More recent studies have shown how deeply social gospelers were involved in racial issues, including in the formation of the NAACP and other organizations for racial reform. Moreover, there was a significant black social gospel movement, whose overriding emphasis obviously lay with issues of social justice. The towering figures here include W. E. B. Du Bois, Ida B. Wells-Barnett, and Richard R. Wright, but there were many others besides.

In some sense, black churches were a natural home for social gospel ideas, for black religious institutions had no choice but to address directly social issues. After Reconstruction, there was no other institution in black communities that could do so. Political outlets for those ideas were very few and mostly powerless.

From possessing an almost frightening power, to languishing as frustrated fellowship, the black church came under scrutiny both for its potential and its problems. Black churches had to be all things to all black people, something no institution could do. Writers and activists such as W. E. B. Du Bois struggled to understand how spiritual power implicit in the black churches could be unlocked and then unleashed into a social world whose entire premise rested on the degradation of African Americans. Philosophers, preachers, and scholars contemplated the black church as a spiritual force, a potential base for power, and a sociological drag on progress. Moreover, from W. E. B. Du Bois forward, those who studied black religious institutions (dominated by black Baptist churches) veered between visions of liberatory potential and sociological explorations of why these poetically powerful institutions so often apparently failed to act as engines of social progress. Du Bois pioneered this in his essays in *Souls of Black Folk* as well as his landmark sociological study *The Negro Church*.

As a scholar and social scientist, Du Bois was often critical of the black church as an institution for its increasing insularity, its focus in the twentieth century on internal growth and power politicking, and its inability before the civil rights movement to utilize its enormous resources effectively on behalf of African American people. At the same time, however, Du Bois as a poet and sensitive essayist understood the kind of powerful work going on in the rituals and the ostensibly "otherworldly" preaching emanating from black pulpits.

The black social gospel movement coalesced around newly formed organizations such as the NAACP, in large "institutional churches" in cities such as Chicago and Atlanta, and with intellectual, college-educated men and women such as Du Bois, John Hope, and Mary Church Terrell. They refused to accept the bounds of habitations handed down to them by American society.

The best example of a southern black institutional church where the minister preached the social gospel was Henry Proctor's 1st

Congregational Church in Atlanta. Seeking to serve the body, mind, and spirit of his congregants, Proctor took the pulpit at First Congregational in 1894. Historically, the church had been a biracial congregation pastored by whites. By Proctor's tenure, however, the congregation was all black, as Congregationalist churches in the South followed the larger pattern of racial separation in religion. Proctor immediately doubled the church membership to four hundred, in part through his efforts at making church activities more relevant to the everyday lives of congregants. He launched a local chapter of the Christian Endeavor Society, a nationwide organization of Christian youth, and a Working Men's Club. Proctor had stayed in Atlanta even during the riots of 1906, when white gangs attacked African Americans on the street and set fires to black neighborhoods. After the brutal melee, he served on a local biracial "Committee on Church Cooperation," where he tried to dispel rumors of race riots that could set tense southern cities ablaze. He condemned the social and political apathy of white ministers and tried to align himself with progressive forces in the white community.

Proctor eventually fled to Atlanta to take up a pulpit in Brooklyn. In doing so, he followed the pattern of the Great Migration of African Americans through the middle years of the twentieth century. The churches such ministers pastored in the North were virtually by definition social gospel, or institutional, churches, as they provided vital help to communities denied access to full job opportunities, citizenship rights, and public services. Those churches met a series of stiff challenges to conventional black Christianity. Some emerged from new institutions such as the African Orthodox Church that came out of the movement engineered in New York City by Marcus Garvey, an advocate for African emigration; others came from a panoply of relatively anonymous religious entrepreneurs, both Christian and others, who offered black folk alternative spiritual visions and homes. One of the most important of those was Holiness/Pentecostalism, the most significant American religious movement of the twentieth century.

EARLY PENTECOSTALS AND RACE

There was another challenge to the bounds of habitations in American religious life, as well. That came not from the intellectual class, but from ordinary men and women seeking an outpouring of the spirit. They burst onto the scene in the Holiness and Pentecostal movement. Their theology insisted on believers achieving a complete purification of the spirit and possession by the Holy Spirit, often evidenced by speaking in tongues and other visible manifestations. While the movements came from many sources and bases, the single most important was the work of William J. Seymour (1870–1922), a black Louisianan who moved to Los Angeles in 1906. From there, he led a series of spiritual revivals that quickly attracted international crowds. More than any single moment, the Azusa Street revivals in Los Angeles sparked the worldwide movement of Pentecostalism.

The relationship between white and black believers in early Pentecostalism emerged most interestingly and ambiguously in one of the fledgling movement's originary moments in Los Angeles. There, Pentecostalism first drew widespread public attention and spread to the rest of the nation. Two key figures in the history of Pentecostalism in the South were present at Azusa: William J. Seymour, a Louisiana native who led the Azusa Street revivals and the early Apostolic Faith Mission; and Charles Harrison Mason, a black Mississippian by birth converted to Pentecostalism at the Los Angeles meetings, and later a founder of the Memphis-based Church of God in Christ.

Born in 1870 in Louisiana, as a young man William J. Seymour traveled frequently, worked odd jobs in Indianapolis and Cincinnati, and contracted the smallpox that permanently damaged his left eye. In 1903, the future prophet began attending a series of meetings in Houston led by Charles Parham, a white holiness preacher. Following a policy of segregation mandated by the location, Parham exiled Seymour to the hallway and generally showed little interest in his black devotee. But Parham's preaching brought Seymour under conviction and persuaded him of the third work of the baptism of the Holy Spirit that would be evidenced by speaking in tongues, the culmination of conversion and sanctification.

In 1906, Seymour answered a call to preach for a congregation in Los Angeles affiliated with the young Church of the Nazarene, a small holiness sect. Upon his arrival, he began teaching the tongues doctrine, the key theological innovation that distinguished Pentecostalism from its holiness antecedent. Fearing heresy, church members prevented him from reentering the church. Seymour took a remnant from the congregation to a series of services he led first in a member's house, and then to a tumbledown building in south central Los Angeles. Using some packing cases as his pulpit, Seymour preached quietly but earnestly for a handful of listeners. "The devotees of the weird doctrine practice the most fanatical rites, preach the wildest theories and work themselves into a state of mad excitement in their peculiar zeal," wrote a *Los Angeles Times* reporter at the scene. "Colored people and a sprinkling of whites compose the congregation, and night is made hideous in the neighborhood by the howlings of the worshipers, who spend hours swaying forth and back in a nerve-racking attitude of prayer and supplication."

After Seymour's reception of the Spirit in April 1906, the movement grew quickly. Seymour's revivals attracted a motley crowd of whites, blacks, Mexicans, Europeans, and Asians. The elaborate homemade network of the Holiness/Pentecostal press helped to further the excitement that "the fire spreads," to use their favorite descriptive metaphor. Seymour established the *Apostolic Faith* to publicize the awakening. Some 50,000 copies of the paper circulated nationally. An early white participant and the revival's most meticulous recorder, William Bartleman, wrote that "Brother Seymour was recognized as the nominal leader in charge. But we had no Pope or Hierarchy. We were brethren."

Seymour attempted to restrain emotions by preaching low-key sermons and insisting on the priority of salvation first over more apparently spectacular demonstrations of spiritual power. He saw the movement of God's spirit as validated first by the evidence of love in the believer. Tongues speech was not the only or even the most important signifier of a true faith. Despite these attempts at deliberate self-control, early participants remembered Azusa as a time when the Spirit broke down intellectualism and ratiocination. As one participant remembered, "and we noticed that those who were down on their knees praying, begun speaking in other tongues. And that was my first introduction in Pentecost . . . nobody trying to urge them on to something, it was just simply God opening the windows of heaven and throwing down upon them, the blessings that they themselves could not contain." As another southern-born participant put it, "I, being southern born, thought it a miracle that I could sit in a service by a colored saint of God and worship, or eat at a great camp table and forget I was eating beside a colored saint, but in spirit and truth God was worshipped in love and harmony."

Seymour's multiethnic movement valued spirit over hierarchy and empowered women, African Americans, and others in marginal status to follow the lead of the Spirit and preach the word. In that sense, Pentecostalism was a spiritual movement which, in its actual early practice, worked against racism and segregation in churches. The interracial nature of Pentecostalism historically has undermined racist practices in Christian churches, not so much intentionally as by the presence of people together seeking the spirit. As was the case with other evangelical movements earlier in history, the eventual institutionalization of churches to carry on the work tended to put in place the kinds of hierarchies (including racial ones) that the religious revolutions had originally moved to combat. Nonetheless, Pentecostalism today remains a massive international phenomenon, with tens of millions of adherents in the "Global South" (Latin America and Africa in particular), and with a religious message that values the action of the spirit foremost. In some cases, moreover, Pentecostal ministers directly confronted racist exercises of power. In Washington, D.C., the leader of one large black Pentecostal congregation held a celebratory "wake" upon the death of Theodore Bilbo, who was a longtime Senator from the state of Mississippi and one of the most egregious racists ever to serve in Congress.

In the early years of southern holiness and Pentecostalism, from the 1880s to the 1920s, dozens of independent evangelists, musical itinerants, and faith healers combed the South. White and black evangelicals joined the new movement, opening up new sanctified churches and denominations. Over time the Church of God in Christ (COGIC) emerged as by far the most influential expression of black Pentecostalism.

It sprang from the work of the evangelist and organizer Charles Harrison Mason (1866–1961). Born to parents who had been slaves, Mason grew up intending to be a minister. "It seemed that God endowed him with supernatural characteristics," his daughter wrote, "which were manifested in dreams and visions that followed him through life." In the early 1900s, Mason walked from town to town in the Mississippi Delta, spreading holiness teachings. Yet he was not satisfied with the second blessing of sanctification. Like other early Pentecostals, he sought a yet more profound spiritual experience. He found it at the Azusa Street revival, where he received the third blessing at the hands of William J. Seymour. During a night of prayer, Mason saw a vision. Upon awaking, he cried out for the culmination of the work of sanctification. Soon he felt himself levitated from his seat. "There came a wave of glory into me," as he described it, "and all of my being was filled with the glory of the Lord. So when He had gotten me straight on my feet there came a light which enveloped my entire being above the brightness of the Sun. When I opened my mouth to say glory, a flame touched my tongue which ran down in me. My language changed and no word could I speak in my own tongue." Upon returning home, he felt that the "Spirit had taken full control of me and everything was new to me. I soon found out the Lord was teaching me and giving me new songs. I asked Him to give me the interpretation of what was spoken in tongues for I did not understand the operation of the spirit." He soon found himself bursting with "all kinds of spiritual utterances."

Early Pentecostals recognized Mason's special powers of discernment. And Mason's preaching skill garnered considerable attention. As he proudly recounted his early career, the Holy Spirit through him "saved, sanctified and baptized thousands of souls of all colors and races." Mason enticed crowds of whites and blacks to see him in action. In Nashville in 1916, for example, he attracted a sizable audience to a city auditorium. "Many of the best white people of the city attended the meeting," Mason claimed. "The Holy Spirit through me did many wonderful things." A series of services in Little Rock in 1919 produced the same effect, as "God so wonderfully wrought His power among both white and black, sanctifying, baptizing, and healing." In 1933, the church's newspaper, *The Whole Truth*, reported that "both white and colored testified of the wonderful healing power of God" at the COGIC annual convention in Rocky Mount, North Carolina.

Mason's creation became a significant force in American cultural life, in large part through its inspiration for new forms of popular music. COGIC meetings resounded with spirited expression and powerfully hypnotic music employing repetitive chanted phrases. The origins of American popular music in the twentieth century come in significant part from the joyful noise in Holiness and Pentecostal churches, where a blue note and a back beat got married to a gospel message and melody. That was a dynamic combination of race and religion, which transformed American culture.

SHERMAN COOLIDGE AND THE PROGRESSIVE INDIAN

Idealists and abolitionists who had led the fight against slavery and in support of black rights after the Civil War increasingly turned their attention to "the Indian" (a term always singularized in that way, much as was done with "the Negro") in the 1880s and 1890s. Native peoples, now clearly subjugated and colonized in the American republic, faced two alternatives: assimilation or extermination. Or so went the dominant thought of many Protestant leaders in the decades after the Civil War. Forming groups such as the "Friends of the Indian," they created Indian boarding schools, intending to teach a younger generation the arts of civilization. They also persuaded Congress to pass the Dawes Act of 1887, which broke up communal property on Indian reservations, allotted plots of land to Indian families for purposes of farming, and sold off or leased the remainder of the land, the proceeds going to fund those same Indian boarding schools. Protestant and Catholic organizations divided up Indian tribes for purposes of mission work, and those with the best reputations for dealing fairly with Indians in the past, the Quakers, took charge of the national missionizing endeavor.

The result mocked the idealism which had motivated Protestant philanthropists. African Americans found ways to turn Christianity into a force for liberation, regardless of the motives of the white Christianizers. For native peoples, however, the idealistic motives of many of the Christianizing groups turned out to have disastrous consequences. The 1890s probably represented the nadir of Native American life and population for all of American history since colonization. The ghost dance episode at Wounded Knee, South Dakota, in 1890, resulting in the massacre of more than two hundred Lakotas at the hands of U.S. Army personnel baffled and frightened by Indian religious ritual, stands as the low point of white-Indian relations in the post–Civil War era.

Native Americans were kept within the bounds of their habitations, usually on reservations. The results were unsatisfactory for those who believed they should be assimilated into the dominant society. For Native Americans in the post–Civil War era, religious resistance appeared increasingly futile, but controversies over religious assimilation tore apart many communities. The Bureau of Indian Affairs repressed native religious practices in Indian boarding schools. There children were punished for "talking Indian," appealing to "medicine men," or otherwise practicing parts of their cultural heritage. Images of the white Jesus, and literally clothing Indian children with the garments and "look" (especially in haircuts) of white civilization, pervaded the behavior norms at the schools. According to novelist Rupert Costo, "When the Christians took the Indian children off to boarding schools, the minister used to lead the children into the chapel and point up to the picture of Jesus, with long flowing hair, and tell the Indian children that they were going to learn how to be just like that man, Jesus. After this statement, the minister would send all the Indian boys off to get their hair cut short."

Government officials also repressed adult Indian religious ceremonies and practices still deemed heathenish. Thus, regulations in the 1920s attempted to delegitimize or stamp out native dances held at Indian Pueblos in New Mexico and Arizona. In 1921, Circular 1665 directed agents of the Bureau of Indian Affairs to discourage or prohibit all types of native ceremonies, particularly including religious ones. While social dancing was certainly acceptable, Commissioner Charles Burke said, immoral or heathenish dances were to be condemned:

> The sun-dance and other similar dances and so-called religious ceremonies are considered "Indian Offences" under existing regulations, and corrective penalties are provided. I regard such restriction as applicable to any dance which involves acts of self-torture, immoral relations between the sexes, the sacrificially destruction of clothing or other useful articles, the reckless giving away of property, the use of injurious drugs or intoxicants and frequent [and] or prolong periods of celebration which bring the Indians together from remote points to the neglect of their crops, livestock, and home interests; in fact any disorderly or plainly excessive performances that promotes superstitious cruelty, licentiousness, idleness, danger to health, and shiftless indifference to family welfare. . . .

During the Progressive Era, a variety of Indian voices tried to clear a path toward Indian respectability and citizenship. They created organizations such as the Society for the American Indian; published books that defended Indian rights; proclaimed their Christianity and urged Indians to leave behind cultural ways no longer appropriate in a modernizing America; and fully aligned themselves with the values of progressive reformers. One of these progressive Native reformers, Etes-che-wa-ah, or "Runs on Top," took the Anglo name Sherman Coolidge and became an exemplar of what many hoped for in terms of Indian life in the Progressive Era. Born in the Northern Arapaho tribe in the early 1860s, he became an Episcopalian minister in the early twentieth century and leader of the Society of American Indians and the Indian Rights Association. Not as well known now as the author Charles Alexander Eastman, author of *The Soul of the Indian* and numerous other works, Coolidge was central to Progressive-Era debates about race, religion, and Indianness. He came to represent a category that, for many, did not exist —an educated and prosperous Native who could interact equally with Christian middle-class leaders of his day.

As a boy, Coolidge's father died in a violent conflict with a rival tribe. A United States Army officer named Charles Austin Coolidge adopted him. As a young man, Coolidge attended an Episcopalian seminary in Minnesota and became an Episcopal Priest in 1885. Later, he took a college degree at Hobart College in New York and subsequently moved to the Shoshone Indian Agency and Episcopal mission at the Wind River Reservation in Wyoming. In 1902, after a courtship of five years, he married Grace Darling Wetherbee, the daughter of a wealthy New Yorker who had come to Wyoming for Indian mission work. Coolidge remained in Wyoming for twenty-six years, pastoring a church at the Shoshone agency and overseeing chapels that ministered to Arapahos on the Wind River Reservation. He also taught at the Wind River Boarding School and took a number of other jobs at the agency. In 1910, he moved to Oklahoma, where he worked in an Episcopal mission among the Cheyenne and Southern Arapaho for three years. He became a founding member of the Society of American Indians. In 1919, he moved to Colorado and pastored the Church of the Good Shepherd in Colorado Springs as well as another congregation in Denver.

Coolidge criticized representations of Native violence in popular culture, charging Buffalo Bill in particular with exploiting Indians and reinforcing "the fear with which all Indians are regarded by children." More importantly, the work of the society took on centuries of perception and distortions of Indian life. At best, members could expect to make only a little headway in counteracting those. He added, "Such pictures of

Rev. Sherman Coolidge (1862–1932)
Source: Photo: BAE GN 00010B 06077500, National Anthropological Archives, Smithsonian Institution.

the pioneer days grossly misrepresent the Indian race. Indians are naturally a peace loving people instead of the cruel savages usually shown in pictures. The red man never killed for the joy of killing. The pioneers they regarded as invaders and the Indian fought to protect his home and family."

Beyond internal conflicts within the organization, there were issues difficult for anyone to manage. Coolidge was an advocate for assimilation, the breakup of reservations, and educating Indians into Anglo-American ways of life and culture. "Don't let our people neglect their opportunities; let them realize that they must compete in life's race, and in the conditions of our American civilization," Coolidge argued, embracing a Darwinian concept of race struggle. He sought to use the Society for American Indians toward the "revitalizing and cherishing of race pride," and to encourage pan-Indian cooperation toward addressing the needs of Indian people.

Regardless of his efforts to promote civilization, and to present himself as the representative Indian man for the new age, Coolidge remained, like all Indians, a curiosity, someone to be observed. And Coolidge's emphasis on progressive citizenship faced the reality that whether Indians could be citizens remained questionable, at best. In the Indian Reorganization Act (sometimes called the Indian New Deal) of 1934, John Collier and other Indian reformers reversed these practices of the last two generations. The Indian New Deal terminated the "allotment" scheme of the Dawes Act and allowed for Indian religious and cultural practices. Here, religion and race were still connected, but in a way that could be valorized rather than condemned. A coming generation of Indian rights activists built upon that foundation, leading to the American Indian Movement and movements for cultural revival a generation later.

THE LATINO SOUTHWEST

After 1848, with the incorporation of huge parts of the Southwest into American territory, including the territory of New Mexico, Protestants saw new home mission territory populated by those who practiced forms of Christianity threatening to the Protestant majority. With Catholic and Jewish immigration dramatically increasing and the incorporation of large portions of Catholic country into the United States, the Protestant future of the country appeared to be under threat. Works such as Josiah Strong's *Our Country* made it clear that Catholicism was a threat to the "fundamental principles and institutions" of the country.

New Mexico could be made a test case. As a writer for the *Rocky Mountain Presbyterian* explained, New Mexicans were American citizens "and yet unassimilated, foreign, and in some measure hostile to the genius of our American institutions." What was required was an "early and persistent introduction of the leaven of Protestantism," especially through public education. Protestants, especially Presbyterians, responded, sponsoring a sizable home missionary effort, including a number of women who made careers out of missions work. They became involved in early efforts to create a social welfare state. Presbyterian schoolteachers explained the dilemmas faced by Latinos trying to decide whether to send their children to public or Protestant mission schools, which were spreading throughout the region: "It must needs take the spirit of a martyr to deny the established religion, the forms and ceremonies of which have been for generations a part of the customs of the people." It required much courage, another wrote, "for these people to stand up against all the manners and customs of the church in which they were born and bred, and in the face of all their relatives declare themselves Christians." The most successful of the teachers became part of the community. They looked to be leaders, teachers, and arbitrators of social conflicts that came up in local communities.

In the twentieth century, church leaders looked increasingly with suspicion on national parishes, fearing they represented too much segregation and reliance on ethnic enclaves. Ironically, it was during the era of segregation in American life that the segregated "national parish" in Catholic life fell out of favor. "It is the wish of the Holy Father that national churches as far as possible be dispensed with in the United States," wrote the chancellor of the diocese of Los Angeles. Many, including Cardinal George Mundelein of Chicago, felt that national parishes simply fed anti-immigrant and anti-Catholic sentiment, because it allowed Catholic immigrants to remain apart from American life and thus vulnerable to attacks from Protestant nativists. Moreover, immigrant children often deserted the church because they saw the national parishes as stuck in an old-world past.

In 1939, Cardinal Francis J. Spellman, New York's archbishop, banned the creation of national parishes, insisting that "integration" should be the desideratum of the Catholic ministry, and that the desertion of home national parishes by the second- and third-generation immigrant children left the church saddled with decaying and emptying church structures. In its stead, the Catholic Church would strive for universality, detached from national traditions and ethnic loyalties. In portions of Texas, New Mexico, and California, however, the sheer preponderance of Mexican American populations created de facto segregated parishes. The church continued to work toward integrated parishes. As one Mexican Catholic official explained it, "We are American Catholics. The Church is one. We must certainly bring the Latin American Catholics to church by means of devotions in Spanish and by contact with priests in their own language, but our aim must ever be to assimilate and incorporate them into parish life." Meanwhile, Mexican American Catholics in San Jose petitioned for a national parish, insisting that they wanted "a church of their own, where they can worship God according to their devotions and customs . . . have easy access to confession in their own language at any time, understand the sermons at Sunday mass, receive the sacrament of matrimony from a priest of their own race, who understands their psychology and customs, and finally where they can feel at ease in a Church of their own, without fear of humiliation due to racial discrimination which unfortunately still exists, even among Catholics." Without national parishes, Mexican American Catholics remained in "missionary status" and had little opportunity to develop their own church leadership. The result, not surprisingly, was friction and tension within parishes that serviced largely Mexican American Catholic populations with Euro-American priests. The historic anticlericalism particularly of Mexican men was only reinforced in such a setting.

In Los Angeles, the Mexican population grew from less than 1,000 in 1900 to nearly 100,000 in Los Angeles proper by 1930, with another 100,000 scattered through Los Angeles county. Nonetheless, despite the population increase, the relative power of Latino Catholicism was in rapid decline. An increasingly segregated Latino population congregated in *barrios*. Catholic priests intent on Americanizing the church and replacing homegrown rituals of Californio days with standard Catholic rites fought with a population who sought to protect the unique blend of customs that made up Latino Catholicism. *Frontera* Catholicism was heavy with rituals not requiring the presence of clergy, which was often an uncertainty in frontier-era California. For example, the practice of *compadrazgo* involved assigning godparents for children to assist in raising the child and adopt him or her in the event of a parent's death. Such communal ties, which could easily incorporate Anglo settlers or other outsiders, bound together community members and remained strong well after the U.S. conquest of California.

In 1936, Mexican Catholics in Los Angeles began publishing *The Guadalupan Voice: Journal of Mexican Culture.* Guadalupe increasingly became a transnational symbol, her meanings being transported from Mexico to East Los Angeles and back again. The first issue came out at the same time as the establishment of a Guadalupe center, and the paper advertised and promoted Guadalupe pilgrimages. Pilgrimage groups came from Mexico to visit Los Angeles. All this came at a time when official religious devotion remained relatively low. A study conducted in Los Angeles in the 1950s showed that parishioners in East Los Angeles attended Mass irregularly, if at all, with the parish clubs and societies mostly kept up by a "few old faithfuls." As one priest told an interviewer, "The old families will light candles before their Guadalupe statue at home, but you'll never see them at Mass on Sunday."

In the World War II era, the Americanization of the church, always incomplete, met up with the continuing streams of immigrants who refreshed Mexican Catholicism. Archbishop Robert Emmet Lucey led a major transition toward connecting Latino Catholics with issues of social justice. As a young priest, Lucey took an active interest in working-class issues, encouraging unions and publicizing the principles favorable to organized labor from *Rerum Novarum* and other official statements of Catholic doctrine. Named archbishop of San Antonio in 1941, he put his energies into pursuing justice for ordinary Mexican Americans. For example, he called a conference for clergy emphasizing issues of social justice that was, as one participant said, "as far to the left as the thinking of the San Antonio Archdiocese had heretofore been to the right." He was especially enthusiastic about his project the Confraternity of Christian Doctrine, whose role it was to spread Catholic doctrine among parishioners who might not have access to Catholic education. He also chaired the Bishop's Committee for the Spanish Speaking, one of the first efforts of the Church to recognize and respond to the special needs of Latino members. Despite criticisms from other bishops, he used the committee to draw attention to the plight of braceros. Lucey and Raymond McGowan of the National Catholic Welfare Conference pressed tirelessly for the needs of Hispano Catholics. In one pastoral letter draft, which other bishops refused to sign, they explained that "the greatest root of the trouble is that the first English-speaking people came here as conquerors and have tried ever since to rule as oppressors . . . instead of as brothers of the Spanish speaking in the development of a civilization that will bring both groups together. Yet the conquering attitude still prevails. . . . Hardly anywhere in the United States is greater or more systematic injustice done to and suffered by the Spanish speaking of our dioceses. . . . The injustice done them is a disgrace." Lucey pressed the church to minister to the Latino community in ways that would respond directly to their needs. Lucey paved the way for the activism generated from the Cesar Chavez generation, a topic covered in the next chapter.

CONCLUSION: OF ONE BLOOD

The 1924 immigration law had tried to resituate Protestantism more securely at the center of America, but Protestant organizations themselves took the lead in advocating a more plural America. Racism and nativism remained powerful forces and significantly affected social life and legislation. The Native Origins Act of 1924 represented the culmination of efforts by a generation of nativists to right the ship (as they saw it) of American immigration toward its historic roots in northern and Western Europe. They sought a renewal of white, Protestant America. The Klan did the same, and the latter-day Klan of the twentieth century focused its animus on Catholics and Jews in northern cities more so than their historic enemies of southern blacks.

The immovable object of racist nativism, however, met the irresistible force of a diversifying America. Immigrants radically transformed demographics, especially of urban America, and even in the heartland of white Protestant America people responded to the reformist sentiments of the social gospel and looked to alternative spiritual expressions. The organizers of the World's Parliament of Religions had sought to contain the riot of religious diversity under the big tent of liberal Protestantism, but the complicated currents of religion and race in American history can never be so easily corralled. And, in the civil rights years, they were about to explode the historical foundations of America's deep-rooted patterns of religious racism.

6

Religion and Civil Rights

The Color of Power

"THEY SAY THAT FREEDOM IS A CONSTANT STRUGGLE," civil rights activists sang during some of the most soul-wrenching movement days in Mississippi. They might well have been describing the long and tortuous journey toward civil and religious freedoms for ethnoracial communities in American history. The African American civil rights movement arose from a long history of struggle and turmoil. The major national figures are well known, if not particularly well understood (especially Martin Luther King, now tamed into a fairly harmless national saint rather than seen as the economic and social radical that he was). Even less known are the heroic efforts of those who fought Jim Crow in the courts and in their own neighborhoods and locales for decades leading up to the critical movement times of the 1950s and 1960s. In doing so, they fought against a long history of religious racism, as narrated in this book.

A long civil rights movement stretched from the black social gospel, discussed in chapter 5, to the late twentieth century. Yet the movement as a self-conscious political force—a *movement*—can still be analyzed in the post–World War II era as a distinct historical phenomenon. The struggle for human and civil rights took a central place in the American consciousness in these years—the *King years*, as historian Taylor Branch calls them. Not surprisingly, for African Americans, Latinos, and Native Americans, religion assumed a central place in quests for freedom.

This chapter narrates a few of those struggles and also covers the growing numbers of whites (many from religious communities) who identified themselves as coworkers in the fight. They understood that when some were not free, all remained in chains. It focuses particularly on the

African American civil rights movement as a dramatic challenge to one long narrative about religion, race, and rights in American history. The chapter also examines Cesar Chavez and the Latino farm workers movement as well, tracing the parallels as well as the divergences of religion, race, and rights among Mexican American Catholics. Biographically, the lens will zoom in here on the theologian and humanist Howard Thurman, his protégé and Congress of Racial Equality founder James Farmer, the longtime feminist activist Pauli Murray, the Mississippi freedom struggle icon Fannie Lou Hamer, the civil rights leaders Martin Luther King and Fred Shuttlesworth, and the Mexican American activist Cesar Chavez. Deploying elements of their religious traditions in distinct ways, all of them transgressed the boundaries of American racial habitations. And all of them staged a constant struggle for freedom.

THE CHURCH AND THE MOVEMENT

Since the early twentieth century, black churches had come under severe fire for being "otherworldly," too concerned with preaching the joys and terrors of the other life to address the pressing concerns of black Americans in this one. Black churches certainly served important functions of sustaining communities in difficult times. They provided necessary social, recreational, and political outlets for a people denied access to public facilities and political power. Yet, in constructing internal defenses against the external ravages of Jim Crow, black churches often became depoliticized, especially compared to the central political role they had played during the heady days of Reconstruction after the Civil War (1865–1877).

And yet it is not so remarkable that the civil rights crusade drew so much of its strength from churches. Or, more accurately, from church people and select ministers. For it took deep religious faith to sustain the thousands of black southerners who stood up in the face of white southern power. It took spiritual sustenance to endure the petty daily harassment as well as more explosive acts of terrorism (beatings, bombings, kidnappings, and lynchings) that stalked activists who sought to "redeem the soul of America," as the manifesto of the Southern Christian Leadership Conference (SCLC) proclaimed as its mission. While many churches, through indifference or fear, closed their doors to the civil rights crusade, church men and women made up the majority of the rank-and-file of the movement. They filled jail cells and engaged in acts of nonviolent civil disobedience. Religious imagery undergirded the movement. Ministers and church activists provided much of its leadership, moral passion, and steely commitment. They empowered a crusade to undermine the historic Christian mythic grounding for destructively hierarchical ideas of whiteness and blackness. For them, black lives mattered spiritually. The historically racist grounding of whiteness as dominant, blackness as inferior was radically overturned in part through a reimagination of the same Christian thought that was part of creating it in the first place. As one female sharecropper and civil rights activist in Mississippi explained in regard to her conversion to the struggle, "Something hit me like a new religion."

Early scholarly studies followed in the wake of media attention given to King, Malcolm X, and movement leaders and celebrities. But scholars soon uncovered the "local people" who did much of the actual work of the struggle. This most especially included women, who made up the bulk of church membership. It also included the long history of civil rights thought that emerged and developed through the twentieth century through figures such as Howard Thurman, James Farmer, and Pauli Murray.

THURMAN, FARMER, AND THE LONG
HISTORY OF CIVIL RIGHTS IDEAS

Howard Thurman and James Farmer were in the generation between "the nadir" of African American life from the 1880s to the 1910s, and the civil rights movement itself. Together with figures such as Benjamin Mays, Richard R. Wright, and John Hope, they educated figures who reshaped the bounds of habitations of race and religion in American history.

Born in 1899 in Daytona, Florida, Thurman's first influence was the Young Men's Christian Association (YMCA). The YMCA functioned as one of the primary vehicles for carrying on the social gospel movement in the early twentieth century. It was a waystation for numerous

Howard Thurman (1899–1981)
Source: Freebase Public Domain.

southern liberals and radicals seeking to apply their Christian training into real-world social problems. The YMCA and YWCA also sponsored numerous speaking tours, international visits, and brought together people from widely varying backgrounds and gave them the opportunity to forge youthful crossracial alliances. Thurman later rejected some of the strictures imposed upon him by the Victorian ethics and conduct required by the YMCA, but it was an important training ground for his growing immersion in social gospel ideas.

Thurman later attended Morehouse College in Atlanta, a city he returned to frequently over the next decades. His bitter experiences with the overt racism of the southern city, which was never "too busy to hate," stayed with him. They soured him even as his training at the historically black Baptist Morehouse College with the likes of Benjamin Mays (who became a lifelong friend) nurtured decades of cooperation and friendship. After receiving theological training in Rochester, New York, he served as a nationally prominent minister and educator at Howard University in the 1930s and 1940s. From his post there, he crisscrossed the country on speaking engagements, began some of his first significant writing, and struggled to balance his thoughts on both the potentialities as well as the limitations of Christianity. In addition, he investigated the dilemmas of the universal message of Christianity and the particular expressions of it within the American racial hierarchy.

One turning point in Thurman's life came in 1935. He traveled with his wife Sue Bailey Thurman as part of the "Negro delegation" of the American Christian Student Movement. At first, he was reluctant. He did not want to be put in the position of defending indefensible practices in American Christianity. Once persuaded, he sought out audiences with prominent Indian thinkers and writers, including Rabindranath Tagore and Mohandas Gandhi. Traveling originally in India, he gave talks in Ceylon. A lawyer there peppered him with questions concerning the racial hypocrisies of American Christianity, and whether other religions might better express the aspirations of black Americans. In February, the Thurmans and a few others conversed with Gandhi for three hours. Arguably, the conversation changed the course of American race relations from that time forward.

Much of the conversation hinged on the meaning of the word non-violence, originally *Ahimsa* in the Sanskrit. Gandhi explained how the word did not come across fully in English, with the negative *non-* at the beginning. In reality, nonviolence was a metaphysical force, a truth that underlay the seemingly endless violence of human life. Always given to a love for the mystical, Thurman was fascinated. Sue Thurman, however, pushed Gandhi on how to apply these ideas in a context where black Americans faced lynching. Much as he replied later when challenged on whether nonviolence had any relevance for Jews facing Nazi exterminationist policies, Gandhi reached for the concept of self-immolation, meaning a complete removal of one's self from contact with the source of the evil. By some accounts, at the end of the talk, Gandhi mused that "if it comes true it may be through the Negroes that the unadulterated message of non-violence will be delivered to the world." By Thurman's own account, Gandhi ended the meeting by pointing out that the greatest enemy of Jesus in the United States was Christianity itself. Either version plausibly expresses Gandhian sentiment, but the former became the tagline that was published in an account of the meeting published the following year. Leaders at the founding meeting of the SCLC two decades later remembered it; they understood themselves to be carrying out Gandhian principles of social struggle.

Coming home from his visit to India, Thurman had new visions for what would be required for racial transformation in American life. After his epic encounter with Gandhi, Thurman kept a heavy teaching and lecturing schedule through the country. At the North Carolina College for Negroes in 1942, he told an audience of the gulf between democracy and the American way of life. Blacks, he believed, would be "largely responsible for the soul of America. We are called at this moment of crisis in our nation's history."

He planned what later became the Church for the Fellowship of All Peoples, founded in 1944 in San Francisco. It was one of the first self-consciously multiracial congregations in American history. Meanwhile, he spread the Gandhian gospel and planted the seeds of what would become the ethic of nonviolent resistance to white supremacy in America. He worked out his ideas, expressed later in *Jesus and the Disinherited*, that Jesus represented the oppressed in American society. Thurman had come to see, during the war, that segregation was in effect a will to dominate, and that it could only be defeated through powerful forces of resistance. His goal, as historians Peter Eistenstadt and Quinton Dixie explain, was to "rip people from their complicity and complacency with evil. Only in this way would people in power relinquish 'their hold on their place. It is not until something becomes movable in the situation that men are spiritually prepared to apply Christian idealism to un-ideal and unchristian situations.'" Full preparation to do nonviolent battle with Jim Crow, Thurman said, would require "great discipline of mind, emotions, and body to the end that forces may not be released that will do complete violence both to one's ideals and to one's purpose."

One of Thurman's most prominent intellectual mentees was Martin Luther King, who frequently quoted Thurman in his sermons. King frequently turned back to Thurman's classic *Jesus and the Disinherited*. In December 1955, at the beginning of the Montgomery bus boycott, King urged the crowed that the protests should be shaped by "the teachings of Jesus," that they must love their enemies, and concluded: "We, the disinherited of this land, we who have been oppressed so long, are tired of going through the long night of captivity. And now we are reaching out for the daybreak of freedom and justice and equality."

Sitting in his class at Howard in the late 1930s, where he was a Divinity school student under Thurman's tutelage, James Farmer, soon to become one of the founding members of the Committee (later Congress) of Racial Equality (CORE), remembered penetrating philosophical questions, the point of which was to challenge students to think beyond becoming complicit in the American racial system of oppression. Born to a family a Texas Methodists, Farmer grew up witnessing the scars of segregation all around him, and determined to do something when he could. With his training from Howard Thurman and others, Farmer became one of the founding members of CORE in Chicago in 1942. From its beginnings, Farmer later remembered, CORE determined that people, not experts or professionals, should lead the struggle for racial justice based on the principles of nonviolent direct action. CORE members helped to spread the practices of sit-ins in the 1940s. They initially focused their efforts on segregated institutions in Chicago. Later, Farmer and a group of others from CORE organized the Freedom Rides of 1961, when groups of integrated passengers boarded buses traveling through the Deep South, intending to test Supreme Court cases mandating segregation in interstate travel. The violence and bombings that met some of the travelers gripped the nation and dramatized the realities of segregation in the region. Two years later, Farmer involved himself in organizing the March for Jobs, Freedom, and Justice in Washington—now known as the March on Washington, when a quarter of a million people heard Martin Luther King deliver his most famous address.

The radical legacy of Thurman, Farmer, and CORE eventually found its way to the ministers and church communities in southern cities who began organizing boycotts and crusades early in the 1950s, leading up to Rosa Parks and the 381-day Montgomery bus boycott from 1955 to 1957. Meanwhile, in some of the toughest, meanest places in the South, individuals such as Fred Shuttlesworth braved years of violent attacks in carrying on the struggle of nonviolent resistance.

Electrified by the *Brown* decision and his sense of God's hand moving in history, Shuttlesworth's civil rights career blossomed in the 1950s. He felt divinely inspired to defy a response to the banning of the NAACP in Alabama imposed by the state authorities. Resisting more senior ministers who urged moderation, Shuttlesworth and his followers organized the Alabama Christian Movement for Human Rights (ACMHR).

He saw the new group as part of a "worldwide revolution which is a divine struggle for the exaltation of the human race." Repeated attempts on his life only enhanced his personal authority and charisma.

In the early 1960s, as movement leaders struggled to find a way to capitalize on their earlier successes, Shuttlesworth led an interracial conference in Birmingham on "Ways and Means to Integrate the South." The success of the gathering convinced Shuttlesworth to pressure King and the SCLC leadership to choose Birmingham for their next crusade. "There are certain places that have symbolic meanings," as one participant put it, including the town infamously known as "Bombingham." After the meeting, true to form, bombers struck Bethel Baptist Church (where Shuttlesworth had preached) for the third time since 1956. Shuttlesworth told black Birminghamians that he possessed no "magic wand to wave nor any quick solution by which the God of segregation can be made to disappear," but had only "myself—my life—to lead as God directs." After suffering a severe beating while trying to enroll his daughter in a school, he lay near death on the ground but heard the voice of God telling him, "You can't die here. Get up. I got a job for you to do." Of his courageous actions, he later reflected, "I really tried to get killed in Birmingham. I exposed myself deliberately, and I felt [that] if I did give my life that the country would have to do something about it." Shuttlesworth placed himself squarely in the "contest for justice and righteousness" from the Old Testament to the present. He saw the biblical parable of good and evil being waged in places like Birmingham. When James Farmer of CORE came to Montgomery during the Freedom Rides, Shuttlesworth escorted him through a mob surrounding a church. Miraculously, the crowd of hostile whites opened up and allowed them to pass. Farmer attributed this to Shuttlesworth's well-deserved reputation for near insanity in pursuit of justice. For Shuttlesworth, it was more akin to God opening up the Red Sea. Reflecting on the years of violence he had experienced, Shuttlesworth predicted the logical conclusion of the white South's course: "whom the gods would destroy, they first make mad. The tragedy of our city and state today is that madness has been substituted for sanity." Yet the movement would not "curse and abuse those who curse and abuse us," for love would prove the superior force. "Water hoses tried in vain to drench a fire that wouldn't go out," Shuttlesworth said of the movement in Birmingham.

PAULI MURRAY AND FANNIE LOU HAMER

Much like Thurman, Farmer, and Shuttlesworth, longtime female activists in the mid-twentieth century indelibly shaped the struggle that would transform the country in the 1960s. Grassroots organization depended on black southerners whose deep religious faith emboldened them to action. As one female activist in 1960s Mississippi put it, "I had found it in the Bible that all men were created equal and I didn't understand that how come that this was my constitutional right and I couldn't have that. I got mad and I was determined that I wasn't gonna take no more. I realized that I was angry and that I had really felt this all of my life." Like so many others, she married the language of evangelicalism ("I had found it in the Bible") with the tenets of the American civil religion, how "this was my constitutional right and I couldn't have that."

They were also inseparable in the mind of Fannie Lou Hamer, who personified the fortitude and vibrant religious imagery of the movement. Daughter of a sharecropper in Ruleville, Mississippi, Hamer rose to prominence in the 1960s as a liaison between "local people" and national civil rights leaders. "Her faith in God is pervasive and in a sense dominates her life," a northern admirer wrote. "There is a prophetic, messianic sense about her— an awareness, an electricity, a sense of mission which is very rarely absent." In 1962, at a Student Non-Violent Coordinating Committee (SNCC) meeting in a rural church, Hamer and a few others volunteered to register for voting. This serious act of political defiance against the state regime earned them a beating in the county jail. Two years later, Hamer eventually won a seat in the Mississippi Freedom Democratic Party's delegation (sent as a protest against the all-white official state delegation) to the Democratic national convention of 1964. Hamer incited Lyndon Baines Johnson's special ire as she delivered an impromptu national address explaining why the Freedom Democratic Party would not settle for the compromise of taking two seats on the official (all-white) state delegation. Queried by reporters, Hamer responded with an impromptu narration of black Mississippians who had risked their lives simply for trying to exercise citizenship rights. Hamer felt that "actually working with these kids that they call radical and far left like SNCC I've seen more Christianity there than I've ever seen in the church."

Hamer's magnetic charisma extended to local people and a national audience, including scores of student volunteers in Mississippi. She used her knowledge of the Bible in public rebukes of the timid. As she told one group of black Mississippians, "We are tired of being mistreated. God wants us to take a stand. We can stand by registering to vote—go to the court to register to vote." Christ would side with the sharecroppers in Mississippi during their struggle. Answering the inevitable charges that civil rights workers were agitators and communists, she retorted, "If Christ were here today, he would be branded a radical, a militant, and would probably be branded as 'red.'" Christ was a "revolutionary person, out there where it was happening. That's what God is all about, and that's where I get my strength." Summing up her life's work, she explained, "We can't separate Christ from freedom, and freedom from Christ."

Fannie Lou Hamer represented a black folk southern religious tradition activated on behalf of civil rights. Another set of activist women came from those with long experience working in the North at the same time as figures such as James Farmer were creating CORE. One was Pauli Murray (1909–1985), who carried on a remarkable career as a civil rights activist, early feminist, scholar, lawyer, teacher, political candidate, author, professor, and finally in her last ten years Episcopalian minister. From the time she wrote a letter of frustration to President Roosevelt in 1938, she was also a correspondent and friend to Eleanor Roosevelt, who was President Roosevelt's emissary to the black community. This was not surprising. She had, after all, applied for graduate school training at the University of North Carolina as early as the 1930s, and spent time in jail in 1940 for protesting outrageous treatment given to black defendants in court cases in Virginia. In 1942, she joined James Farmer and others to form CORE and remained active in the movement in the subsequent decades.

In the 1960s, Murray attended law school at Yale. During the civil rights years, she combined her twin interests in advancing the status of African Americans and of women, In the 1970s, she felt called to take ordination orders in the Episcopal Church and entered intensive study in seminary at the age of 63 to pursue this final calling. She and other early female ministerial applicants raised a storm of controversy in the Episcopal Church and other denominations, but Murray was no stranger to controversy, nor to rejected applications and conservative resistance. Murray received her ordination in 1977, becoming the first female

Pauli Murray in 1946
Source: Library of Congress Prints and Photographs Online Catalog, http://www.
loc.gov/pictures/item/94500294/.

Episcopal minister, made the more remarkable given her status as an African American, her age, and her varied career that led her to this point. In her memoir, Murray reflected on the frustrations she experienced as a believer denied full privileges in her communion and at the same time on the solace and strength that her faith afforded.

As she later recollected, it was her "growing feminist consciousness" that led to her "battle with the Episcopal Church over the submerged position of women in our denomination." To challenge inequality in the church took on questions that were insulated from attack because of faith. For example, "an aura of immutability surrounded the exclusion of women from the clergy, reinforced by a theology which held that an exclusively male priesthood was ordained by almighty God." In March 1966, this became intolerable to her: "I do not know why this familiar spectacle suddenly became intolerable to me one Sunday morning in March 1966. I doubt that Rosa Parks could explain why on

December 1, 1955, she rebelled against the segregation she had endured all her life. I remember only that in the middle of the celebration of the Holy Eucharist an uncontrollable anger exploded inside me, filling me with such rage I had to get up and leave. I wandered about the streets full of blasphemous thought, feeling alienated from God. The intensity of this assault at the deepest level of my devotional life produced a crisis in faith."

She felt raw wounds and refused to attend the Episcopal General Conference in 1973 for fear of an outburst of anger. After being rejected for ordination at one service, she turned around with other female candidates and "walked with bowed heads in solemn procession down the center aisle. No funeral procession could have been more sorrowful." The incident split the seminary she attended, and some who had supported the women "now railed against using a 'civil rights demonstration' tactic which, they felt, had no place in the solemn liturgy of the church. Others contented themselves with hostile stares at those of us who supported the women deacons by our presence at the ordination service. I learned that disputes among the faithful, although usually fought with polite words, can be as acrimonious in their language as a street brawl." Later, though, she received ordination in a black congregation in Philadelphia: "Symbolically, the rejected opened their arms to the rejected." She felt vindicated, and that the arc of her life had reached some completion.

THE FREEDOM SONGS AND THE STRUGGLES
IN BIRMINGHAM AND MISSISSIPPI

Nowhere is the philosophy of the movement better articulated than in two very different sets of documents: the freedom songs and King's "Letter from a Birmingham Jail." One represents the energy, creativity, and spiritual sustenance that empowered the rank-and-file of the movement; the latter stands as the single most concise and powerful intellectual manifesto of the philosophy of nonviolent resistance produced by a movement participant.

Religious music centrally shaped racial justice work. From the mid-eighteenth century forward, for example, Christian evangelicals began to write songs that expressed opposition to slavery. The slave spirituals of the nineteenth century formed a fundamental base for American

religious music that has sustained social justice struggles. In the twentieth century, activists and troubadors transformed many of those spirituals into "freedom songs" of the civil rights movement. Twentieth-century
gospel music, originating in northern urban black churches in the 1920s
and 1930s, also fed into social crusades. The great black gospel singer
Mahalia Jackson (1911–1972), for example, sang gospel tunes such as
"Precious Lord, Take My Hand," at numerous mass meetings. Revivalist
fervor, and a vision of interracialism encapsulated in the idea of the
beloved community, infused the culture of the movement. It arose out
of a religious culture steeped in the rituals of mass meetings, revivalis-
tic preaching, and sacred singing. As was true throughout the history of
black Christianity, music inspired new visions of freedom. During the
civil rights movement, black protestors unified themselves through freedom songs, bringing local people to organizing on behalf of the larger
political aims of the struggle (including the passage of the Civil Rights
Act of 1964 and the Voting Rights Act of 1965).

While the freedom songs provided the soundtrack for the movement,
"Letter from a Birmingham Jail" was its ninety-five theses nailed to
the door of the white southern churches. In his searching letter, written
while King sat in jail during the spring 1963 campaign in Birmingham,
King severely chastised his white church brethren and other southern
"moderates." They had settled for order rather than fighting for justice. King also employed his theological training in his exposition of just
and unjust laws, as explained in Paul's letter to the Romans. Just as Paul
and Silas sat in jail for breaking unjust Roman laws, so King and his
cohorts sat in jails for breaking the unjust laws of the Jim Crow South.
King's letter soon achieved the status of a classic of American literature,
just as his great speech of that August, "I Have a Dream," has assumed a
canonical place in American oratory. Perhaps most important for King's
own thinking, it represented a significant shift from his views about the
role of white moderates. In the 1950s, King frequently expressed hope
in the reasonable and moderate class of southern whites to stand up and
lead the region into a more just future. He assumed that white southern
Christians would pave the way. By 1963, it was all too evident that that
was not the case. King's writings condemned the "moderates," more so
than the Klansmen, as the biggest obstacle to achieving justice, precisely
because they would always settle for order over justice.

In the 1950s, the boycott of buses in Montgomery, Alabama provided the impetus for the formation of the SCLC, and propelled Martin Luther King to his fame and leadership. SCLC was an organization of ministers, arising directly from black churches. In 1960, SCLC asked its organizing secretary, Ella Baker, to bring together students to form a youth auxiliary. Meeting at a historically black institution in North Carolina in April, 1960, just as the student sit-in movement was springing up through southern cities, the students instead opted to form their own organization, the SNCC.

SNCC's language in its early days was deeply theological. Its real impulse involved more than integration, one participant explained, for beyond that lay the "redeemed community and the Kingdom of God." Racial prejudice, wrote one SNCC idealist, was a "judgment on the lie we have been living. . . . For though the days of lynching may be over, the lynching of personhood continues. It is a spiritual issue." The non-violent character of the movement exhibited a "noble, dignified understanding of oneself," one that could "deal with the rabid segregationist as a person." The final goal of the student movement, the editor of SNCC's paper *The Student Voice* explained, was the "retaining and creating of personhood," a task made difficult given that mass movements were "necessary to save the South and America." The radical organization's "distinctively idealistic belief that fortitude, determined action, and fearlessness would result in momentous social change," white SNCC worker Mary King later reminisced, "stemmed to a great degree from the Protestant upbringings of most of its workers." She connected her vision specifically to Wesleyan theology, that "through grace and redemption each person can be saved." This view reinforced the belief that the "good in every human being could be appealed to, fundamental change could correct the immorality of racial segregation, and new political structures could be created." Christian SNCC organizers felt a higher power and respected the "spirit" of the deeply evangelical local people with whom they worked. The young students who integrated lunch counters in Greensboro and inspired the original SNCC organizing conference also grew up in black churches.

The police state tactics of the Mississippi establishment intimidated many civil rights organizations. It would be more productive to focus on locales where some victories could be secured, they reasoned.

The students in SNCC would not be intimidated, however. Early in the 1960s, SNCC sent organizers to Mississippi, the heart of southern segregationism. In 1964, SNCC and other groups organized Freedom Summer, which brought over eight hundred volunteers from around the country to Mississippi. Freedom Summer arose from SNCC's efforts to publicize the difficulties of voter registration for tens of thousands of black Mississippians. The white Mississippi establishment lived up to its reputation, forming its own Sovereignty Commission as a state-sanctioned way to harass the "outside agitators." The fact that many churches and ministers shrank from the conflict did not spare them from being targeted. In mid-summer 1964, three black churches burned in Pike and Amite counties, despite the fact that the parishioners in these congregations had not been politically active.

Violence targeting civil rights centers continued well beyond Freedom Summer and the congressional civil rights acts of the mid-1960s. McComb, Mississippi gained a reputation as the "bombing capital of the world," with numerous violent attacks during and after Freedom Summer. Attempting to separate COFO from its local support base, segregationists employed indiscriminate violence against African Americans in McComb. A SNCC worker surveyed the damage to both buildings and spirit:

> Who now? My mother, father, sister, brother. God damn, how much blood do they want. They got the church—Society Hill—the movement church. Its doors were closed this summer, but it has always been the center of the movement in South McComb. . . . The NAACP holds its meetings there. I spoke there this summer. SNCC workers were there the past Sunday and the Sunday before. . . . The church is demolished. It was a terrible blast. The police are here, certain again to see that all clues are removed and destroyed.

In 1964, over 1000 movement activists were arrested; dozens suffered beatings. COFO and SNCC members pondered painful questions. Could the sacrifice be justified? "We had told a lot of people to put down their guns and not be violent in Mississippi," SNCC organizer Dave Dennis later recalled, "and I wasn't so sure that the nonviolent approach was the right approach anymore. And I had to do a lot of soul searching about that." For many in the movement, the beatings administered the next year to John Lewis and scores of others attempting to march across the Edmund Pettis bridge in Selma, Alabama, marked the nadir for the philosophy of nonviolence and soul force. One SNCC worker reported of talking with a civil rights leader in Lee County and trying to determine "how to convince him (or to decide whether we should convince him) to leave his pistol home when he comes to mass meetings. After an intensive discussion of non-violence at one of our meetings, [he] told me, 'I believe in the Bible, the Lord, and my 30–30.'"

This man spoke for the fact that, for many, nonviolence could serve its purpose as a useful tool, but violence in the name of self-defense had to be in the arsenal of options as well. The rise to fame in the 1960s of Malcolm X (largely through his searing autobiography, as told to Alex Haley) came in part through his capturing of the rhetoric of self-defense that already long had been part of black communities. Born Malcolm Little in Omaha, Nebraska, this orator of black power and pride grew up the hard way in Boston. After a career in petty crime, he was finally caught and sentenced for his criminal activity. While in prison in the early 1950s, Malcolm engaged in an intense period of self-study that resulted in his conversion to black Islam. He became a follower of Elijah Muhammad, a black man from Detroit who was the prophet of the movement and a protégé of the movement's founder, Wallace Fard. As was the custom among many converts, Malcolm rejected his given "white" name of Little and took the name "Malcolm X," signifying the lost names of his black ancestors brought during slavery.

Through the 1950s and early 1960s, Malcolm emerged as the Nation of Islam's foremost spokesman, attracting thousands to his passionate speeches. Malcolm rejected integration as a solution. In its place, he argued for black power, self-defense, and economic autonomy, and supplied his followers with the Nation of Islam's own "history" of the evil doings of the white devil in history. Critics labeled the Nation of Islam a "cult" and criticized Malcolm's ideas as "black supremacy" akin to the white supremacy he fought against. CBS News produced a famous documentary, *The Hate that Hate Produced*, that purported to expose the workings of the cult.

Malcolm's real following, however, came not so much for his offering of orthodox Nation of Islam doctrines as for his insistence that oppressed

African Americans had to defend their rights "by any means necessary." He attracted admirers throughout black America for his eloquence in defending his positions and insisting on racial pride. In the early 1960s, Malcolm was disillusioned by corruption and thievery within the Nation of Islam organization; he broke with the formal organization and, late in his life, began the Organization of Afro-American Unity. This corresponded also with a broadening of Malcolm's vision, from one of strict black separatism to one that embraced a more universalist notion of Islam. Malcolm was assassinated in 1965, but not before he had captured the imagination of a younger generation and provided an alternative answer to the nexus of race and religion in America, and black Americans' response to that.

MEXICAN AMERICANS AND THE CHURCH IN THE CIVIL RIGHTS ERA

While black Americans in the 1960s captured the attention of the nation through the mass protests of the civil rights movement, Latinos, a smaller and less visible minority group, began their own movement toward freedom. The religious impulses of the civil rights movement soon inspired activists in other ethnic groups that had been denied first-class citizenship. Other theologians and activists took up the mantle of liberation theology, whose most prominent advocates came from Latin America. They argued that God was in solidarity with oppressed peoples everywhere. For black theologian James Cone, this meant that God was "black," a term he meant metaphorically rather than phenotypically. For Latino Christians, God was living among the struggling farmworkers, denied decent housing or minimal health care, exposed to pesticides and disease, paid miserable wages for long hours of uncertain seasonal work, and turned away even at the door of the one true Church. Latinos took action to desegregate and implant an ethic of social justice into an ethnically divided Catholic Church.

Cesar Chavez, a Latino Catholic and farm laborer, organized farmworkers in the Central Valley of California. He took his inspiration from a highly personal and mystical folk Catholicism, both drawing from and reacting to his own tradition in a way much like Martin Luther King did with his black Baptist upbringing. "We raise two things in Delano: grapes and slaves," he said in 1969, at the height of the struggle. "But we will win with two weapons: dedication and disciplined sacrifice." Chavez organized a series of farm worker strikes in the produce fields in the 1960s, where migrant laborers of Mexican descent toiled for low pay in terrible conditions. Migrant workers had briefly captured the attention of the nation in the 1930s when the "Okies," whites from the American South and Southwest, migrated to California in search of work and often ended up picking produce in the fields. Mexican migrant laborers historically had been exploited with impunity and had difficulty organizing, since farm laborers had been exempted from many of the formative labor laws of the New Deal era.

Chavez had grown up in Arizona, the child of struggling Mexican parents who once had been landowners. As a young man, he labored in the fields and later served in the military during World War II. After the war, he worked crops in California's Central Valley. Prior to his leadership of the United Farm Workers, Chavez began to work with Catholic priests and organizers. He learned about the history of Catholic social justice thought from the traditional writers such as St. Francis of Assisi, as well as Gandhi. In his work with members of the Catholic left in the 1950s and early 1960s, Chavez was exposed to *Rerum Novarum* and other documents central to the history of Catholic thought on labor organizing. Issued in 1891 by Pope Leo XIII, *Rerum Novarum*, subtitled "Rights and Duties of Capital and Labor," decried "the misery and wretchedness pressing so unjustly on the majority of the working class," defended the rights of laborers to organize unions, and set a pattern for Catholic economic social teaching over the next century.

Chavez began to marry his political consciousness of the oppression of farm workers together with his religious faith in the worth of even the lowest toilers. In the early 1960s, seeking to unionize farm workers but finding the Community Services Organization resistant to labor organizing of that type, Chavez turned his attention to what became the United Farm Workers. Cesar Chavez deployed much the same philosophy and techniques of nonviolence that had worked successfully in the black civil rights struggle but added to it religiously based protest rituals such as fasts.

Chavez drew on the rich legacy of the social teachings of the Church, and of Latino spirituality, to empower *La Causa*. Chavez experienced resistance from the Catholic establishment but knew that the church could be a powerful force on behalf of justice for farm workers. Chavez asked the Church to "sacrifice with the people," to exert true servant-hood. Some of Chavez's associates took his call further. Figures such as Chicano activist Reyes Lopes Tijerina led groups who squatted on land they believed still rightfully belonged to Hispanic settlers who had been there centuries before the white American arrival in the Southwest. Other local Latino leaders occupied Catholic churches, insisting on Latino representation and the appointment of Latino Catholic priests to oversee ethnic parishes dominated by Latinos. Other voices from within the Latino Catholic community attacked the historic devaluing of the Latino presence in the Church. Their vision of social justice built on left Catholic traditions that emphasized community and God's identification with the poor.

Chavez developed a redemptive faith in nonviolence that was a Chicano Catholic version of Martin Luther King's black Baptist faith. From Gandhi, for example, Chavez learned "moral jujitsu," the art of "keeping the opponent off balance while adhering to your own princi-ples." Nonviolence called for organizing mass numbers of small actions, which is how Chavez saw Gandhi's genius. "Strategy for nonviolence takes a tremendous amount of our time—strategy against the opposition, and strategy to strengthen our support. We can't let people get discour-aged. If there's no progress, they say nonviolence doesn't work. They begin to go each and everywhere. And it's only when they are desperate that people think violence is necessary"—as Chavez witnessed a number of times during the movement. "The churches had to get involved in the struggle," the devout Catholic had put it. "Everything they had taught for two thousand years was at stake in this struggle."

Chavez put his own words into action in 1968. His most striking pub-lic protest was the penitential fast. After the Delano grape strike had dragged on for over two years, and some militant strikers were found with guns, he informed his staff the he would take a penitential fast, an act to repent of the sins of the movement and renew the spirit of non-violence. Chavez told the National Council of Churches that his fast was "informed by my religious faith and by my deep roots in the Church. It is not intended as a pressure on anyone but only as an expression of my own deep feelings and my own need to do penance and be in prayer." In 1968,

Chavez walked out of the Filipino Hall in Delano and to the UFW head-quarters, which soon became itself a site of pilgrimage. Mark Day, a Franciscan priest and Chavez supporter, celebrated Mass there each day and commented that "the huge banner of the Union is against the wall, and the offerings the people make are attached to the banner: pictures of Christ from Mexico, two crucifixes, a large picture of Our Lady of Guadalupe—the whole wall is covered with offerings." Another witness described it as a "monastic cell" for Chavez. As both an authentic witness and a brilliant maneuver to bring attention to the movement, the social fast was a combination of Gandhian struggles of resistance, the tradition of self-denial and civil disobedience of figures such as Henry David Thoreau, and the suffering servant popular in Mexican American piety.

Chavez's close associate and dynamic organizer, Dolores Huerta, noted the extent of opposition to not only the fast but also the Mexican Catholic symbols that pervaded the movement. Some in the union strongly opposed the influence of religion. "I know it's hard for people who are not Mexican to understand," Huerta later said, "but this is part of the Mexican culture—the penance, the whole idea of suffering for something, of self-inflicted punishment. It's a tradition of very long standing. In fact, Cesar has often mentioned in speeches that we will not win through violence, we will win through fasting and prayer." In 1968, calling a meeting of Mexican and Filipino farm workers, he said that "I was going to stop eating until such time as everyone in the strike either ignored me or made up their minds that they were not going to be committing violence." During the fast, he lay in bed, continuing to work and taking communion and resisting pressures on him both internally and externally to quit the fast. "Very few people could see all the spiritual and psychological and political good that was coming out of it," he later recounted. Examining his past closely, he concluded that "if I'm going to save my soul, it's going to be through the struggle for social justice."

The fast came to an end in March 1968, as Chavez broke bread with Senator Robert F. Kennedy and others. He then concluded with his famous statement:

When we are really honest with ourselves we must admit that our lives are all that really belong to us. So, it is how we use our live that determines what kind of men we are. It is my deepest belief that only by giving our lives do we find life. I am convinced that the truest act of courage, the strongest act of manliness is to sacrifice ourselves for others in a totally non-violent struggle for justice. To be a man is to suffer for others. God help us to be men!

The farm workers saw the connection between the black civil rights movement and the Mexican American farm workers' struggle. When Chavez sensed, at the beginning of his struggles, that staff people "didn't thoroughly understand the whole idea of nonviolence," he requested volunteers who had been involved with CORE and SNCC in the South. They proved to be "very good at teaching nonviolent tactics." He also enlisted student volunteers from the Free Speech Movement and other settings. "If we were nothing but farm workers in the Union now," he ruminated, "we'd only have about 30 percent of all the ideas that we have. There would be no cross-fertilization, no growing. It's beautiful to work with other groups, other ideas, and other customs. It's like the wood is laminated."

From that time until the 1970 contract between laborers and growers in the Delano area, Chavez employed his combination of mystical Catholicism, the philosophy of nonviolence, and creative strategies of action and defiance. In the process, he captured national attention. Like the black Protestants who dominated parts of the civil rights movement, Chavez drew on Latino spiritual traditions to empower his cause. Steeped in the traditions of Mexican popular religion, Chavez picked up on a suggestion from a farm worker who asked to bring a statue of Our Lady of Guadalupe to a march in Oxnard in 1969. Soon, *La Morenita*, with her deep resonance of what it means to be a Mexican Catholic, appeared at the front of most of the marches of *La Causa*. In other areas, *altarcitos* and nightly prayer vigils provided a setting for meetings and union card signings. Often Catholic masses were offered at the end of strike days, followed by union organizing meetings and prayers directed toward seeking the will of God toward the future action of the unions. Chavez put into action *religion casera*, "homespun religion," the kind of mixture of official and popular Catholicism that was theorized by the Latino theologians, especially Virgilio Elizondo, in the 1970s. As Chavez himself put it, concerning the idea of holding prayer vigils with makeshift altars near the fields during the course of strikes, "The ideas came from the workers themselves. When you search out these ideas from among the people you can get out of almost any jam. This is the real meaning of nonviolence, as far as I'm concerned." In his Good Friday letter of 1969, he expressed his philosophy that "We advocate militant nonviolence as our means for social revolution and to achieve justice for our people . . . we shall overcome and change" the farm laborer system "not by retaliation or bloodshed but by a determined nonviolent struggle carried on by those masses of farm workers who intend to be free and human."

Chavez experienced resistance from the Catholic establishment (not unlike what Martin Luther King had seen in the Protestant establishment). As he once put it, referring to the movement in Delano, "The church has been such a stranger to us, that our own people tend to put it together with all the powers and institutions that oppose them." But he knew that the church could be a "powerful moral and spiritual force which cannot be ignored by any movement." For Chavez, as for liberation theologians generally, the church was spiritually mandated to side with the poor. He asked the Church to "sacrifice with the people," to exert true servanthood.

Chavez's piece "The Mexican-American and the Church," later widely reprinted, contains some of his most compelling ruminations on the relationship of spirituality, social organizing, and the organized church. Chavez recounted how he gradually had learned to involve the Church in the struggle of rural working-class Mexican Americans. At first, it was with the California Migrant Ministry, who implemented the kind of liberation theology that, in Mississippi, bore fruit as the Delta Ministry of the National Council of Churches. Chavez commented a number of times on the degree to which Protestants were more active than the Church itself, especially through the activism of the California Migrant Ministry, which mobilized Protestant clergy who were on the front lines of the Delano strike and were often arrested with the farm workers. This compelled Chavez to raise the question of "why OUR Church was not doing the same. We would ask, 'Why do the Protestants come out here and help the people, demand nothing, and give all their time to serving farm workers, while our own parish priests stay in their churches, where only a few people come, and usually feel uncomfortable?'" Local priests were recalcitrant even about loaning a building for a strike. Later, the Church appointed sympathetic priests, such as Mark Day, to minister for the workers.

Chavez believed there was a "deep need for spiritual advice" when workers were struggling in a protracted conflict: "Without it we see families crumble, leadership weaken, and hard workers grow tired. And in such a situation the spiritual advice must be given by a *friend,* not by the opposition. What sense does it make to go to Mass on Sunday and reach out for spiritual help, and instead get sermons about the wickedness of your cause?" He called on Mexican American groups not to ignore the power of the Church, and for workers to defend priests who might get themselves into trouble because of their commitment to seeing justice. "What do we want the Church to do?" Chavez concluded. "We don't ask for more cathedrals. We don't ask for bigger churches or fine gifts. We ask for its presence with us, beside us, as Christ among us. We ask the Church to *sacrifice with the people* for social change, for justice, and for love of brother. We don't ask for words. We ask for deeds. We don't ask for paternalism. We ask for servanthood."

For all his various and diverse influences, Chavez was, as one writer and observer put it at the time of his death, "essentially a lay Catholic leader," with his origins less in community-organizing radicalism than in the cursillos, the lay Catholic revival movement which spread from Spain to the United States in the 1950s and taught ordinary Catholics of social justice. "What many of the liberals and radicals on the staff of the union could never understand," he concluded, "was that all the fasts, the long marches, the insistence on personal sacrifice and the flirting with sainthood were not only publicity gimmicks, they were the essential Chavez." The same could be said for Martin Luther King and the other (lesser-known) figures traced in this chapter. All of them found in religious tradition the right teachings about and sustenance for overturning America's racial and economic order. Religion radicalized them to confront racism dramatically and effectively. In doing so, they reoriented many people into conceptualizing what "religion" and "race" even meant as social phenomena, because they disrupted the bounds of habitation that those terms had long defined.

CONCLUSION: THE INTERNATIONAL IMPACT OF THE MOVEMENT

The rich history and historiography of the American civil rights movement grows even richer when the broad implications of the freedom struggle domestically and internationally are understood. That is even more true when the diversity of characters and impulses, religious and otherwise, that drove the movement forward are considered fully. The story grows in complexity and significance, for example, when including the Latino civil rights movement, one which drew from a Catholic symbology and leadership as deeply as did the southern black civil rights movement on evangelical Protestantism. The international impact of the civil rights movement is also impressive, as gauged particularly through figures such as Allen Boesak and Desmond Tutu in South Africa, and even into contemporary political heroes such as Aung San Suu Kyi in Myanmar. In effect, the language and movement culture of the black American civil rights movement has become a kind of international script for the working of freedom struggles everywhere.

The limitations of religiously based social movements have to be acknowledged, as well. In the post–civil rights era, some suggested that America had moved into a "post-racial" era, despite the overwhelming statistics documenting racial inequality in American society. In particular, both the black American civil rights movement and the antiapartheid crusade in South Africa helped grow a black middle class. At the same time, structural inequalities of opportunity, income, education, and life prospects remained relatively immune to the morally impassioned calls of the civil rights crusades. As a result, the movements transformed attitudes and opened up some opportunities, but religiously based crusades would have marginal impact on structural inequalities and institutionally racist patterns of the distribution of wealth and power that were deeply embedded in the United States. Contemporary versions of civil rights movements, notably including the #blacklivesmatter uprising, have begun to address those issues. Thus, activists who have mined the connection between religion, civil rights, and social justice will have plenty of work to do in the future. But as theologians and activists discovered in the late twentieth century, liberation theologies would struggle to have a real-world impact in an age of political conservatism and hardening economic divisions.

7

Liberation Theologies and Problems of Religious Freedom in a Conservative Age

THE CIVIL RIGHTS MOVEMENTS TRANSFORMED AMERICA socially and politically. Those changes became law in the Civil Rights Act of 1964, the Voting Rights Act of 1965, and the significant extensions of the New Deal, such as Medicare and Medicaid, signed into law under Lyndon Johnson. At the same time, although much less noticed at the time, the Hart-Celler Immigration Act of 1965 dramatically altered the country demographically over the next five decades. The 1960s proved to be as revolutionary as proclaimed not in the much-vaunted student movements or headline-grabbing brief-lived organizations, but in providing the legal foundations for an America that never before had existed—an America based on the legal principle (if not the de facto reality) of racial equality. By the millennium, the effect of these changes was apparent and would continue remaking the country socially into the twenty-first century.

Another equally significant transformation came out of the 1960s and 1970s as well. This was the rise of modern conservatism. For our purposes, this most notably includes the burgeoning of the religious right as a significant force in American politics. Obviously much of this can be attributed to a reaction to the social changes wrought by the movements of the 1960s. It also originated from a deeper sense of what the right-wing political operative Patrick Buchanan later referred to as the "war for the soul of America." The religious right emerged in part from the same people (such as Jerry Falwell) who had articulated the fears of many conservative church people about what a racial revolution would do the country. In the 1960s, they blasted Martin Luther King, established "segregation academies" associated with churches in response to the mandatory desegregation of public educational institutions, and decried what they believed to be a moral decline that would lead to the downfall of America. Initially resistant to political activism, they moved significantly on that issue in the 1970s. Richard Nixon courted them with his "silent majority" and "southern strategy" campaigns in 1968 and 1972. The movement reached its apex, and found its unlikely hero, in the election of former actor Ronald Reagan in 1980. Two decades later, religious conservatives found their champion in one who was truly more of their own: former Texas governor and reformed alcoholic and true evangelical believer George W. Bush. In particular, Bush's very narrow 2004 electoral victory over Senator John Kerry came in large part due to votes in Ohio drawn out by the state's Definition of Marriage Amendment, mandating in the state's constitution that only marriages between one man and one woman could be recognized by the state.

These two forces—the liberation theology emerging from the civil rights movement and the conservative uprising of the religious right— shaped American religious life, and political debate, over the ensuing decades. The rise of theologies emanating from the civil rights struggles, as traced in this chapter, ironically came simultaneously to the decline of 1960s-style liberalism and the triumph of modern conservatism politically, and to some degree in the intellectual world. Moreover, as churches broke through historic barriers to interracial relations, Americans divided up socially and politically into red and blue states; those political colorings came with distinct racial associations and social polarization. A multiethnic, multireligious America emerged and flowered just as social and political rifts deepened, income inequalities worsened over the stretch from about 1974 to 2016, and movements such as Black Lives Matter drew attention to continued racial disparities in American life.

This chapter traces some of the main elements of theologies that came out of the civil rights and farm workers' movements of the 1960s. It then looks at recent court battles involving Native American religious practices and suggests why the kinds of liberation theologies that have been empowering for other groups have less resonance for them. Finally, the chapter examines recent religioconservative figures who have articulated theologies of purity that have resurrected older hierarchies of race and religion in American history. The paradox of the rise of liberation theology in religion and the cresting of conservative movements in the sociopolitical world illuminates much about current American political cleavages, racial tensions, and socioeconomic inequalities and divisions. The story also suggests much about the racialized bounds that continue to mark Americans' religious habitations and practices.

BLACK POWER, BLACK THEOLOGY, AND THE CHURCH

By 1969, black Christian authors and theologians exposed the unspoken assumptions and practices of white racism that pervaded the American Christian establishment. The "black theology" movement of the 1960s, led by figures such as James Cone, Vincent Harding, and Jacquelyn Grant highlighted the implicit racism they saw running through the Western theological tradition. Corresponding with these theological developments came radical acts and public displays that shocked many white Christians, who had become accustomed to nonviolent street protests. Their work from this era drove the continued civil rights agenda after the "civil rights movement" as it normally is historically conceived had come to an end with the assassination of Martin Luther King in 1968.

Themes of the blackness of God, developed initially by Henry McNeal Turner in the nineteenth century and pursued by a variety of folk artists and poets and writers during the Harlem Renaissance and after, reappeared in the 1960s in the phenomenon of black theology. A professor at Union Theological Seminary in New York City since 1969, James Cone became its best-known exponent. First announced in his book *Black Theology of Liberation*, Cone followed this work with a series of treatises on themes in African American religious history, including the groundbreaking 1972 text *The Spirituals and the Blues*. Heavily influenced originally by German modernist theologians that he read in his graduate training, Cone later rejected reliance on white theologians and terminology. He argued that black Christians would have to devise their own understandings freed from a dominant theological tradition too entangled in racism and colonialism.

In reflecting on the course of black theology, Cone noted that "my reflections on God were defined by the great contradiction of racism in the U.S. as mirrored in U.S. history and the freedom movements of the

1950s and 60s." God is black, Cone said (inspiring also the title of Vine Deloria's classic of a few years later, *God is Red*). By that, Cone meant not that God had a particular skin color, but rather that God always and by definition aligns Himself with the oppressed and against the oppressors. Black people in the United States were thus a chosen people. He sought to bring together Martin Luther's King stress on beloved community with Malcolm X's emphasis on justice for the oppressed and judgment on the oppressor. God is black, he said, because he "freely chooses to be known as the One who liberates victims from their oppression." After his original articulation of black theology, he was more convinced than ever that God could only be known among the oppressed struggling for justice. He found no place for a "colorless God in a society where human beings suffer precisely because of their color."

Knowing God meant siding with the oppressed and participating in their liberation. Asking "'How can white persons become black?' was analogous to the Philippian jailer's question to Paul and Silas, 'What must I do to be saved?'" The fallacy was thinking it could be achieved through work, rather than understanding that "blackness, or salvation (the two are synonymous) is the work of God, not a human work. It is not something we accomplish; it is a gift." Cone challenged the notion of a "raceless" Christ: "For whites to find him with big lips and kinky hair as offensive as it was for the Pharisees to find him partying with tax-collectors. But whether whites want to hear it or not, *Christ is black, baby,* with all of the features which are so detestable to white society."

Others who had been closely involved with Martin Luther King and the civil rights movement turned to the insights of black theology to comprehend their experiences in the 1960s. In "Black Power and the American Christ," the civil rights organizer and Mennonite minister Vincent Harding interpreted black theology for a largely white and liberal Protestant leadership; Harding insisted that the open expression of black fury was far healthier than the silent anger that had broiled underneath the surface for so long. When blacks saw whites fleeing cities in racial transition, "leaving their stained glass mausoleums behind them," black power advocates found ample material for their critiques of white America. In place of the "redemptive suffering" preached by SNCC, black power could be the "redemptive anger" that would bring down judgment on white American power:

The ideology of blackness surely grows out of the deep ambivalence of American Negroes to the Christ we have encountered here. . . . If the American Christ and his followers have indeed helped to mold the Black Power movement, then might it not be that the God whom many of us insist on keeping alive is not only alive but just? May he not be attempting to break through to us with at least as much urgency as we once sensed at the height of the good old "We Shall Overcome" days? Perhaps he is writing on the wall, saying that we Christians, black and white, must choose between death with the American Christ and life with the Suffering Servant of God. Who dares deny that God may have chosen once again the black sufferers for a new assault on the hard shell of indifference and fear that encases so many Americans?

In this rendering, black power was a response to the white Christ foisted on people of color in American history.

Harding had been involved with the National Committee of Negro Churchmen, which served as a liaison between black civil rights leaders and the white Protestant establishment. Harding and other black churchmen on the committee perceived a persistent problem that had faced America since the arrival of the first slave ship in 1619. They saw the fundamental distortion in American life derived from imbalances of wealth and power between whites and blacks. This "distortion" then justified the assumption that whites could exercise power while blacks should appeal to the conscience and not seek to use the mechanisms of power to advance their agenda. But discussions of power were central to the Christian tradition, for a more equitable sharing of social goods was a prerequisite for "authentic human interaction." Key in that would be blacks finding self-love, for "as long as we are filled with hatred for ourselves we will be unable to respect others." It meant also building from power bases already established in black communities.

On May 4, 1969, James Forman, formerly of SNCC, stormed the pulpit of Riverside Church in New York City, one of the country's most prestigious (and socially conscious) congregations. Forman's act, and the resulting document the "Black Manifesto," put into practice the assumptions explicit in academic black theology. Forman presented the "black manifesto," which was a product of the National Black Economic Development Conference in April of that year. In his address, Forman connected the black struggle in America to the cause of colored people around the world. "Caution is fine," he warned, "but no oppressed people ever gained their liberation until they were ready to fight, to use whatever means necessary, including the use of force and power of the gun to bring down the colonizer." Forman argued that the churches were sustained "by the military might of the colonizers," and called on "black people to commence the disruption of the racist churches and synagogues throughout the United States."

Performative acts such as those of Forman coincided with a national hysteria about like actions by the Black Panthers and student radical groups. Public reaction to them significantly fed growing support for "law and order" and "silent majority" political candidates who spoke to fears about the breakdown of social order. Martin Luther King himself, later in his life, also had raised power relations, economic inequalities, and colonialist military interventions abroad as a central part of his critique of American society. But by that time, the "classic" period of the civil rights movement already had solidified into the kind of nostalgia Vincent Harding portrayed, and advocates of black power demonized by comparison. Local church people in places such as Cairo, Illinois, made up the grassroots of black power crusades, but nationally the movement was perceived to have moved away from the Christian base of the civil rights freedom struggle.

Advocates of "black theology" soon found themselves under critique, namely from black women who perceived the old false god of patriarchy barely hidden under the theoretically revolutionary rhetoric of black power. A young black feminist theologian named Jacquelyn Grant articulated major themes of black women's theology. She insisted that "black theology cannot continue to treat Black women as if they were invisible creatures who are on the outside looking into the Black experience." Given that women made up the majority of members of black churches (a demographic also true of white Protestant churches), a true liberation theology would have to address the freeing of black women from sexism, as well as the unshackling of black people in America from racism. Sexism remained a reality in black communities as well as white. While black men sought to expose stereotypes and identify with the oppressed, they could ignore the same conditions imposed on women.

Western ideals of beauty and ugliness, stereotypes of black hypersexuality, combined with Christian teachings blaming women for the fall of man into sin, all combined to degrade black women, she argued. The injustices could be seen in the male-dominated structure of black churches, where men monopolized the professional ministry just as was the case in white churches.

The black theology articulated by Cone, Wilmore, Grant, and others eventually fed into a worldwide movement of liberation theology in the 1980s. By that time, it was associated increasingly with radical priests in Central America who were confronting grotesque violence at the hands of right-wing paramilitaries trained in and funded by the United States. Later, after a long hiatus, black theology exploded on the national scene during the presidential election of 2008. Reverend Jeremiah Wright was the pastor of a large black congregation in Chicago, and Senator Barack Obama, the Democratic frontrunner, was one of its members. Wright gained infamy when snippets of his sermons and his rhetorical phrase "God damn America" went viral. Openly supporting Obama, Wright turned to the Bible and pronounced that "Jesus was a poor black man who lived in a country and who lived in a culture that was controlled by rich white people."

Obama himself quickly distanced himself from his former pastor, insisting that Wright's condemnations failed to recognize the progress that had been made since the 1960s. Commentators pointed to Wright's roots in the black theology movement of the 1960s. Yet those seeking to explain the phrase "God damn America" recounted a truncated history of black theology. This short history of black liberation theology failed to explain the deep-seated anger within Wright's preaching or his nod to much longer histories of racial oppression. They failed to witness the longer histories of liberation theology going back over generations of black religious thought and action. Narrowing that history to the recent past alone ignored the variety of ways (including in music and art, as well as formal theology) that African Americans had challenged the connection of whiteness and divinity in American history. Many of the examples raised in previous chapters of this book suggest the long life and power of black theology in the everyday religious lives of black Americans for centuries.

LA RAZA AND THE CHURCH

Black liberation theology found a counterpart in Latino Catholic activist thought during this same period. The parallels and differences between a mostly Protestant black liberation theology and a mostly Catholic Latino one suggested much about possibilities for alliances as well as differences that naturally emerged from such divergent intellectual backgrounds and social experiences.

Following Cesar Chavez's leadership of the strikes of farm workers from 1965 forward, the Catholic Church increasingly appeared to be on the side of established economic forces. From Pope Leo's 1891 encyclical *Rerum Novarum* forward, Catholic workers found theological support for labor organizations. Despite such support of the pontiff, growers in California enlisted allies in the Catholic hierarchy to suspend priests engaged in pro-Union activity during the farm workers' movement. Recognizing how little the welfare of American Latinos mattered to the Catholic Church establishment, organizers sympathetic to the work of Chavez demanded that the Church address the issue of Latinos, particularly the Mexican and Central Americans who represented the largest single ethnic group of Catholics in San Diego. As one writer put it in *La Verdad* (The Truth), a movement newsletter, charged that the Catholic Church had been "milking the Mexican American barrio since the day of the conquistadors." The church had accepted generations of contributions from the people, but had done little or nothing for them.

Leaders of *Católicos por la Raza* (CPLR) asked the people of the barrio, "How many churches, let alone million-dollar churches, did Christ build?" While Catholic leaders built showplaces, its people suffered. Latino Catholics had watched the church in the Southwest become "no longer a church of blood, a Church of struggle, a Church of sacrifice. It is our fault because we have not raised our voices as Catholics and as poor people for the love of Christ. We can't love our people without demanding better housing, education health, and so many other needs we share in common."

The founding activists of CPLR made their Catholic theologies and sympathies clear, but insisted that the Church had failed to serve its Latino constituents. They demanded that church leaders come to the barrio, just as Jesus met the people where they were, and align themselves with *la gente*. In November 1969, meeting at a Catholic campground just east of San Diego, a group of Latino Catholics and students seized the area, renamed it *Campo Cultural de la Raza*, and sent a list of thirteen grievances to the bishop. They insisted on fair pay for Latino employees of the Church, that Catholic schools provide free admittance and texts for Chicano children, that Latino laymen and priests be considered for positions of authority in the Church, and that the church support the Delano grape boycott and Chavez's United Farm Workers Organizing Committee. On Christmas Eve 1969, more than three hundred Latino activists attempted to enter St. Basil's Church on Wilshire Boulevard in Los Angeles. While James Frances Cardinal McIntyre led elite parishioners in a chorus of "O Come All Ye Faithful," those from CPLR were locked out of the church. Off-duty policemen attacked the protestors, twenty of whom were arrested for disturbing the peace.

After the Christmas Eve event at St. Basil's Church in Los Angeles, Latino church activists learned what could happen when they stood their ground and articulated their demands. Their very presence drew out liberals in the Church and sympathetic priests and nuns who realized they had to stand either with the Church or with CPLR. After the event, Cardinal McIntyre was compelled to retire. His replacement proved more open to hearing Latino voices in the Church. Not long afterward, Patricio Flores became the first Mexican American bishop. Nonetheless, leaders of CPLR saw continued challenges. Euro-American priests continued to preach the same sermons dwelling on outdated themes of individual behavior, ignoring the cries of people for social justice. Priests insisted on faithful attendance of Mass and close study of the catechisms, "instead of urging that people become action-oriented in the selfless service of their own people and others less fortunate."

Latino activists also pressed for culturally appropriate worship and theology in the Church. For Latinos, as one priest expressed it, this meant the "human intersection of two histories, two nations, two cultures, two languages converging, colliding, blending, embracing, depending on one's location within the human geography evolved by one and a half centuries of relentless interaction." Another Latino Catholic priest pointed to the history of national parishes in the American Catholic system. Historically, the system afforded opportunities for the faithful to "practice Catholicism in their own cultures and not make acculturation blackmail to receive the redemptive act of Christ." Injustices committed against Latino believers had to be acknowledged, and the Church had to rectify the injustices. "Why do many want to de-Hispanicize and to Americanize us?" asked one Latino layperson in 1974. "What crime is there in being Hispano?"

Latino Catholic priests and leaders in the 1970s and 1980s pursued power within the church walls through the organization of PADRES, short for *Padres Asociados para los Derechos Religiosos, Educativos, y Sociales* (Priests Associated for Religious, Educational, and Social Rights). For women, *Las Hermanas* ("The Sisters") served a parallel function. Following the example of Chicano/a student activism in groups such as MEChA, as well as ad hoc protest groups such as CPLR, which had formed around specific issues of Latino inclusion and exclusion in major Latino Catholic areas, PADRES came from the efforts of Ralph Ruiz and other priests who gathered originally in San Antonio to share their experiences in the church and discuss ways to meet the needs of Chicano Catholics. At a press conference following the first meeting in 1970, they vowed to transmit the "cry of our people to the decision-makers of the Catholic Church in America." Writing to the archbishop of San Antonio, Ralph Ruiz explained that they could serve as spokesmen for a disaffected Latino church membership, because they had come from the people themselves. The Latino priests pointed out the neglect of their people by the institutional Church. Juan Romero of Los Angeles recalled that in his first parish, in Los Angeles, he could not celebrate the Mass in Spanish even though almost everyone who came to confession spoke Spanish. Some newly trained priests during those years withdrew as they concluded that the promise of the Church was a "total lie and a doublecross." PADRES could provide them with an alternative.

At the first national PADRES meeting in Tuscon in 1970, controversies over whether there would be lay membership in the group generated splits. Those who sought to limit full membership to Mexican American priests insisted that the Church itself would listen to a group of priests far more readily than an organization diluted with clerical and lay and Chicano and white members. PADRES focused especially on the issue of Latino bishops and other Latinos in positions of church authority, but some argued it should be less worried about placing Latino bishops than pushing a political program to help the poor. PADRES saw an early success with the appointment of Patricio Flores as the first Mexican American bishop in 1970. Meanwhile, in 1972, PADRES helped to form the Mexican American Cultural Center in San Antonio. It proved to be a fertile ground for theologians such as Virgilio Elizondo and others who began to articulate what they referred to as a mestizaje theology. They emphasized the mixing of cultures and ideas in forming Latino/a identity.

Juan Romero, one of the founding members, noted that groups such as PADRES were deliberately temporary creations to make visible the Latino presence and to "provide a support system for Mexican-American priests who often felt isolated and tended toward burn-out during the hard days of the movimiento." Ironically, it was in part the success of groups such as PADRES that ultimately led to their decline, as Latino priests increasingly found themselves appointed to positions within the church hierarchy.

Like black women, who wrote of the double bind of race and sex, Chicanas (a term for Mexican American women that came to be preferred among politically active Latinos in the 1960s) came to realize that they struggled with the same dilemmas of race and gender. In the Catholic Church, home for the large majority of Mexican American Christians, women were viewed as submissive. Mexican American women who entered religious orders could not simply leave behind their cultural heritage. The politically and culturally aware Mexican American nun, Sister Teresito Basso argued, would be compelled to recognize the urgency of La Raza even to the point of building her life in the Church around it. Basso's struggles within the church may be compared to those of Daniel Berrigan, who addressed the question of how to engage in civil disobedience against the Vietnam War even while remaining true to the Church and Order (the Jesuits) that he loved.

Basso was one of the founding members of *Las Hermanas* an organization of Spanish-speaking religious women serving in the Church in the United States. *Las Hermanas* provided a means to pursue the larger good of the Latina community even while serving the Church as an institution. Mexican American sisters, she said, had to

> choose whether to identify with her people as "Chicana" or remain an acculturated Mexican-American. If she chooses to be known as "Chicana" it is because she is consciously aware of herself, her power of self-determination, as well as proud of her cultural heritage and experiences.

Within her religious commitment, the people of La Raza will take priority while she seeks basic institutional changes because she senses the urgency and immediacy of bringing about this change.

She would see the shortcomings of the Church in providing the spiritual and material sustenance the people needed or in addressing the demands for social justice. As the Mexican American community pursued its aims of improving neighborhoods, job opportunities, and educational institutions, Latina sisters could no longer wait for an indifferent church or inequitable governmental structures to recognize the plight of the people.

Las Hermanas had a longer life than PADRES, in large part because they could hold out no such hope for advancement within the church (meaning also that the church authorities could do little to discipline or stifle the sisters). They too faced controversies on limited versus open membership and whether non-Spanish speakers would be given full membership. *Las Hermanas* took on a structure like that of PADRES, in which Spanish-speaking priests and lay religious were full members and associate membership was open to others, including Anglos, who worked in Latino communities or expressed sympathy with the organization. In the early 1970s, *Hermanas* leaders pointed to statistics that the Catholic population was more than one-quarter Latino, while the Catholic episcopacy had less than one percent Hispanic representation. By contrast, Irish Americans made up seventeen percent of American Catholics but controlled over half of the bishop positions.

In one of its earliest statements from the founding conference in Houston in 1971, the fifty nuns from eight states who gathered to form *Hermanas* said that Latina sisters had seen a gap between what they hoped to achieve for their people and what they actually had done within the Church. An early document by two founders of *Las Hermanas* lamented that sisters had not served the people as they wished, while some who had tried found themselves in trouble with members of their own congregations or with leaders of the Church. "We, as Spanish-speaking Sisters, are greatly concerned with the plight of La Raza especially and are determined to better our efforts to meet their needs." While PADRES and *Las Hermanas* issued statements about social struggles (such as farm workers' strikes), their most concentrated activism was within the Church itself. *Las Hermanas*, for example, blasted the Church for using cheap Mexican labor in Church institutions. "Is it necessary to profess vows to be a wait-ress or a house maid?" two members of *Las Hermanas* rhetorically asked of the low pay extended to domestic workers in the Church.

Much like PADRES, founding members of *Hermanas* debated the degree to which they should focus on reforming the Church from within versus investing energies in social struggles around them. One found-ing member who had grown up in South Texas, Sister Yolanda Tarango, remembered it this way. Her reflections capture the movement of many Latino/a activists toward engagement with social justice issues:

> I think that we changed from initially like being concerned about the ministry with the folks, and then as you get involved with the ministry of the folks you get involved with the justice issues. And so like one of the first justice issues was, for example, the farm workers. When we had the third national assembly in California, there was a real chal-lenge of 'Do we sit here and meet, or do we get out on the streets and march with the farm workers?' And so it was like a big tension. And the result was saying, 'We need to be out there; we need to be out in the trenches.' And so a few people stayed and kind of did the business of the work, and others you know packed their bag and went and joined the farm workers. The farm workers who were and continue to be for, well for Hermanas and for the Church, a wonderful, what do I say, educational call to the Church to be who we say we are and to be with the people. And so anyway, so we started with the farm workers and more Hermanas getting involved in demonstrations and joining the farm workers and just really making that our issue in addition to the ministry area.
>
> And then our issue became feminism, and looking at how do you [or] how do we deal with feminism among Latinas.

In the 1970s and 1980s, the Catholic Church attempted to respond in some tentative way to the growing predominance of Latinos in the American church. "This Hispanic presence challenges us all to be more *catholic*, more open to the diversity of religious expression," one bishop wrote. Recognizing that the Church historically was an immigrant church, the bishops saw the "pastoral needs" of Hispanic Catholics as great, with a strong tradition of faith in communities being challenged by pressures of assimilation into American society. The bishops endorsed the turn in Catholic teaching toward being specific about defining social justice and looking into issues of nutrition, health crises, poor housing, unemployment, and substandard education. They also encouraged attention to issues close to the lives of Latino constituents, including voting, immigration rights, and access to bilingual citizenship materials. "The Church embraces the quest for justice as an eminently religious task," they concluded.

In stark contrast to the response of the church to Chavez's crusades in the mid-1960s, the bishops devoted a special section to the needs of farm workers, including a sociological paragraph detailing the streams of migrant workers in various parts of the country. They decried the poor treatment of migrant workers and urged support of the right of migrant laborers to engage in collective bargaining through unions. They perceived the lingering problems of racism, despite the strides made in targeting prejudice and discrimination. The bishops also noted that the practice of ordinary Latino Catholics "imbues them with a spirit of sacrifice. It can lead to an acute awareness of God's attributes, such as his fatherhood, his providence, and his loving and constant presence."

Since the 1970s, a combination of immigration patterns from Mexico and Central America together with declining and aging Euro-American populations in Catholic parishes in cities soon made it evident that the future of the American Catholic Church lay with its growing Latino population. With a current Catholic constituency in North America of just over forty percent Latino, a figure soon to be well over fifty percent based on current demographic patterns and birth rates, American Catholicism will undergo another of its transformations that has in American history periodically reshaped it. The struggles of Latino activists from this period began to compel Euro-American authorities within the Church to acknowledge this rapid transformation.

NATIVE AMERICANS AND DILEMMAS OF RELIGIOUS FREEDOM

Deliberately modeling his work on James Cone's pronouncement that "God is black," Vine Deloria, a friend of Cone's and a scholar of Native American history and religions, published his now-classic *God is Red* in 1973. The work arrived just on the heels of a standoff between Indian activists in the American Indian Movement (AIM) and federal authorities at Wounded Knee in South Dakota. AIM had occupied the town, in part, as a symbolic redemption of the 1890 massacre there that had killed some two hundred ghost dancers of the plains.

Spiritually reared in Indian and Episcopalian ways and educated in a Lutheran seminary, Deloria developed a wide familiarity with varieties of religious thought. In the 1960s and 1970s, he rejected the Western biblical tradition as beholden to a linear religious and historical narrative that was time oriented. This, he suggested, devalued native modes of placing space and geography at the center of religious understanding. Western Christians claimed that God works in history, Deloria suggested, but tribal religions "bound as they are to some specific places and particular ceremonies, do not need to rely upon the compiled arguments of history. It is only necessary that people experience the reality of the sacred. . . . A Sweat Lodge, a Vision Quest, or a Sing performed in a sacred place with the proper medicine man provides so much more to its practitioners than a well-performed Mass, a well-turned sermon argument, or a well-organized retreat." Christianity taught that Jesus "made the one supreme sacrifice," Deloria wrote, but "the rest of creation is involved in the Crucifixion only by logical extension and does not participate in the same way that Indian ceremonies involve it. . . . Traditional Indians do not see that sacrifice necessarily involves a sinful nature; rather, it is the only way that humans can match the contribution of other forms of life." Deloria endeavored to shift the sacred from the person of Jesus and his actions in the past to the places of existence and experience connected to Indian geographies and sacred lands.

By critiquing the entire Western religious tradition, Deloria found a way to understand and contextualize his training in it and move beyond it. But the nexus of race, religion, and freedom always has been a troubled one for Native Americans. Native traditions historically have valued and sacralized land—space and geography—rather than sacred texts. Native religions have been more about practices and stories than "beliefs" in the Protestant American sense. Partly as a result, attempts to apply First Amendment law to Native American cases often have met with frustration. As a result, religious practices have met racial barriers created through the lens of ostensibly neutral court decisions.

The court's reliance on Western theological definitions of God—such as the concept of "ultimate concern" as outlined by theologian Paul Tillich and cited in Supreme Court cases—also has hindered protection of Native American practices. Plaintiffs in these cases must meet standards of sincerity and centrality; in other words, they must show that their religious beliefs and practices are sincerely held and that the practices themselves are central and fundamental to the expression of the religion. If and when they can meet those tests, then the state is required to meet a compelling interest test when those religious interests may be abrogated or violated in some way. These tests have often not been applied, or have been applied in ethnocentric ways, in cases where Native American sacred land usages have interfered with development projects or with administrative needs. Congress has responded with symbolic gestures such as the American Indian Religious Freedom Restoration Act of 1994, but the ways that "religion" is defined for the purposes of legal proceedings make it difficult to defend Native practices within the context of a "compelling interest" test.

The stage was set for contemporary Native American religious freedom jurisprudence in the 1971 case, *Lemon v. Kurtzman*. In the *Lemon* case, the court enunciated its three tests of constitutionality for church-state laws. Laws that might impinge on religious practice should have a secular legislative purpose, neither advancing nor inhibiting religion, and there should be an avoidance of an "excessive government entanglement with religion." The court also recognized, however, that "judicial caveats against entanglement must recognize that the line of separation, far from being a 'wall,' is a blurred, indistinct, and variable barrier depending on all the circumstances of a particular relationship."

The principle of neutrality, and the *Lemon* principle of avoiding excessive entanglement of religion, would appear to work in favor of the Native American religious freedom, but the net effect has been the opposite. The test was whether government action violated a person's religious beliefs or practices, which could be proven to be deep, compelling, and fundamentally religious. If those tests could be met, then only a compelling state interest could override them.

In the most important case of the last quarter century, however, *Employment Division, Department of Human Resources of Oregon v. Smith* (here abbreviated as *Smith v. Oregon*), the court moved in the direction of expanding the sphere of what constituted "state interest." The court ruled that generally applicable legislation was permissible even in the case where it might incidentally affect the religious practice of one group, provided it was not aimed at that practice. In this case, Galen Black and Alfred Smith, one an Indian and one white, lost their jobs in a drug rehabilitation program because of their use of peyote. They could not collect unemployment compensation because they had been fired for "misconduct." After a complicated history in the Oregon courts, the case made its way to the Supreme Court. In the majority opinion, which held for the State of Oregon's dismissal of the two employees, Justice Antonin Scalia insisted that the court had "never held that an individual's religious beliefs excuse him from compliance with an otherwise valid law prohibiting conduct that the state is free to regulate."

Requiring Oregon to make an exemption to its laws prohibiting the use of drugs because of the religious beliefs of this particular group of respondents would create a "private right to ignore generally applicable laws," Scalia said. "Respondents urge us to hold, quite simply, that when otherwise prohibitable conduct is accompanied by religious convictions, not only the convictions but the conduct itself must be free from governmental regulation." But this was not the case, Scalia insisted. To allow individuals to selectively obey laws, and to argue for free exercise when they chose not to, would indeed permit them to become a law unto themselves, which contradicted "both constitutional tradition and common sense." There was no "private right to ignore generally applicable laws," something that was well recognized on issues of race or free speech, for example. It was true, Scalia acknowledged, that this ruling would tend to "place at a relative disadvantage those religious practices that are not widely engaged in; but that unavoidable consequence of democratic government must be preferred to a system in which each conscience is a law unto itself or in which judges weigh the social importance of all laws against the centrality of all religious beliefs." While concurring with the decision, Justice Sandra Day O'Connor vigorously dissented from the rejection of the "compelling interest" test. "There is nothing talismanic about neutral laws of general applicability or general criminal prohibitions," she wrote, "for laws neutral toward religion can coerce a person to violate his religious conscience or intrude upon his religious duties just as effectively as laws aimed at religion." Freedom of religion was a constitutional norm, not an "anomaly." O'Connor considered Oregon to have just enough compelling state interest in this case to make its law valid, although the matter was close. The dissenters in *Smith* likewise insisted on maintenance of the compelling state interest test and found no reason to believe that making an exemption for the sacramental use of peyote would unduly burden the state.

In other cases as well, Indian religious rights have been superseded by state interests, in part because the court has interpreted religious practices as cultural or traditional in nature. The case of *Sequoyah* also illustrates this point. The court held that constructing a dam in the Tennessee River valley, in lands held to be sacred by the Cherokees, would not violate First Amendment rights. The Cherokees had not demonstrated the "centrality and indispensability" of the valley: "The overwhelming concern of the affiants appears to be related to the historical beginnings of the Cherokees and their cultural development. It is damage to tribal and family folklore and traditions, more than particular religious observances, which appears to be at stake. The complaint asserts an 'irreversible loss.' . . . Though cultural history and tradition are vitally important to any group of people, these are not interests protected by the Free Exercise Clause of the First Amendment."

Sequoyah and other similar cases led to the most significant of these decisions, *Lyng v. Northwest Indian Cemetery Protective Ass'n*, a case involving the government building a forest road in Northern California through lands held sacred by three tribes in the area. The court held that the government's compelling interest in eminent domain for the roads did not violate First Amendment protections. The court reasoned, first, that the "Free Exercise Clause simply cannot be understood to require the Government to conduct its own internal affairs in ways that comport with the religious beliefs of its particular citizens." The building of the road did not ask individuals to violate their beliefs, and it did not penalize them for practicing their religion. The key phrase in the First Amendment was "prohibit," the court pointed out, and the government was not doing any prohibiting in this case, while individual religious practitioners were demanding relief from a government that was not to be involved with religion. This was notably true in a previous case involving building a logging road through lands considered sacred by one tribe. In that case, the court held that the land was not "central" to the religious practices of the Indian group. The court was unpersuaded as to the centrality of the place, in part because there was no set or fixed body of doctrine that it could point to as a basis for ruling on the First Amendment.

Thus, just as Deloria had perceived in *God is Red*, the nature of Indian religious belief and practice simply does not fit well into what American society perceives and defines as "religion." Such a definition generally involves a sacred text, particular institutions and the practices performed within those institutions, and clear lines of religious authority. Arising from traditions that predated such a separation of sacred from secular, and lacking what Americans looked for when they sought out something perceivable as "sacred," Native American traditional practices were bound to have a difficult time within First Amendment church and state cases. Ironically, their very struggles, and congressional action resulting from them in the 1990s, ended up benefiting most those who began to argue for "religious liberty" from government edicts regarding access to contraception. The most obvious beneficiaries of Native struggles for recognition of their religious practices, in other words, turned out to be members of the religious right, who themselves organized initially in hostile response to civil rights uprisings of the 1960s.

RACE, RELIGION, AND THE RIGHT

In the 1950s and 1960s, the long history of race and religion in the South ran through segregationist theology and deeply shaped the consciousness of white southern churchgoers. But in the civil rights era, the base assumptions underlying the white southern Christian narrative lay bare. In the harsh light of national public disgust and attack by denominational leaders even within the region, the intellectual edifice of the white southern religious framework crumbled.

But the social power of the religious right came in recapturing historic white southern themes and recasting them in politically potent ways. The movement of the religious right from criticism of civil rights activism to their own forms of politically potent organizing occurred rapidly in the 1970s. Originally opposed to religious involvement in civil rights on the basis of the "spirituality of the church," but embarrassed by public

spectacles of expelling prospective worshippers and espousing racist rhetoric, white religious conservatives had to reinvent tradition for a new day.

In a famous (if later disowned) sermon on "Ministers and Marches"
from 1965, Jerry Falwell explained the opposition of many white evangelicals toward deliberate political activism (here directed at Martin Luther
King and black civil rights ministers of that era): "Preachers are not called
to be politicians but to be soul winners. . . . If as much effort could be put
into winning people to Jesus Christ across the land as is being exerted
in the present civil rights movement, America would be turned upside
down for God." By the late 1970s, however, a surge of activism fueled the
religious right. Angered by IRS rulings against some of its prized institutions (such as Bob Jones University in South Carolina, which had continued its racially discriminatory practices), morally offended by *Roe v. Wade*
and legalized abortion, concerned about a perceived national decline in
defense and economic strength, and bewildered by a moral revolution
that seemed to assault their deepest values, a generation of evangelical
leaders energized a constituency in defense of traditional values. This
was a national movement, with pockets of strength across the country,
but especially in the South, where the Republican Party benefited from
anger at the civil rights acts passed by Democratic administrations in the
mid-1960s. Activists from the religious right intentionally invested hopes
in the conventional means of politics to rescue Christian America from
the forces (such as humanism and the decline of the "traditional family")
that conservatives believed undermined Christian morality.

By the 1970s, many white southern believers accommodated themselves to the demise of legal segregation. Thus, in the recent controversies
within southern church organizations, race has been one of the very few
items usually *not* in dispute. Since the 1960s, southern religious conservatives, for the most part, have repudiated the white supremacist views of
their predecessors.

Yet the standard biblical arguments against racial equality, now
looked upon as an embarrassment from a bygone age, have found
their way rather easily into the contemporary religious right's stance
on gender. A theology that sanctifies gendered hierarchy has become
for the post–civil rights generation what whiteness was to earlier generations of believers. For religious conservatives generally, patriarchy has

supplanted race as the defining first principle of God-ordained inequality. Ultimately, leaders of the religious right mobilized a large segment of white evangelicals across the country and turned them into the most reliable base of the conservative wing of the Republican Party. As a force for political mobilization, that was an impressive achievement, given the relatively skeptical view evangelicals held before then toward what could be accomplished through politics. As an indicator of the continued power of race and religion, it was a significant symbol of how Americans could still be divided by faith, into racial religiopolitical blocs.

CONCLUSION

Liberation theologies arose as formal statements in an age when conservative political movements gained strength, and then power. They emerged too in an age when newfound black political power met economic realities of declining tax bases in cities that blocked the realization of dreams for which civil rights activists had fought. And liberation theologies showed their limits, too, when applied to the issues most affecting Native Americans, for whom Christian language and symbols could prove troublesome or damaging to their interests.

In the complicated tangle of these stories, we see something of the continued importance of divisions of religion and race in an increasingly multicultural America. The rapid growth of pluralism in American life since 1965, in both the composition of population and in the growth of religious traditions outside the Judeo-Christian framework (or outside the "Abrahamic" tag given to the Judeo-Christian-Islamic triad), is in the process of transforming American life. But the United States remains a country where whites remain a majority in demography and Christians a large majority in terms of religious adherence. In that sense, American history is meeting the American future, fueling both social conflicts and suspicions, as well as remarkably rapid adaptations. While many insist on preserving America's character as a "Christian nation," political figures publicly recognize celebrations of Eid (the end of the Muslim holy month of Ramadan), host Diwali (Hindu festival of lights) festivals, and warn against responding to acts of violence and terrorism with religious bigotry. The tension between the American religious past, and its future, provides fodder for political debates, social conflicts, and cultural experiments in public pluralism. This seems especially evident when applied to the case of Muslims and other immigrant groups in twenty-first-century America.

Epilogue

Contemporary Dilemmas of Pluralism

A PEW RESEARCH CENTER STUDY released in 2015 calculated that, since the 1965 Hart-Celler Immigration Act, about fifty-nine million immigrants (documented and undocumented) had come to the United States over the past fifty years. The largest number came from Mexico, the Philippines, Korea, the Dominican Republic, India, Cuba, the former Soviet Union, and Vietnam. Unlike previous eras, when Europeans dominated immigrant-sending countries, from 1965 to 2015, just twelve percent of immigrants were from Europe. As late as 1970, Europe had remained the largest source of immigrants, but the situation changed quickly thereafter. Taking the totals from 1965 to 2015 cumulatively, approximately half of the total immigrant wave came from Latin America (including documented and undocumented immigrants from Mexico and Central America), about twenty-five percent from Asia (including South, Southeast, and East Asia), and about eight percent from Africa. This contrasts starkly with the other great period of immigration from 1880 to 1920 discussed in chapter 5, when just under ninety percent of immigrants originated in Europe. Immigration peaked in the period from 2000 to 2005, when about eight million people entered the country; since then, the figure from 2008 to 2013 is about six million. Immigration, both legal and illegal, from Latin America peaked in the 1990s, and has since declined; since 2011, Asian immigrants have taken the lead in terms of total numbers per year. Overall, immigrants accounted for fifty-five percent of American population growth during this fifty-year period, and the foreign-born population of the country rose from five percent in 1965 to fourteen percent in 2015.

Juxtaposing this wave of immigration with statistics about the religious affiliations of Americans (and how those break down racially and geographically) suggests much about the ongoing tensions between the Christian history and pluralist present of the United States. Recent surveys from the Pew Research Center have shown that America remains a predominantly Christian country, but that the share of those self-identifying as "Christian" is in decline, from about seventy-eight percent in 2007 to seventy percent in a 2014 survey. The numbers claiming "no religious affiliation," often referred to as "nones," are growing markedly, from a figure of sixteen percent in 2007 to over twenty-two percent in 2014. Meanwhile, those claiming non-Christian traditions—Jews, Muslims, Hindus, Buddhists, Sikhs, and others—have risen as a share of the population from just over four percent in 2007 to nearly six percent. And the share of racial and ethnic minorities within various Christian traditions is soaring—forty-one percent of American Catholics in 2014 (as compared to thirty-five percent in 2007), twenty-four percent of American evangelical Protestants (as compared to nineteen percent in 2007), and fourteen percent of mainline Protestants (as compared to nine percent in 2007). The majority of "new" immigrants since 1965, in fact, are Christian, and as these figures show they are remaking American Christian churches, as part of what one scholar has called the "de-Europeanization of American Christianity." As he concludes, "race and religion are increasingly decoupling." Another scholar analyzing demographic data has described what he calls "the end of white Christian America." Images of Christianity in America, church leaders have pointed out, must incorporate Asians in Bible studies, Mexicans conducting Passion Plays during Holy week, and Ethiopians gathering in Eastern Orthodox congregations.

Because census takers are not allowed to gather religious data, these figures come from surveys that sample the population. Thus, they should be understood as very approximate numbers with a considerable margin of error. Moreover, the numbers themselves change depending on how terms are defined—for example, are Methodists counted as "mainline" or "evangelical" Protestants? And how do you count "nones" who nonetheless also self-describe as "spiritual but not religious"? How about those born Jews who incorporate Buddhist practices into their daily lives? Surveys always suggest much about the conceptions the survey takers themselves bring to the enterprise.

Caveats aside, putting together the impressive numbers on immigration statistics over the last fifty years, and the data on religious affiliations and attitudes suggested by surveys, raises important questions about the future of religion and race in American history. What will race and religion "look" like in an increasingly multiracial and plural society, one still "divided by faith" in terms of race but one in which race no longer defines religion in the ways that it historically has?

Events in the very recent past have provided much fodder for both the optimistic and pessimistic views of the interaction of race and religion in American history.

On a June evening in 2015, a young white man named Dylann Roof came to the Wednesday evening prayer meeting at the Emanuel African Methodist Episcopal Church in Charleston. He sat for an hour that evening with a small group of congregants. They were led in Bible study by Clementa Pinckney, their pastor who also served as a South Carolina State Senator. After that hour, Roof rose up and began shooting, while allegedly declaring, "I have to do it. You rape our women, and you're taking over our country. And you have to go." He murdered the pastor and eight others, an event with an eerie connection to violent attacks on this church in its past.

Emanuel AME (known under a different name in the nineteenth century) had a long and storied history, dating from the 1810s and its connection with Denmark Vesey, a free black man who allegedly was the ringleader of a narrowly aborted revolt in 1822 in Charleston. The backlash to the Vesey Revolt ended in the church being burned down and the organization of the African Methodist Episcopal Church banished from the state. The church returned after the Civil War, its physical construction being supervised by Denmark Vesey's son, a carpenter by trade. By the 1960s, it housed civil rights organizing meetings. In 1969, the church served as a gathering point for striking black hospital workers, who heard a message from the widow of Martin Luther King, slain a year earlier while in Memphis to preach to striking garbage workers. By 2015, Emanuel AME stood squarely within Charleston's thriving tourist district. By that time, the governor of the state was Nimrata (Nikki) Randhawa Haley, the daughter of a family of Indian Sikh immigrants who had launched a career as a conservative Tea Party insurgent in the state Republican establishment.

Ghosts of the violent past of race and religion in American history rose up in the guise of troubled young men like Roof and in the Confederate symbols and monuments pervasively visible throughout the region. Prior to his act, Roof had immersed himself in racist hate literature. He had compiled material from the "Council of Conservative Citizens," a politically well-connected group descended from the White Citizens' Councils of the civil rights era. Commentators pointed out the irony of how the Confederate flag rose at full height outside the State Capitol grounds in Columbia, even as the American flag stood at half-staff. A horse-drawn carriage pulling the coffin of the Reverend Clementa Pinckney rolled under that Confederate battle flag, an emblem that still flew in numerous public locales throughout the region as an emblem of "heritage."

Yet unlike so many other white supremacist crimes in southern history, this time, interracial gatherings mourned the dead. President Barack Obama's eulogy for Clementa Pinckney alluded to the traumas of that southern past, but also the evidence of God's grace seen in the transformations of the region. Pinckney had said that "Across the South, we have a deep appreciation for history. We haven't always had a deep appreciation of each other's history." But, Obama added, he also "understood that justice grows out of recognition of ourselves in each other, that my liberty depends on you being free," and that "history can't be a sword to justify injustice or a shield against progress." Obama's address expertly wove the theme of "grace," throughout, punctuated with an impromptu singing of "Amazing Grace." After the funeral, local politicos pivoted quickly to distance themselves from the Confederate battle flag which flew over the procession of the Reverend Pinckney in Columbia. Televised scenes from the courtroom showed family members of the victims in the Charleston shooting express their grief but also their forgiveness toward the presumed perpetrator. Russell Moore, a denominational official within the conservative-led Southern Baptist Convention, wrote in a post responding to Charleston that "the cross and the Confederate flag cannot coexist without one setting the other on fire." Governor Haley, flanked by South Carolina's black Republican Senator Tim Scott, declared that the flag had been an important part of South Carolina's past, but had no place in its future. Some perceived this as a turning point, at least symbolically, in race, religion, and southern history.

A few months later, the leading Republican candidate early in the primary season for the 2016 presidential election, the businessman and real

estate mogul Donald Trump, announced to enthusiastic crowds his proposal to build a wall between the United States and Mexico and ban the
entry of all Muslims into the country until "we know what the hell is
going on." Not to be outdone, his closest rival for the Republican nomi-
nation, Ted Cruz, urged systematic surveillance of "Muslim neighborhoods" in the United States and a stringent regime of deportation even
for sons and daughters of those who had crossed the border illegally. At
one campaign event, an audience member told the crowd, "We have a
problem in this country. It's called Muslims," as Trump nodded and said
"Right." "We know our president is one. You know he's not even an
American," the person concluded, to no contradiction from the crowd
or the candidate. Polls and surveys demonstrated that, even at the end of
Obama's presidency, nearly a third of Americans either thought Obama
(a Protestant Christian) was a Muslim, or were "not sure"; for Republican
primary voters, the figure was over fifty percent.

As was normal with his campaign, Trump's suggestions were less policy proposals than symbolic statements articulating the historic prejudices
of great numbers of Americans, who feared immigrants generally, and
the decline of white American nationalism particularly. Since the tragedy of September 11, 2001, many had perceived the threat of terrorism
associated with Islam in general and Muslim immigrants to America in
particular. No amount of statistics pointing out that average Americans
were more likely to die in a lightning strike than in a terrorist incident,
or that right-wing white domestic terrorism had resulted in more deaths
since September 11 than all incidents related to terrorism arising from
those motivated by violent interpretations of Islam, could persuade those
who already had made the connection. And a steady stream of hate crimes
directed against those perceived to be Muslims (including Sikhs, who come
from an entirely different tradition) and against their institutions (such as
hate graffiti sprayed on mosques) resulted in part from the connections.

THE RACIALIZATION OF MUSLIM AMERICANS

The contemporary Muslim-American experience of (at once) freedom,
surveillance, and suspicion reflects much of the long history of race, religion, and "difference" in American history. The fears expressed here
harkened back to nativist movements familiar in American history, most

especially to the Know-Nothing Party of the 1850s, which tried to ban Catholic immigration and perceived Catholics as a dire threat to the American Republic, just as many Americans perceived Muslims in the 2016 electoral cycle. Perhaps most important, it suggested the ways in which "Muslim" elided categories or both race and religion and stirred up deep-rooted American tropes of the bounds of racial and religious habitation.

Islam has had a long history in the United States, dating from the large-scale importation of slaves from Islamic regions of West Africa in the seventeenth and eighteenth century. Later, in the nineteenth and early twentieth century, sizable populations from what later came to be called the Middle East, particularly Lebanese, began to arrive. Since the Hart-Celler Act of 1965, Muslim immigrants have come in large numbers particularly from South Asia (Pakistan), Southeast Asia (particularly Indonesia), and the Middle East and North Africa, coinciding with a dramatic diversification of the immigrant population generally.

The main factor differentiating contemporary Muslim Americans is their racial diversity. As one careful demographic study from 2011 indicated, of the approximately 2.75 million Muslims residing the United States, "No single racial or ethnic group makes up more than 30% of the total" population. Thirty percent described themselves as "white," slightly over twenty percent as Asian, six percent as Hispanic, and nineteen percent as "other" or "mixed race." Part of this statistic derives from the fact of many Muslims from the Middle East describing themselves as white or mixed race, while South Asian Muslims typically signify themselves as "Asian." More native-born Muslims self-identified as "black" (forty percent did so), while eighteen percent identified as white, ten percent as Asian, and twenty-one percent as "other." Interestingly, an unusually high concentration (almost sixty percent) of third-generation Muslims (born in the United States or of parents from the United States) self-reported as black.

This sets the context for the cultural conversation of the role of Islam in America and its status as a "minority" religion, or an "ethnic" religion, or a racialized religion. For the demographic reasons just noted here, it is impossible to see Muslims as a "race," despite the mistaken propensity of many white Americans to identify "Muslim" with "Arab." At the same time, the rising hostility toward Islam among a sizable minority of white

Christians in the 2010s, and the nativist sentiments held by many, suggest the continued racialization of suspicious religious subjects in contemporary American life.

Ironically, at the same time, Islam in America faced its own dilemmas of race and religion, most particularly in divisions between African American versus immigrant Arabic or South Asian Muslims. Most American mosques remain essentially monocultural, just as do the majority of American Christian (especially Protestant) congregations. The same differences in language, worship practice, socioeconomic status, neighborhood residentially organized religious institutions, and other factors that kept American Christians apart racially (even when they deliberately strove to break down those barriers) had a parallel effect on American Muslim institutions. This suggests the degree to which racial inequalities in America are deeply rooted structurally and institutionally, such that they are reproduced in schools, churches, and neighborhood organizations, even when participants in those organizations actively fight against them.

DIVIDED BY FAITH

Optimists about race and religion frequently point to the important role religion has played historically in movements such as abolitionism and civil rights. And certainly, movements toward racial equality historically have had a strong religious base, as has been discussed previously in this book.

Yet one primary challenge to the thesis that churches will point the way to racial equality came in the important 2001 work *Divided by Faith*, authored by the religious sociologists Michael Emerson and Christian Smith. The title captured their thesis. Emerson and Smith showed that contemporary white and black evangelicals believed on the one hand in a racially egalitarian church, but were fundamentally divided on issues of how racial inequalities could best be addressed in society. White evangelicals continued to insist that conversion and "heart change" would be sufficient to address deep-rooted social problems such as racial inequality. Meanwhile black, Latino, and other evangelicals of color perceived structural barriers to racial inequality. They insisted that an activist government was necessary to address the deeply embedded racial inequalities of American society. A simple "heart change" was not sufficient.

White evangelicals, Emerson and Smith found, held one of three views. The first was that racial problems resulted from the sin of personal prejudice. The second was that a perception of "race problems" resulted from members of minority groups who harped on racial prejudice and blew up random individual incidents into systemic problems. Related, many evangelicals felt that there was no race problem, but only something ginned up by a racial grievance industry that capitalized on racial rhetoric to advance its own agenda. Even evangelicals who recognized the reality of racial inequality, they suggested, interpreted this through an individualistic theology, which made them unable to see structural and institutional discrimination written into the history of American neighborhoods. As they summarized it, "white evangelicals' cultural tools and racial isolation direct them to see the world individualistically and as a series of discrete incidents. They also direct them to desire a color-blind society." Black evangelicals tend to see the racial world very differently, through the lens of systemic discrimination enforced less by personal prejudice than by the workings of institutions and by a gulf in generational wealth accumulated disproportionately by whites.

Since this work, scholars have examined the "Divided by Faith" thesis in a variety of contexts, most particularly within the rise of multiethnic churches in American society. Difficult issues of how churches may address social change in America come in part because of the long evangelical emphasis on "heart change" over social change. On the other hand, religion in America often has been at the forefront of the most dramatic and sweeping movements of equality, from abolitionism in the nineteenth century to the civil rights movement in the twentieth. Thus, churches have shown how they can work effectively "in the world" without sacrificing their spiritual message, precisely by *applying* their spiritual message to the world. The increasingly pluralization of American society is reflected in the growing multiethnic church movement and the very self-conscious ways churches and ministers have acted as mediators and interpreters of contemporary social conflicts involving race.

MULTIETHNIC CHURCHES

Over the last two decades, a growing effort to intentionally foster and establish multiethnic churches has taken hold among a significant minority of American Christians. Sometimes this happens without that much conscious intent, as in the case of suburban megachurches which draw huge crowds from their surrounding areas, and thus attract multiethnic congregations more or less by default. In other cases, religious leaders have consciously fostered multiethnic settings in urban congregations in an attempt to recapture the church's potential for easing or overcoming human divisions through the power of bodies worshipping together.

In the wake of controversies over the highly publicized shootings of young black men in Missouri, New York, and elsewhere in 2014, a group of multiethnic church leaders wrote the following, expressing their vision of what the church could accomplish that other institutions in society could not by themselves:

> At its core the scourge of racism presents a spiritual crisis with real life and death repercussions. And while government and educational programs, together with the efforts of countless individuals, groups and agencies, have long-sought to eliminate prejudice and the disparaging consequences of systemic racism still deeply embedded within our society, it is long-past time to recognize that systemic racism cannot be overcome apart from the establishment of local churches which intentionally and joyfully reflect the love of God for all people beyond the distinctions of this world that so often and otherwise divide.

They noted as well that current statistics demonstrate that over eighty-six percent of churches have less than twenty percent diversity in their congregations, showing how far American churches had to go on this issue. Groups such as the "Mosaix Global Network," founded by a pair of pastors in 2004 to "catalyze" the growing multiethnic church movement, aimed to move American churches toward a goal of twenty percent congregational diversity in twenty percent of American churches by 2020. They described the importance of their work as follows: "Apart from ethnically and economically diverse relationships, we will not fully encounter the condition of those different than our own . . . we are less

likely to get involved in genuine community transformation. Without
involvement, nothing changes, and, thus, systemic inequities are perpetu-
ated unintentionally by sleeping giants; namely the evangelical churches
of America."

However, the degree to which even multiracial churches will move
evangelicals to embrace more structural ways of interpreting inequality remains in some question. A recent close study of the issue, focusing
on the "racial healing" movement, and especially on "racial reconcilers
of color," found them ambivalent on the question of whether race problems were in fact just *sin* problems. After well-publicized incidents in
Missouri, Chicago, and elsewhere demonstrated persistent problems of
systematic targeting of minority communities by local police and government, a football player for the New Orleans Saints (Benjamin Watson,
himself an African American) posted the following reflections:

> I'M ENCOURAGED, because ultimately the problem is not a SKIN
> problem, it is a SIN problem. SIN is the reason we rebel against
> authority. SIN is the reason we abuse our authority. SIN is the reason
> we are racist, prejudiced and lie to cover for our own. SIN is the reason
> we riot, loot and burn. BUT I'M ENCOURAGED because God has
> provided a solution for sin through . . . Jesus and with it, a transformed
> heart and mind. One that's capable of looking past the outward and
> seeing what's truly important in every human being. The cure for the
> Michael Brown, Trayvon Martin, Tamir Rice and Eric Garner trag-
> edies is not education or exposure. It's the Gospel. So, finally, I'M
> ENCOURAGED because the Gospel gives mankind hope.

One extensive study of the "Evangelical Racial Change" movement over
the last generation of American evangelical history, based on years of
interviews and participant-observation of efforts, quotes a reconciler of
color concluding: "A lot of times the reconciliation issue is focused on
Anglos making it right, but it's from both sides, from all sides. It's not
just white/black or white/brown; it's sometimes black/brown and Asian/
Asian, brown against brown and so forth. So it isn't a matter of skin, it's
a matter of sin. So I get forgiveness of my sin and you get forgiveness
for your sin and we forgive each other and we're forgiven of God, then

we can start on a clean slate." This reinforced the reflections of Watson and others. The study showed that the "racial reconcilers" often saw racism not as a social problem, but as an individual affliction of sin, and that government attempts to address racism at systematic and structural levels would therefore fail. This view resonated not only among white evangelicals but was also characteristic of "reconcilers of color." The reconcilers of color may be more sensitive to the social causation of racial inequality, but they often tend to turn to individual solutions, including moments of personal reconciliation that evangelicals experience as social miracles. Ultimately, they too see it as a *sin* problem.

Even the most politically conscious of these newly emerging multiethnic churches remain ambivalent, at best, about addressing political rather than personal solutions. Evangelicals remain resistant to examining the structural roots that frame racial encounters unequally. Many multiracial churches would have to avoid such discussions because their members would divide up into racially defined voting blocs. At one particularly successful Pentecostal megachurch, Redemption Church in Greenville, South Carolina, one member noted that in a church with the motto "Where the Many Become One," the church was de facto divided between liberals (nearly all black) and conservatives (nearly all white), and "it's like never the twain shall meet." As a result, political discussions were taboo. Redemption Church thus represents a living symbol of progress toward a multiracial society, even while it stands as a representative of the deep divisions that will continue to define race and religion in America. Members of various religious traditions—evangelicals, Catholics, Muslims, and others—truly believe that of one blood God made all nations, but find it difficult, for deep historical and institutional reasons, to break the bounds of America's racial habitations.

* * *

This book has attempted to balance the terms "religion" and "race" over the long duration of (North) American history. I have aimed to show how they remained always contested and yet ultimately solidified into social formations that fundamentally shaped American religions in terms of ideology, organization, and practice. However constructed "race" may be, it acts as a real force in history, and however much the term "religion" is always being redefined and reformed, it has been a central ordering force in individual lives, in social policies, and in vast social movements. This book has been a highly selective glimpse at just a handful of the stories that could be told. And yet, the half has never been told.

A Note on Sources

This book may be best accompanied by Paul Harvey and Kathryn Gin Lum, eds., *The Oxford Handbook to Race and Religion in American History* (New York: Oxford University Press, forthcoming 2017). For acute theological accounts of race and religion, see J. Kameron Carter, *Race: A Theological Account* (New York: Oxford University Press, 2008), and Willie Jennings, *The Christian Imagination: Theology and the Origins of Race* (New Haven, CT: Yale University Press, 2011). Reginald Horsman, *Race and Manifest Destiny: The Origins of American Racial Anglo-Saxonism* (Cambridge, MA: Harvard University Press, 1981), is an essential study of the rise of "whiteness" thought in American history, as is Winthrop Jordan, *White Over Black: American Racial Attitudes Toward the Negro, 1550–1812* (Chapel Hill: University of North Carolina Press, 1968). On race and Mormonism, see W. Paul Reeve, *Religion of a Different Color: Race and the Mormon Struggle for Whiteness* (New York: Oxford University Press, 2015).

Important for theoretical conceptualizations of the constructions of race, Michael Omi and Howard Winant's *Racial Formation in the United States: From the 1960s to the 1990s* (New York: Routledge, 1994) remains a classic. See also Ian Haney-Lopez, *White by Law: The Legal Construction of Race* (New York: New York University Press, 2996), and the collection of essays in Craig R. Prentiss, ed., *Religion and the Creation of Race and Ethnicity* (New York: New York University Press, 2003).

For an important and irreplaceable anthology of primary sources from the entirety of African American religious history, see Milton Sernett, ed., *African–American Religious History: A Documentary Witness* (2nd ed. Durham, North Carolina: Duke University Press, 1998). A quick survey of African American religious history from the slave trade to the present may be found in Paul Harvey, *Through the Storm, Through the Night: A History of African American Christianity* (Lanham, MD: Rowman & Littlefield, 2011). A recent synthesis which proposes a new paradigm for the field is Sylvester Johnson, *African American Religions, 1500–2000: Colonialism, Democracy, and Freedom* (Cambridge: Cambridge University Press, 2015). Another useful survey may be found in Bettye Collier-Thomas, *Jesus, Jobs, and Justice: African American Women and Religion* (New York: Knopf, 2010). See also Barbara Savage, *Your Spirits Walk Beside Us: The Politics of Black Religion* (Cambridge, MA: Harvard University Press, 2008). Savage's work may be read alongside Mark Noll, *God and Race in American Politics: A Short History* (Princeton, NJ: Princeton University Press, 2008), a useful introductory survey to that subject. More specific to the American South, see the synthetic surveys in Paul Harvey, *Christianity and Race in the American South: A History* (Chicago: University of Chicago Press, 2016), and Randy Sparks, *Religion in Mississippi* (Jackson: University Press of Mississippi, 2001).

For surveys and interpretations of Native Americans and religion, see James L Sullivan, *Native Religions and Cultures of North America* (New York: Continuum, 2000), and George Tinker's more polemical *Missionary Conquest: The Gospel and Native American Cultural Genocide* (Minneapolis: Fortress Press, 1993). For Natives, a sweeping collection of primary documents may be found in Colin Calloway, ed., *First Peoples: A Documentary Survey of American Indian History* (4th edition, Boston: Bedford Books, 2011). For Asian American religions, the outstanding primary source documentary history is Thomas A. Tweed and Stephen Prothero, eds., *Asian Religions in America: A Documentary History* (New York: Oxford University Press, 1999).

For accounts of religion, race, and politics in African American life, see Frederick Harris, *Something Within: Religion in African American Political Activism* (New York: Oxford University Press, 1999), and Vincent Harding, *There is a River: The Black Struggle for Freedom in America* (New York: Houghton Mifflin Harcourt, 1993). Quinton Dixie and Juan Williams, *This Far by Faith: Stories from the African American Religious Experience* (New York: William Morrow, 2003), is an excellent survey text. For a useful primary source compilation, see Judith Weisenfeld and Richard Newman, eds., *This Far By Faith: Reading in African American Women's Religious Biography* (New York: Routledge, 1995). Advanced scholarly arguments in the field are taken up in Sylvester Johnson, *African American Religions, 1500–2000: Colonialism, Democracy, and Freedom* (Cambridge, MA: Harvard University Press, 2015); Albert J. Raboteau,

A Fire in the Bones: Reflections on African-American Religious History (Boston: Beacon Press, 1995) and Michael Gomez, *Black Crescent: The Experience and Legacy of African Muslims in the Americas* (Cambridge: Cambridge University Press, 2005). The best history of black Catholics in the United States is Cyprian Davis, *The History of Black Catholics in the United States* (New York: Crossroad, 1990). Humanism and alternative religious thought in African American communities has been explored in Anthony Pinn's *African American Humanism: A Documentary History* (New York: New York University, 2003), and *Humanism: Essays on Religion, Race, and Cultural Production* (London: Bloomsbury, 2015). The ways in which African American humanism might function as a religious orientation is presented in Pinn's *African American Humanist Principles* (New York: Palgrave Macmillan, 2004).

Columbia University Press has a series of books on particular religious traditions that are exceedingly helpful introductions, including Jane Smith, *Islam in America* (New York: Columbia University Press, 2012) and Richard Seager, *Buddhism in America* (New York: Columbia University Press, 2012). Peter Manseau's *One Nation, Under Gods: A New American History* (New York: Little, Brown, & Company, 2015), is a sweeping reinterpretation of American religious history and pluralism, focusing on lesser-known or forgotten stories.

R. Marie Griffith, ed., *American Religions: A Documentary History* (New York: Oxford University Press, 2007), provides an excellent primary source overview of the entirety of American religious history and Larry Murphy, ed., *Down by the Riverside: Readings in African American Religion* (New York: New York University Press, 2000), as well as Cornel West and Eddie Glaude, eds., *African American Religious Thought: An Anthology* (Westminster: John Knox Press, 1993) do the same in the form of secondary reading essays that anthologize the richness of the scholarship in African American religious history.

Atlases can provide particular lenses to envision the history of race and religion in America. The classic "big" atlas of American religious history, with loads of information specific to the topic of race and religion, may be found in Edwin Gaustad, ed., *New Historical Atlas of Religion in America* (New York: Oxford University Press, 2001). For a shorter and more user-friendly version, see Bret E. Carroll, *The Routledge Historical Atlas of Religion in America* (New York: Routledge, 2000).

A number of recent collections look at episodes of race, religion, and politics in American life. See, for example, Robin Dale Jacobson and Nancy D. Wadsworth, *Faith and Race in American Political Life* (Charlottesville: University of Virginia Press, 2012) and Valerie Martinez Ebbers and Manochehr Dorraj, ed., *Perspectives on Race, Ethnicity and Religion: Identity Politics in America* (New York: Oxford University Press, 2009). Jonathan Kahn and Vincent Lloyd, eds., *Race and Secularism in America* (New York: Columbia University Press, 2016) is a pioneering work in addressing race squarely within secularism. See also Anthony Cook, *The Least of These: Race, Law and Religion in America* (New York: Routledge, 1997).

A full survey of how American racial preconceptions were literally written "onto" the body and physical appearance of Christ may be found in Edward J. Blum and Paul Harvey, *The Color of Christ: The Son of God and the Sage of Race in America* (Chapel Hill: University of North Carolina Press, 2012). Stephen Prothero, *American Jesus, How the Son of God Became a National Icon* (New York: Farrar, Strauss, and Giroux, 2004) and Richard Wightman Fox, *Jesus in America: Personal Savior, National Hero, Cultural Obsession* (New York: HarperOne, 2005), also both devote considerable attention to race and the formation of ideas about the body and meaning of Jesus in American life.

CHAPTER 1

For Puritan New England, this volume relied heavily upon a vast older literature on New England Puritans dating from Perry Miller's *The New England Mind: The Seventeenth Century* and *The New England Mind: From Colony to Province* (repr. ed., Cambridge, MA: Belknap Press of Harvard University Press, 1983), and newer classics such as David Hall's *Worlds of Wonder, Days of Judgment: Popular Religious Belief in Early New England* (Cambridge, MA: Harvard University Press, 1990). For newer perspectives, incorporating more of the histories of Native peoples and of African Americans, see especially Richard Bailey's *Race and Redemption in Puritan New England* (New York: Oxford, 2011) and Linford Fisher's powerful reinterpretation in *An Indian Great Awakening: Religion and the Shaping of Native Cultures in Early America* (New York: Oxford, 2013).

Much of the thinking about John Eliot and his crusade to translate the Bible into Indian languages comes from Richard Cogley's *John Eliot's Mission to the Indians Before King Philip's* War (Cambridge, MA: Harvard University Press, 1999). Neal Salisbury, *Manitou and Providence: Indians, Europeans, and the Making of New England, 1500–1643* (New York: Oxford University Press, 1983) looks at Puritan-Indian relations from the perspective of Indian peoples in New England. Jill Lepore, *In the Name of War: King Philip's War and the Origins of American Identity* (New York: Knopf, 1999) and Mary Beth Norton, *In the Devil's Snare: The Salem Witchcraft Crisis of 1692* (New York: Norton, 2012) are key recent interpretations of the largest war in seventeenth-century America, and of the Salem witchcraft episode, particularly in terms of its racial implications.

On the Jesuits in New France, a convenient and user-friendly introduction, a sort of "greatest hits" compilation of the multivolume *Jesuit Relations* of the seventeenth century, is Allen Greer, ed., *The Jesuit Relations: Natives and Missionaries in Seventeenth–Century North America* (Boston: Bedford Books, 2001). On Kateri Tekakwitha, the key work is Allan Greer, *Mohawk Saint: Catherine Tekakwitha and the Jesuits* (New York: Oxford University Press, 2005).

On the Spanish and their missionaries in New Mexico, the classic work is Ramón Gutiérrez, *When Jesus Came, the Corn Mothers Went Away: Marriage, Sexuality, and Power in Northern New Mexico, 1500–1846* (Stanford: Stanford University Press, 1991). For Florida, see Daniel Murphee, "Race and Religion on the Periphery: Disappointment and Missionization in the Spanish Floridas, 1566–1763," in *Race, Nation, and Religion in the Americas*, edited by Henry Goldschmidt and Elizabeth McAlister (Oxford: Oxford University Press, 2004), 35–59.

For religion, Natives, and multicultural interactions and colonialism in early America, see James Brooks, *Captives and Cousins: Slavery, Kinship, and Community in the Southwest Borderlands* (Chapel Hill: University of North Carolina Press, 2002); Julianna Barr, *Peace Came in the Form of a Woman: Indians and Spaniards in the Texas Borderlands* (Chapel Hill: University of North Carolina Press, 2007); Andrew Knaut, *The Pueblo Revolt of 1680: Conquest and Resistance in Seventeenth-Century New Mexico* (Norman, OK: University of Oklahoma Press, 1997); David Weber, ed., *What Caused the Pueblo Revolt of 1680* (Boston: Bedford/ St. Martin's, 1999); and David Roberts, *The Pueblo Revolt: The Secret*

Rebellion that Drove the Spaniards Out of the Southwest (New York: Simon & Schuster, 2005).

John Thornton's works on the connection of Africa and the Americas during the era of the slave trade are vital. See especially, *Africa and Africans in the Making of the Atlantic World, 1400–1680* (Cambridge, England: Cambridge University Press, 1992). The interpretation of the Stono Rebellion presented here comes from Thornton, "African Dimensions of the Stono Rebellion," *The American Historical Review* 96 (1991): 1101–13, and the primary documents collected in Mark Smith, ed., *Stono: Documenting and Interpreting a Southern Slave Revolt* (Columbia: University of South Carolina Press, 2005). The document from 1723 quoted in chapter 1 comes from Thomas N. Ingersoll, "Releese Us out of This Cruell Bondegg: An Appeal from Virginia in 1723," *William and Mary Quarterly,* Third Series, 51 (October 1994): 776–82.

CHAPTER 2

Sylvia Frey and Betty Wood, *Come Shouting to Zion: African American Protestantism in the American South and British Caribbean to 1830* (Chapel Hill: University of North Carolina Press, 1998), provides a central and sweeping interpretation of the rise of black Protestantism through the Great Awakening and revolutionary period. In *Exchanging Our Country Marks: The Transformation of African Identities in the Colonial and Antebellum South* (Chapel Hill: University of North Carolina Press, 1998), Michael Gomez provides a stimulating reinterpretation of the transition from African to African American identities in the eighteenth and early nineteenth centuries, including the contested role of religion in that process; James Sidbury provides a complementary analysis in *Becoming African in America: Race and Nation in the English Black Atlantic, 1760–1830* (New York: Oxford University Press, 2007).

Joel Martin's work is especially important for Native religions from the mid-eighteenth to the mid-nineteenth century. For a more general history, see Martin's *The Land Looks After Us: A History of Native American Religion* (Oxford, UK: Oxford University Press, 2001) and "Indians, Contact, and Colonialism in the Deep South: Themes for a

Postcolonial History of American Religion," as well as Laurie Maffly–Kipp, "Eastward Ho! American Religion from the Perspective of the Pacific Rim," both in Thomas Tweed, ed., *Retelling U.S. Religious History* (Berkeley: University of California Press, 1997), 127–181. More specifically about the Redstick revolt, see Joel Martin, *Sacred Revolt: The Muskogees' Struggle for a New World* (Boston: Beacon Press, 1991). There are a number of excellent recent works on Native writers and thinkers. Laura Murray's *To Do Good to My Indian Brethren: The Writings of Joseph Johnson, 1751–1776* (Amherst: University of Massachusetts Press, 1998) and Joanna Brooks's *The Collected Writings of Samson Occom, Mohegan: Leadership and Literature in Eighteenth-Century Native America* (New York: Oxford University Press, 2008) are excellent compilations of key writings, indispensable for future scholarship. For secondary accounts, see Kristina Bross's *Dry Bones and Indian Sermons: Praying Indians in Colonial America* (New York: Cornell University Press, 2004) and Rachel Wheeler's *To Live Upon Hope: Mohicans and Missionaries in the Eighteenth-Century Northeast* (Ithaca, NY: Cornell University Press, 2013). Joanna Brooks, *American Lazarus: Religion and the Rise of African-American and Native American Literatures* (New York: Oxford University Press, 2007) is a critical reinterpretation of the writings of blacks and natives. David Silverman, *Red Brethren: The Brothertown and Stockton Indians and the Problem of Race in Early America* (Ithaca, NY: Cornell University Press, 2010), is an excellent social history.

Christopher Cameron's *To Plead our Own Cause: African Americans in Massachusetts and the Making of the Antislavery Movement* (Kent: Kent State University Press, 2014) shows how African Americans in Massachusetts helped to build an antislavery movement on religious convictions. In *Black Puritan, Black Republican: The Life and Thought of Lemuel Haynes, 1753–1833* (New York: Oxford University Press, 2002), John Saillant provides a key study of an early black abolitionist.

Important studies for race and religion in the South include Cynthia Lynn Lyerly, *Methodism and the Southern Mind, 1780–1910* (New York: Oxford University Press, 1998); Jon Sensbach, *A Separate Canaan: The Making of an Afro-Moravian World in North Carolina, 1763–1840* (Chapel Hill: University of North Carolina Press, 1998); Rhys Isaac, *The Transformation of Virginia, 1740–1790* (Chapel Hill: University of North Carolina Press, 1982); Allan Gallay, *The Formation of a Planter Elite:*

Jonathan Bryan and the Southern Colonial Frontier (Athens: University of Georgia Press, 1989); and Emily Clark, *Masterless Mistresses: The New Orleans Ursulines and the Development of a New World Society, 1727–1834* (Chapel Hill: University of North Carolina Press, 2007). On the Great Awakening, see Thomas Kidd, *The Great Awakening: The Roots of Evangelical Christianity in Colonial America* (New Haven, CT: Yale University Press, 2009), and Kidd, *The Great Awakening: A Brief History with Documents* (Boston: Bedford Books, 2007).

CHAPTER 3

Lawrence Levine's *Black Culture and Black Consciousness: Afro American Folk Thought from Slavery to Freedom* (New York: Oxford University Press, 1977) has what is still the single best discussion of the meaning of the spirituals in African American life. The absolutely central book in the field of slave religion remains Albert Raboteau, *Slave Religion: The Invisible Institution in the Antebellum South* (New York: Oxford University Press, 1978). Accompanying that would be an older and very much underappreciated classic, Mechal Sobel's *Trabelin' On: The Slave Journey to an Afro-Baptist Faith* (Westport, Connecticut: Greenwood Press, 1978).

The list of outstanding works on race, religion, and slavery in the South is long and deep. Notable titles include Erskine Clarke's Bancroft-prize winning work *Dwelling Place: A Plantation Epic* (New Haven, CT: Yale University Press, 2004); Donald Mathews, *Religion in the Old South* (Chicago: University of Chicago Press, 1977); David Bailey, *Shadow on the Church: Southwestern Evangelical Religion and the Issue of Slavery* (Ithaca, New York: Cornell University Press, 1985); John Boles, ed., *Masters and Slaves in the House of the Lord: Race and Religion in the American South, 1740–1870* (Lexington: University Press of Kentucky, 1988); Margaret Washington Creel, *A Peculiar People: Slave Religion and Community Culture Among the Gullahs* (New York: New York University Press, 1988); Dena J. Epstein, *Sinful Tunes and Spirituals: Black Folk Music to the Civil War* (Urbana: University of Illinois Press, 1977); Eugene Genovese, *Roll, Jordan, Roll: The World the Slaves Made* (New York: Pantheon Books, 1974); Nathan Hatch, *The Democratization of American Christianity* (New Haven, CT: Yale University Press, 1989); Walter Pitts, *Old Ship of Zion:*

Afro-Baptist Ritual in the African Diaspora (New York: Oxford University Press, 1993); Mechal Sobel, *The World They Made Together: Black and White Values in Eighteenth-Century Virginia* (Princeton, NJ: Princeton University Press, 1987); Randy Sparks, *On Jordan's Stormy Banks: Evangelicalism in Mississippi, 1763–1877* (Athens: University of Georgia Press, 1994); Janet Duitsman Cornelius *Slave Missions and the Black Church in the Antebellum South* (Columbia, South Carolina: University of South Carolina Press, 1999); Christine Leigh Heyrman, *Southern Cross: The Beginnings of the Bible Belt* (New York: Knopf, 1997); Michael Pasquier, *Fathers on the Frontier: French Missionaries and the Roman Catholic priesthood in the United States, 1789–1870* (New York: Oxford University Press, 2012); and Charles Irons, *The Origins of Proslavery Christianity: White and Black Evangelicals in Colonial and Antebellum Virginia* (Chapel Hill: University of North Carolina Press, 2008). Daniel L. Fountain, *Slavery, Civil War, and Salvation: African American Slaves and Christianity, 1830–1870* (Baton Rouge: Louisiana State University Press, 2010) makes the case that Christianity became a dominant force in African American cultural life after, rather than before, emancipation. For a penetrating study of the meaning of the "Ham curse" in American theology, see Stephen Haynes, *Noah's Curse: The Biblical Justification of American Slavery* (New York: Oxford University Press, 2002).

David Brion Davis, *In the Image of God: Religion, Moral Values, and Our Heritage of Slavery* (New York: Oxford University Press, 2001), presents the results of a lifetime of research in the rise of slavery and anti-slavery thought in the Western world. Joanne Pope Melish, *Disowning Slavery: Gradual Emancipation and "Race" in New England, 1780–1860* (Ithaca, New York: Cornell University Press, 2000) examines the slow and contested process of emancipation in the North. A wonderful collection of primary documents articulating black responses to antebellum American racism may be found in Patrick Rael, et al., eds., *Pamphlets of Protest: An Anthology of Early African American Protest Literature* (New York: Routledge, 2001). See also Rael's monograph *Black Identity and Black Protest in the Antebellum North* (Chapel Hill: University of North Carolina Press, 2002). For a broad survey of African American social and cultural institutions in the antebellum era, see John Ernest, *A Nation Within a Nation: Organizing African American Communities Before the Civil War* (Chicago: Ivan Dee, 2011). Eddie Glaude, *Exodus! Religion,*

Race, and Nation in Early Nineteenth-Century Black America (Chicago: University of Chicago Press, 2000), is a profound theological study.

For a compelling study of California, see Douglas Monroy. *Thrown Among Strangers: The Making of Mexican Culture in Frontier California* (Berkeley: University of California Press, 1991), which insightfully discusses interaction of religious worldviews of California Indians, Spanish missions, and incoming Yankee Protestants. On Nativism, the older classic is still vital: John Higham, *Strangers in the Land: Patterns of American Nativism, 1860–1925* (New Brunswick: Rutgers University Press, 1955).

Study of missionaries has taken off in recent historiography. One particularly compelling recent study of the conceptions of the first generation of American missionaries is Emily Conroy-Krutz, *Christian Imperialism: Converting the World in the Early American Republic* (Ithaca: Cornell University Press, 2015). A few other studies of particular analytical acuity include Patricia Grimshaw, *Paths of Duty: American Missionary Wives in Nineteenth-Century Hawaii* (Honolulu: University of Hawaii Press, 1989), and Joel Martin, "Almost White: The Ambivalent Promise of Christian Missions among the Cherokee," in *Religion and the Creation of Race and Ethnicity*, edited by Craig R. Prentiss (New York: New York University Press, 2003), 43–60. Much of the material about the conceptualization of "Oriental religions" in this chapter comes from the primary source compilation *Asian Religions in America* (cited above) and from Mike Altman, "Imagining Hindus: India and Religion in Nineteenth-Century America" (PhD diss., Emory University, 2014; forthcoming from Oxford University Press under the title *Heathen, Hindoo, Hindu*).

Anthony F. C. Wallace, *The Death and Rebirth of the Seneca* (New York: Vintage Books, 1972), is the seminal text on Native American religion in the New Republic, based on "revitalization" theory in anthropology. Henry Warner Bowden, *American Indians and Christian Missions: Studies in Cultural Conflict* (Chicago: University of Chicago Press, 1981), is an older but still essential work on that topic.

CHAPTER 4

James Campbell, *Songs of Zion: The African Methodist Episcopal Church in the United States and South Africa* (New York: Oxford University

Press, 1998), surveys the rise of the most important African American religious institution in the nineteenth century. Evelyn Brooks Higginbotham, *Righteous Discontent: The Women's Movement in the Black Baptist Church, 1880–1920* (Cambridge, MA: Harvard University Press, 1993), is a pioneering work of African American women's religious organizations in this period. Derek Chang's *Christians of a Christian Nation: Evangelical Missions and the Problem of Race in the Nineteenth Century* (Philadelphia: University of Pennsylvania Press, 2010) is an important comparative work looking at missions among African Americans in the South and Chinese Americans in California in the later nineteenth century. Josh Paddison focuses specifically on California, in his work *American Heathens: Religion, Race, and Reconstruction in California* (Berkeley: University of California Press, 2013). Charles Reagan Wilson's memorable work *Baptized in Blood: The Religion of the Lost Cause* (Athens, Georgia: University of Georgia Press, 1980) is the indispensable source for white southern "Lost Cause" religion.

Race, religion, and the Civil War and Reconstruction era has been a key theme of much recent scholarship. A thoughtful short analysis of the inability of American Christianity to resolve the problem of slavery is explored in Mark Noll, *The Civil War as a Theological Crisis* (New York: Oxford University Press, 2007), and the postwar turn toward white American nationalism in Edward J. Blum, *Reforging the White Republic: Religion, Race, and American Nationalism* (Baton Rouge: Louisiana State University Press, 2003). See also the essays on race, religion, and Reconstruction collected in Edward J. Blum and W. Scott Poole, eds., *Vale of Tears: New Essays on Religion and Reconstruction* (Macon, Georgia: Mercer University Press, 2005). Emily Clark's *A Luminous Brotherhood: Afro-Creole Spiritualism in Nineteenth-Century New Orleans* (Chapel Hill: University of North Carolina Press, 2016) is a wonderful study of the conjunction of radical religion and politics in postwar New Orleans, through the venue of Spiritualism. See also James Bennett, *Religion and the Rise of Jim Crow in New Orleans* (Princeton, NJ: Princeton University Press, 2005); Yvonne P. Chireau, *Black Magic: Religion and the African American Conjuring Tradition* (Berkley: University of California Press, 2003); and Claude F. Jacobs and Andrew J. Kaslow, *The Spiritual Churches of New Orleans: Origins, Beliefs, and Rituals of an African-American Religion* (Knoxville: University of Tennessee Press, 1991).

On religion and race in the postwar South, Paul Harvey's *Freedom's Coming: Religious Cultures and the Shaping of the South from the Civil War through the Civil Rights Era* (Chapel Hill: University of North Carolina Press, 2005) is a broad study, as is William E. Montgomery, *Under Their Own Vine and Fig Tree: The African-American Church in the South 1865–1900* (Baton Rouge: Louisiana State University Press, 1993), while John Giggie's *After Redemption: Jim Crow and the Transformation of African American Religion in the Delta, 1875–1915* (New York: Oxford University Press, 2007) provides an analytical focus on religion and the marketplace. Glenda Gilmore, *Gender and Jim Crow: Women and the Politics of White Supremacy in North Carolina, 1896–1920* (Chapel Hill: University of North Carolina Press, 1996), is a crucial study of that subject. James Melvin Washington, *Frustrated Fellowship: The Black Baptist Quest for Social Power* (Macon, Georgia: Mercer University Press, 1986), was a pioneering narrative of black Baptists. A wonderful compilation of primary documents may be found in Stephen Angell, ed., *Social Protest Thought in the African Methodist Episcopal Church, 1862–1939* (Knoxville: University of Tennessee Press, 2000); accompanying it is Angell's indispensable biography *Bishop Henry McNeal Turner and African American Religion in the South* (Knoxville: University of Tennessee Press, 1994). Laurie Maffly-Kipp, *Setting Down the Sacred Past: African American Race Histories* (Cambridge, MA: Harvard University Press, 2010), surveys the historical writings of educated African American religious leaders. For broader studies and surveys, reliable works include Laurie Maffly-Kipp, *Religion and Society in Frontier California* (New Haven, CT: Yale University Pres, 1994); Joe Richardson, *Christian Reconstruction: The American Missionary Association and Southern Blacks, 1861–1890* (Athens: University of Georgia Press, 1986); and Joseph O Jewell, *Race, Social Reform and the Making of a Middle Class: The American Missionary Association and Black Atlanta, 1870–1900* (New York: Rowman & Littlefield, 2007).

More excellent recent works on African American Christianity, missions, and popular culture include David Wills and Richard Newman, eds., *Black Apostles at Home and Abroad: Afro-Christians and the Christian Mission from the Revolution to Reconstruction* (Boston, MA: G. K. Hall & Co., 1982); Lerone Martin, *Preaching on Wax: The Phonograph and the Shaping of Modern African American Religion* (New York: New York University Press, 2014); and Edward R. Crowther and Keith Harper, eds., *Between Fetters and Freedom: African American Baptists Since Emancipation* (Macon: Mercer University Press, 2015). Joel Williamson, *A Rage for Order: Black-White Relations in the American South Since Emancipation* (New York: Oxford University Pres, 1986), is a condensed and more reader-friendly form of his longer *Crucible of Race* and provides a searching study of diverse varieties of racial thought among whites and blacks in the postwar South. Stephen Ochs, *A Black Patriot and a White Priest: Andre Cailloux and Claude Paschal Maistre in Civil War New Orleans* (Baton Rouge: Louisiana State University Press, 2000), and Peter Hinks and Stephen Kantrowitz, eds., *All Free Men and Brethren: Essays on the History of African American Freemasonry* (Ithaca: Cornell University Press, 2013), provide histories of alternative African American religious institutions (such as the Masons) and some white allies (as in the case of the white radical priest Claude Maistre).

On Natives, Wovoka, and the ghost dances, the best academic account is Gregory Ellis Smoak, *Ghost Dances and Identity: Prophetic Religion and American Indian Ethnogenesis in the Nineteenth Century* (Berkeley: University of California Press, 2008). It can be compared to much older ethnography from the time done by the pioneering scholar James Mooney, such as *The Ghost Dance Religion and Wounded Knee* (repr. ed. New York: Dover Books, 2011). For a compilation of primary documents from Indians in the Progressive era, see Frederick Hoxie, ed., *Talking Back to Civilization: Indian Voices from the Progressive Era* (Boston: Bedford Books, 2001).

CHAPTER 5

A fine compilation of essays exploring issues of religion, race, and nationalism in this period can be found in Elizabeth McAlister and Henry Goldschmidt, ed., *Race, Nation, and Religion in the Americas* (New York: Oxford University Press, 2004).

The black social gospel and conceptions of "black religion" more generally have been the subject of much fine recent scholarship. Ralph Luker's *The Social Gospel in Black and White: American Racial Reform, 1885–1912* (Chapel Hill: University of North Carolina Press, 1991) and Gary Dorrien's *The New Abolition: W. E. B. Du Bois and the Black Social*

Gospel Movement (New Haven, CT: Yale University Press, 2015) remain two central and complementary studies showing the close relationship of the social gospel movement to race. They should be read alongside the older classic by Ronald C. White, *Liberty and Justice for All: Racial Reform and the Social Gospel, 1877–1925* (San Francisco: Harper & Row, 1990), and Curtis Evans, *The Burden of Black Religion* (New York: Oxford University Press, 2008), which shows how much of the concept of there being a "black religion" in the first place was a construct of twentieth-century sociologists. For a provocative interpretation religion and race in the 1920s and the Great Depression, see Kelly J. Baker, *Gospel According to the Klan: The KKK's Appeal to Protestant America* (Lawrence: University of Kansas Press, 2011), and Alison Greene, *No Depression in Heaven: The Great Depression, the New Deal, and the Transformation of Religion in the Delta* (New York: Oxford University Press, 2015). Issues surrounding religion, race, and labor movement are explored provocatively in Ken Fones-Wolf and Elizabeth A. Fones-Wolf, *Struggle for the Soul of the Post-War South: White Evangelical Protestants and Operation Dixie* (Urbana: University of Illinois Press, 1015); Erik Gellman and Jarod Roll, *The Gospel of the Working Class: Labor's Southern Prophets in New Deal America* (Urbana: University of Illinois, 2011); and Jarod Roll, *Spirit of Rebellion: Labor and Religion in the New Cotton South* (Urbana: University of Illinois Press, 2010). Mary G. Rolinson, *Grassroots Garveyism: The Universal Negro Improvement Association in the Rural South, 1920–1927* (Chapel Hill: University of North Carolina Press, 2007), finds a religious enthusiasm for the ideas of Marcus Garvey extending out into the southern countryside.

   Black urban religion, and the making of new religious traditions and sounds, emerges as a major theme in Nick Salvatore, *Singing in a Strange Land: C. L. Franklin, the Black Church, and the Transformation of America* (New York: Little, Brown & Company, 2005), and in Bernice Johnson Reagon ed., *We'll Understand It Better By and By: Pioneering African American Gospel Composers* (Washington, DC: Smithsonian Institution Press, 1992). A classic older study of black religious life in the urban North in this period is St. Clair Drake and Horace R. Cayton, eds., *Black Metropolis: A Study of Negro Life in a Northern City* (New York: Harcourt, Brace, 1945). Their study is updated and black urban religions and the quest for identity given entirely new meanings in three more recent works: Milton Sernett, *Bound for the Promised Land African American Religion and the Great Migration* (Durham: Duke University Press, 1997); Wallace D. Best, *Passionately Human, No Less Divine: Religion and Culture in Black Chicago, 1915–1952* (Princeton, NJ: Princeton University Press, 2007); and Judith Weisenfeld, *New World A-Coming: Black Religion and Racial Identity During the Great Migration* (New York: New York University Press, 2016). A parallel cultural study may be found in Suzanne Smith, *To Serve the Living: Funeral Directors and the African American Way of Death* (Cambridge, MA: Harvard University Press, 2010). On race, religion, and film more specifically, see Judith Weisenfeld, *Hollywood Be Thy Name: African American Religion in American Film, 1929–1949* (Berkeley: University of California Press, 2007). On music, particularly black gospel music, start with Michael Harris, *The Rise of the Gospel Blues: Thomas Andrew Dorsey and the Music of the Urban Church* (New York: Oxford University Press, 1992). Randal Maurice Jelks, *Benjamin Elijah Mays: Schoolmaster of the Movement, A Biography* (Chapel Hill: University of North Carolina Press, 2012), is a biography of a man who eventually became a key tutor and mentor to Martin Luther King, Jr.; this may be compared with the story told in Jacqueline Anne Rouse, *Lugenia Burns Hope: Black Southern Reformer* (Athens: University of Georgia Press, 2004).

Explorations of alternative black religious identities and racially progressive institutions in the urban North have been a staple of recent scholarly studies. See Jacob S. Dorman, *Chosen People: The Rise of American Black Israelite Religions* (New York: Oxford University Press, 2013), and Jill Watts, *God, Harlem, U.S.A.: The Father Divine Story* (Berkeley: University of California Press, 1995). For African Americans and the YMCA/YWCA, see Nina Mjagkij, *Light in the Darkness: African Americans and the YMCA, 1859–1946* (Lexington: University Press of Kentucky, 1994); Judith Weisenfeld, *African American Women and Christian Activism: New York's Black YWCA, 1904–1946* (Cambridge, MA: Harvard University Press, 1997); and Nancy Robertson, *Christian Sisterhood, Race Relations, and the YWCA, 1906–1946* (Urbana: University of Illinois Press, 2007).

Religion, race, and politics in the Depression and World War II era come alive in Patricia Sullivan, *Days of Hope: Race and Democracy in the New Deal Era* (Chapel Hill: University of North Carolina Press, 1996), and Kevin Schultz, *Tri-Faith America: How Catholics and Jews Held Postwar America to Its Protestant Promise* (New York: Oxford University Press, 2011).

On the rise of Holiness and Pentecostalism in this era, see Cheryl Sanders, *Saints in Exile: The Holiness-Pentecostal Experience in African American Religion and Culture* (New York: Oxford University Press, 1999); Gaston Espinosa, *William J. Seymour and the Origins of Global Pentecostalism* (Durham: Duke University Press, 2014); Grant Wacker, *Heaven Below: Pentecostals and American Culture* (Cambridge, MA: Harvard University Press, 2001); Randall Stephens, *The Fire Spreads: Holiness and Pentecostalism in the American South* (Cambridge, MA: Harvard University Press, 2008); and Anthea Butler, *Women in the Church of God in Christ: Making a Sanctified World* (Chapel Hill: University of North Carolina Press, 2007).

The American missionary movement from the Civil War era to World War II has received close attention in much excellent recent scholarship, much of which emphasizes the connections of missionaries and the literature they produced to changing racial attitudes at home. See Patricia Hill, *The World Their Household: The American Women's Foreign Mission Movement and Cultural Transformation, 1870–1920* (Ann Arbor: University of Michigan Press, 1985); Brian Masaru Hayashi, *For the Sake of Our Japanese Brethren: Assimilation, Nationalism, and Protestantism Among the Japanese of Los Angeles, 1895–1942* (Stanford: Stanford University Press, 1995); Jane Hunter, *The Gospel of Gentility: American Women Missionaries in Turn-of-the-Century China* (New Haven, CT: Yale University Press, 1984); John King Fairbank, ed., *The Missionary Enterprise in China and America* (Cambridge, MA: Harvard University Press, 1974); William Hutchison, *Errand to the World: American Protestant Thought and Foreign Missions* (Chicago: University of Chicago Press, 1987); Clifton Phillips, *Protestant America and the Pagan World: The First Half-Century of the American Board of Commissioners for Foreign Missions, 1810–1860* (Cambridge, MA: East Asian Research Center at Harvard University and Harvard University Press, 1969); Sylvia Jacobs, ed., *Black Americans and the Missionary Movement in Africa* (Westport, CT: Greenwood Press, 1982); Lian Xi, *The Conversion of Missionaries: Liberalism in American Protestant Missions in China, 1907–1932* (University Park: Pennsylvania State University Press, 1997). For a broader intellectual history, see Henry Yu, *Thinking Orientals: Migration, Contact, and Exoticism in Modern America* (New York: Oxford University Press, 2001). Other important studies include Eliza F. Kent, *Converting Women: Gender and Protestant Christianity in Colonial South India*. Oxford: Oxford University Press, 2004; Susan Haskell Khan, "From Redeemers to Partners: American Women Missionaries and the 'Woman Question' in India, 1919–1939," in *Competing Kingdoms: Women, Mission, Nation, and the American Protestant Empire, 1812–1960*, edited by Barbara Reeves-Ellington, Kathryn Kish Sklar, and Connie A. Shemo (Durham, NC: Duke University Press, 2009), 141–63; Karen Seat, *Providence Has Freed Our Hands: Women's Missions and the American Encounter with Japan* (Syracuse, NY: Syracuse University Press, 2008); Brian Stanley, "From 'the Poor Heathen' to 'the Glory and Honour of All Nations': Vocabularies of Race and Custom in Protestant Missions, 1844–1928," *International Bulletin of Missionary Research* 34 (2010): 3–10; and Yumi Yasutake, *Transnational Women's Activism: The United States, Japan, and Japanese Immigrant Communities in California, 1859–1920* (New York: New York University Press, 2004).

On conceptions of Asians and Asian religions, see Stephen Prothero, *The White Buddhist: The Asian Odyssey of Henry Steel Olcott* (Bloomington, IN: Indiana University Press, 1996); and Thomas Tweed, *The American Encounter with Buddhism (1844–1912): Victorian Culture and the Limits of Dissent* (Bloomington: Indiana University Press, 1992). Jennifer Snow's *Protestant Missionaries, Asian Immigrants, and Ideologies of Race in America, 1850–1924* (New York: Routledge, 2012), points out the important but ultimately ineffective voice of missionaries against the rise of anti-Asian racism during the late nineteenth century. Other key works include Michihiro Ama, *Immigrants to the Pure Land: The Modernization, Acculturation, and Globalization of Shin Buddhism, 1898–1941* (Honolulu: University of Hawaii Press, 2011); Eiichiro Azuma, *Between Two Empires: Race, History, and Transnationalism in Japanese America* (Oxford: Oxford University Press, 2005); Anne M Blankenship, *Christianity, Social Justice, and the Japanese American Incarceration during World War II* (Chapel Hill: University of North Carolina Press, 2016); Wakoh Shannon Hickey, "Two Buddhisms, Three Buddhisms, and Racism," In *Buddhism Beyond Borders: New Perspectives on Buddhism in the United States*, edited by Scott A. Mitchell and Natalie E. F. Quli (Albany: State

University of New York Press, 2005), 35–56; Michael K Masatsugu, "Beyond This World of Transiency and Impermanence": Japanese Americans, Dharma Bums, and the Making of American Buddhism during the Early Cold War Years," *Pacific Historical Review* 77 (2008): 432–451; Richard H Seager, *The World's Parliament of Religions: The East/West Encounter, Chicago, 1893* (Bloomington: Indiana University Press, 2009); Wesley Woo, "Chinese Protestants in the San Francisco Bay Area," In *Entry Denied: Exclusion and the Chinese Community in America, 1882–1943*, edited by Sucheng Chan (Philadelphia: Temple University Press, 1991), 213–245; and David K. Yoo, *Contentious Spirits: Religion in Korean American History, 1903–1945* (Stanford, CA: Stanford University Press, 2010).

The racialization of the conception of immigrants and their lives becomes clear in Matthew Frye Jacobson, *Whiteness of a Different Color: European Immigrants and the Alchemy of Race* (Cambridge, MA: Harvard University Press, 1998), and Jacobson, *Barbarian Virtues: The United States Encounters Foreign Peoples at Home and Abroad, 1876–1917* (New York: Hill and Wang, 2001). See also Peter Schrag, *Not Fit for Our Society: Immigration and Nativism in America* (Berkeley: University of California Press, 2011).

Important work on Native American religions for this period include Omer Call Stewart, *Peyote Religion: A History* (Norman: University of Oklahoma Press, 1987); Tisa Wenger, *We Have a Religion: The Pueblo Indian Dance Controversy and American Religious Freedom* (Chapel Hill: University of North Carolina Press, 2009); and Angela Tarango, *Choosing the Jesus Way: American Indian Pentecostals and the Fight for the Indigenous Principle* (Chapel Hill: The University of North Carolina Press, 2014).

CHAPTER 6

The single most important compilation of primary sources for specifically religious speeches and sermons on the civil rights movement may be found in the magnificent two-volume collection of Davis Houck and David Dixon, eds., *Rhetoric, Religion, and the Civil Rights Movement* (Waco, Texas: Baylor University Press, Vol. I, 2007; Vol. II, 2014). The literature on religion and the civil rights movement is vast. One great place to start in terms of a strongly argued and highly opinionated work is David Chappell, *A Stone of Hope: Religion and the Death of Jim Crow* (Chapel Hill: University of North Carolina Press, 2004). For studies of the impact of civil rights on two important denominations, see Joel L. Alvis, *Religion and Race: Southern Presbyterians, 1946–1983* (Tuscaloosa: University of Alabama Press, 1993), and Gardiner H. Shattuck, *Episcopalians and Race: Civil War to Civil Rights* (Lexington: University Press of Kentucky, 1994). Charles Marsh, *God's Long Summer: Stories of Faith and Civil Rights* (Princeton, NJ: Princeton University Press, 1997), remains an outstanding theological study of the ideas both of the civil rights movement as well as figures from the radical segregationist right. An essential theological text, written by one of Martin Luther King's most important influences, is Howard Thurman, *Jesus and the Disinherited* (Boston: Beacon Press, 1948). On Fannie Lou Hamer, there are several good biographies and analyses, but the most effective analysis of the effect of her rhetoric is Meagan Parker Brooks, *A Voice that Could Stir An Army: Fannie Lou Hamer and the Rhetoric of the Freedom Movement* (Jackson: University Press of Mississippi, 2014), and an accompanying volume of essays titled *The Speeches of Fannie Lou Hamer: To Tell It Like It Is* (Jackson: University Press of Mississippi, 2011). Clayborne Carson has headed the team that is annotating and publishing the papers of Martin Luther King; see Carson et al., eds., *The Papers of Martin Luther King*, 4 vols and continuing (Berkeley: University of California Press, 1992–). A useful collection of King's writings and speeches may be found in James Melvin Washington, ed., *A Testament of Hope: The Essential Writings of Dr. Martin Luther King, Jr.* (New York: Harper & Row, 1994). James Cone and Gayraud Wilmore, eds., *Black Theology: A Documentary History* (Maryknoll: Orbis Books, Vol. I 1979; Vol. II 1993), remains the central primary source anthology for the subject and shows how much growth and change happened as a result of the entrance of black female theologians into a conversation formerly dominated by men. On the music of the movement, particularly the freedom songs, see Guy Carawan and Candie Carawan, *We Shall Overcome: Songs of the Southern Freedom Movement* (New York: Oak Press, 1963); Guy Carawan and Candie Carawan, *Freedom Is a Constant Struggle: Songs of the Freedom Movement* (New York: Oak Press, 1968); and Pat Watters, *Down to Now: Reflections on the Southern Civil Rights Movement*

(New York Pantheon, 1971). The classic CD compilation of freedom songs is *Voices of the Civil Rights Movement: Black American Freedom Songs, 1960–1966* (Washington, DC: Smithsonian institution Folkways Recording, 1980). Women in this era receive particular attention in Vicki Crawford, et al., eds., *Women in the Civil Rights Movement: Trailblazers and Torchbearers, 1941–1965* (Bloomington: Indiana University Press, 1993), and Charles Payne, *I've Got the Light of Freedom: The Organizing Tradition and the Mississippi Freedom Struggle* (Berkeley: University of California Press, 1995). Two excellent primary source compilations are Clayborne Carson, et al., eds., *The Eyes on the Prize Civil Rights Reader: Documents, Speeches, and Firsthand Accounts from the Black Freedom Struggle* (New York: Penguin, repr. Ed., 2001); and David Howard-Pitney, ed., *Martin Luther King, Malcolm X, and the Civil Rights Struggle of the 1950s and 1960s: A Brief History With Documents* (Boston: Bedford St. Martin's, 2004). The movement produced some excellent memoir literature, including these three notable titles: James Farmer, *Lay Bare the Heart* (New York: Arbor House, 1985); John Lewis, *Walking With the Wind: A Memoir of the Movement* (New York: Mariner Books, 1999); and Andrew Young, *An Easy Burden: The Civil Rights Movement and the Transformation of America* (rev. ed. Waco: Baylor University Press, 2008).

Aldon D. Morris, *The Origins of the Civil Rights Movement: Black Communities Organizing for* Change (New York: Free Press, 1984), is a still-vital study of black communities in the 1950s. For examinations of white southern religious reactions to the civil rights movement, see Jane Dailey, "Sex, Segregation, and the Sacred After Brown," *Journal of American History* 91 (June 2014): 119–144, and Carolyn Dupont, *Mississippi Praying: White Southern Evangelicals and the Civil Rights Movement, 1945–1975* (New York: New York University Press, 2014). Mark Newman, *Divine Agitators: The Delta Ministry and Civil Rights in Mississippi, 1945–1995* (Athens: University of Georgia Press, 2004), is a solid study of the ministry that came out of Freedom Summer. On Methodist women's civil rights activism, see Alice G. Knotts, *Fellowship of Love: Methodist Women Changing American Racial Attitudes, 1920–1968* (Nashville: Abingdon Press, 1996). An excellent compilation of primary documents related to the Montgomery Bus Boycott, demonstrating memorably how key churchwomen were in organizing it, is Stewart Burns, ed., *Daybreak of Freedom: The Montgomery Bus Boycott* (Chapel Hill: University of

North Carolina Press, 1997). Stephen Haynes, *The Memphis Kneel-Ins and the Campaign for Southern Church Desegregation* (New York: Oxford University Press, 2012), is a memorable account of the church pray-ins and kneel-ins in Memphis and their long range effect on the Presbyterian churches (and Rhodes College) there.

Other important studies of religion and the movement include the following: Jay MacLeod, ed., *Minds Stayed on Freedom: The Civil Rights Struggle in the Rural South, An Oral History* (Boulder, Colorado: Westview Press, 1991); Jacquelyn Dowd Hall, "The Long History of the Civil Rights Movement and the Political Uses of the Past," *Journal of American History* 91 (March 2005): 1233–1263; Quinton Dixie and Peter Eisenstadt, *Visions of a Better World: Howard Thurman's Pilgrimage to India and the Origins of African American Nonviolence* (Boston: Beacon Press, 2011); James F. Findlay, *Church People in the Struggle: The National Council of Churches and the Black Freedom Movement, 1950–1970* (New York: Oxford University Press, 1993); and Jonathan Rieder, *The Word of the Lord is Upon Me: The Righteous Performance of Martin Luther King, Jr.* (Cambridge, MA: Harvard University Press, 2008).

Important works on Cesar Chavez and *la causa* include Jacqueline Levy, *Cesar Chavez: Autobiography of La Causa* (Minneapolis: University of Minnesota Press, 2007), and Susan Ferriss and Richard Sandoval, *The Fight in the Fields: Cesar Chavez and the Farmworkers Movement* (New York: Mariner Books, 1998). Both are largely admiring accounts of the rise of the United Farm Workers. More recently, Miriam Pawel, *The Union of Their Dreams: Power, Hope and Struggle in Cesar Chavez's Farmworker Movement* (New York: Bloomsbury Press, 2010), and *The Crusades of Cesar Chavez* (New York: Bloomsbury Press, 2015), both provide empathetic, but also critical and at times myth-busting, accounts emphasizing Chavez's foibles and late-life attraction to the Esalen movement and difficulties maintaining relations with those he had worked with for so long. One of those was longtime activist Dolores Huerta, who was as instrumental to the movement as was Chavez; there is no standard biography of her, but a good primary source compilation is Mario Garcia, ed., *A Dolores Huerta Reader* (Albuquerque: University of New Mexico Press, 2008). For broader studies of Latino activism and its relationship to religion, see Gastón Espinosa et al., eds., *Latino Religions and Civic Activism in the United States* (Oxford, 2005); and Gaston Espinosa,

Mexican American Religions: Spirituality, Activism, and Culture (Durham: Duke University Press, 2008).

CHAPTER 7 AND EPILOGUE

Michael Emerson and Christian Smith, *Divided by Faith: Evangelical Religion and the Problem of Race in America* (New York: Oxford University Press, 2001), is perhaps the single most discussed and debated text in contemporary studies of race, religion, and evangelicalism. The thesis presented by Smith and Emerson is explored and tested in J. Russell Hawkins and Philip Sinitiere, eds., *Christians and the Color Line: Race and Religion after Divided by* Faith (New York: Oxford University Press, 2014). James Cone, *The Cross and the Lynching Tree* (Boston: Orbis Books, 2013), is a recent updating of key themes in black liberation theology. The impact of religion in the black power movement is detailed for one locale in Kerry Pimblott, *Between the Bible and The Gun in Little Egypt: Black Power and Black Theology in Cairo, Illinois, 1969–74* (Lexington: University Press of Kentucky, 2016). On religion, African Americans, and popular culture, see Kathryn Lofton, *Oprah: The Gospel of an Icon* (Berkeley: University of California Press, 2009).

Important contemporary works on Latinos and Catholicism include, Peter Casarella, ed., *The Hispanic Presence in the American Catholic Church* (New York: Crossroad Publishers, 1998); Allan Figueroa Deck, *Frontiers of Hispanic Theology in the U.S* (Maryknoll: Orbis Books, 1992); Ada Maria Isasi-Díaz and Yolanda Tarango, *Hispanic Women: Prophetic Voice in the Church* (Minneapolis: Fortress Press, 1992); Ada Maria Isasi-Diaz, *Mujerista Theology: A Theology for the Twenty-First Century* (Boston: Orbis Books, 1996); and Isidro Lucas, *The Browning of America: The Hispanic Revolution in the American Church* (Chicago: Fides/Claretian, 1981). A critical and groundbreaking collection of primary documents may be found in Antonio Stevens–Arroyo, ed., *Prophets Denied Honor: An Anthology on the Hispano Church of the United States* (New York: Orbis Books, 1997), and a good bibliography in Antonio Stevens-Arroyo, ed., *Discovering Latino Religion: A Comprehensive Social Science Bibliography* (New York: Bildner Center for Western Hemisphere Studies, 1995). A good general history is Moises Sandoval,

On the Move: A History of the Hispanic Church in the United States (Maryknoll, NY: Orbis Books, 1990).

Works on contemporary immigration and religion are exploding. For the immigration statistics cited in the epilogue, see "Modern Immigration Wave Brings 59 Million to U.S., Driving Population Growth and Change Through 1965," at http://www.pewhispanic.org/2015/09/28/modern-immigration-wave-brings-59-million-to-u-s-driving-population-growth-and-change-through-2065. On immigration and religion, see, for example, Ihsan Bagby, *The American Mosque 2011: Activities, Administration, and Vitality of the American Mosque* (Islamic Society of North America, 2012); Wendy Cadge and Elaine Howard Ecklund, "Immigration and Religion," *Annual Review of Sociology* 33 (2003): 359–79; Carolyn Chen, *Getting Saved in America: Taiwanese Immigration and Religious Experience* (Princeton, NJ: Princeton University Press, 2014); Korrie L. Edwards, *The Elusive Dream: The Power of Race in Interracial Churches* (New York: Oxford University Press, 2008); Prema Kurien, *A Place at the Multicultural Table: The Development of an American Hinduism* (New Brunswick, NJ: Rutgers University Press, 2007); Peggy Levitt, *God Needs No Passport: Immigrants and the Changing American Religious Landscape* (New York: New Press, 2007); Gerardo Marti, *A Mosaic of Believers: Diversity and Innovation in a Multiethnic Church* (Bloomington: Indiana University Press, 2005); Pyong Gap Min and Sou Hyun Jang, "The Diversity of Asian Immigrants' Participation in Religious Institutions in the United States," *Sociology of Religion* 76 (2015): 253–74; and Robert Wuthnow, *Boundless Faith: The Global Outreach of American Churches* (Berkeley: University of California Press, 2010). Two excellent compilations of essays on religion, immigration, and pluralism in contemporary America are Stephen Prothero, ed., *A Nation of Religions: The Politics of Pluralism in Multireligious America* (Chapel Hill: University of North Carolina Press, 2006), and Karen I. Leonard, et al., eds., *Immigrant Faiths: Transforming Religious Life in America* (New York: AltaMira Press, 2005). See also Diana Eck, *A New Religious America: How a 'Christian Country' Has become the World's Most Religiously Diverse Nation* (San Francisco: HarperSanFrancisco, 2001); Yvonne Haddad et al., eds., *Religion and Immigration: Christian, Jewish, and Muslim Experiences in the United States* (Walnut Creek, CA: Altamira, 2003); and Bruce B. Lawrence, *New Faiths, Old Fears: Muslims and Other Asian Immigrants in American*

Religious Life (New York: Columbia University Press, 2002). Other outstanding recent works in Asian American religion include Khyati Joshi and Jigna Desai, *Asian Americans in Dixie: Race and Migration in the South* (Chapel Hill: University of North Carolina Press, 2013); Khyati Joshi, *New Roots in America's Sacred Ground: Religion, Race, and Ethnicity in Indian America* (New Brunswick: Rutgers University Press, 2006); and David Yoo, ed., *New Spiritual Homes: Religion and Asian Americans* (Honolulu: University of Hawai'I Press, 1999).

Vine Deloria, *God is Red: A Native View of Religion* (Rev. ed., Golden, CO: Fulcrum Press, 1994), is the seminal text from a contemporary Native American scholar of religion. Other important works on Native Americans and religion in contemporary America include James Treat, ed., *Native and Christian: Indigenous Voices on Religious Identity in the United States and Canada* (New York: Routledge, 1996); Clara Sue Kidwell, *A Native American Theology* (Boston: Orbis Books, 2001); George Tinker, *Spirit and Resistance: Political Theology and American Indian Liberation* (Minneapolis: Fortress Press, 2004); and Andrea Smith, *Native Americans and the Christian Right: The Gendered Politics of Unlikely Alliances* (Durham, NC: Duke University Press, 2004).

Index

A.M.E. Church Review, 61

abolitionists, 6, 62, 66–70, 75, 77–78, 82–85, 116, 148, 211–12

Adams, Hannah, 73, 85–87

Adams, John, 85

Africa: civil rights movement's impact in, 182; colonization of African Americans to, 59, 63, 78, 105–6; enslaved people from, 5–6, 26, 210; immigration from, 205, 210; missions to, 59; Pentecostalism in, 146; white perceptions of, 26–28

African Americans: and black churches, 43, 45, 58–61; and Christianity, 33, 35–36, 57–63, 65, 79–82; and civil rights movement, 159–75; and the Great Awakening, 35–36, 41; and Islam, 12, 174–75, 210–11; racialization of, 28–33; during Reconstruction, 100–110; and slave rebellion, 33–35, 44, 63, 74–75, 77, 103, 207; and slavery, 28, 43–45, 79–82. *See also* African Methodist Episcopal Church; race; slavery

African Methodist Episcopal Church (AME), 43, 45, 58–61, 80, 103, 105, 207

African Methodist Episcopal Zion Church (AMEZ), 58, 61

Ahimsa, 163

Alabama, 50, 165, 172, 174

Alabama Christian Movement for Human Rights (ACMHR), 165

Algonquian (language), 23

Allen, Richard, 43, 45, 58, 60, 61, 80

An Alphabetical Compendium of the Various Sects Which Have Appeared from the Beginning of the Christian Era to the Present Day (1784), 85

Altman, Mike, 87

Amat y Brusi, Thaddeus, 122, 125

American Board of Commissioners for Foreign Missions (ABCFM), 52, 88

American Christian Student Movement, 163

American Colonization Society (ACS), 59, 63, 105

American Home Missionary Society, 113

American Indian Movement (AIM), 152, 197

American Indian Religious Freedom Restoration Act (1994), 198

American Missionary Association, 117

American Revolution, 14, 41, 44–46, 57, 63, 65

Andover Seminary, 88

Anglicans, 11, 12, 14, 30–35

antislavery, 35, 60, 66, 73, 82–84. *See also* abolitionists

Apess, William, 54–56

Apostolic Faith, 145

Apostolic Faith Mission, 144–45

Appeal to the Coloured Citizens of the World (1829), 43–44, 61, 63–65

Augusta Baptist Institute, 107. *See also* Morehouse College

Austin, Stephen F., 93–94

Azusa Street Revivals, 144–46

Baker, Ella, 172
Ball, Charles, 79
Bancroft, Hubert Howe, 93
Bannock (Indians), 118
Baptists, 5, 77, 93–94, 101, 208; black, 74, 102, 106–9, 142, 162, 166, 175–77; and the Great Awakening, 36; missionaries, 45, 51; and Nat Turner's rebellion, 74–75; northern and southern, 83. *See also* National Baptist Convention; Southern Baptist Convention
Barbados, 26, 30
Barrows, John Henry, 130
Bartleman, William, 145
Basso, Teresita, 193
Battle of Little Bighorn, 120, 121. *See also* Custer, George Armstrong
Berrigan, Daniel, 193
Bethel African Methodist Episcopal Church (Philadelphia), 58–60
Bethel Baptist Church (Birmingham), 166
Bilbo, Theodore, 146
Birth of a Nation (1915), 132, 140, 141
Bishop's Committee for the Spanish Speaking, 155
Black, Galen, 199
black colleges, 6, 61, 107, 162, 164. *See also* Howard University; Morehouse College
Black Lives Matter, 182, 184
blackness, 13, 28–29, 76, 106, 161, 185–87
Black Panthers, 188
A Black Theology of Liberation (1970), 185–86
Bob Jones University, 202
Boesak, Allen, 182
Boudinot, Elias, 53
Brahmanism, 91, 92
Brainerd, David, 36, 37–38
Brainerd School, 51

Branch, Taylor, 159
Bray, Thomas, 31
Brown, Michael, 214
Brown v. Board of Education (1954), 165
Buchanan, Patrick, 183
Buddhism, 73, 85, 87, 92, 130, 135
Buddy, Charles, 122
Buffalo Bill, 150
Bureau of Ethnology, 119
Bureau of Indian Affairs, 148–49
Burke, Charles, 149
Burroughs, Nannie, 109
Bush, George W., 184
Bushnell, Horace, 84

Cailloux, Andre, 99
California, 93, 100, 112–14, 125–26, 131, 136, 154–55, 175–76, 180, 190, 195, 200
California Migrant Ministry, 180
Calvinism, 21, 36
camp meetings, 44
Campo Cultural de la Raza, 191
Canada, 5, 19, 21–22
Cane Ridge, Kentucky, 44
Caribbean, 8, 26, 33. *See also* Barbados
Carlisle School, 117
Cartwright, Peter, 44
Cass, Lewis, 53
Cather, Willa, 96–97
Catholics, 7, 12, 31, 41, 77, 99, 152–54, 206, 210, 125; and the civil rights movement, 175–81; Latino Catholics, 92–97, 100, 111–12, 121–26, 154–56, 160, 175–81; and liberation theology, 190–96; missions to Native Americans, 15, 18–22, 148; and the Pueblo Revolt, 15–17; and the Stono Rebellion, 34–35
Católicos por la Raza (CPLR), 190
Central America, 7–8, 189–90, 196, 205

Cercle Harmonique, 99
Channing, William Ellery, 84
Chauchetière, Claude, 20, 21
Chavez, Cesar, 156, 160, 175–81, 190, 191, 196
Cherokee Phoenix, 53
Cherokees, 48–49, 51, 52–54, 200
Cheyenne, 120, 150
Chicago World's Fair (1893), 129–31. *See also* World Parliament of Religions
Child, Lydia Maria, 89–92
Chinese Exclusion Act (1882), 7, 92, 113, 116, 136
Christian Endeavor Society, 143
Christian Recorder, 61
Church for the Fellowship of All Peoples, 164
Church of God in Christ (COGIC), 144, 146–47
Church of Jesus Christ of Latter-day Saints. *See* Mormons
Church of the Good Shepherd, 150
Church of the Nazarene, 144
Circular 1665, 149
citizenship, 57, 66, 98, 99–103, 110, 112, 113, 115, 116–21, 132, 136, 143, 149, 152, 167, 175, 196
Civil Rights Act (1875), 105
Civil Rights Act (1964), 171, 173, 183, 202
civil rights movement, 7, 142, 157, 181–82, 183–88, 202, 212; and African Americans, 159–75; and Mexican Americans, 175–81
Civil War, 43, 60, 65, 71, 78–80, 82, 92, 97–98, 100–4, 108–9, 117, 124, 141, 148, 207. *See also* Confederate States of America
The Clansman (1905), 138, 139, 140
Clarke, James Freeman, 89–91
Coker, Daniel, 59, 61–62
Collier, John, 152

Colorado, 95, 96, 150
Community Services Organization, 176
compadrazgo, 123, 155
comparative religion, 73, 85, 89, 91–92
Cone, James, 175, 185–86, 189, 196
Confederate States of America, 45; flag, 61, 208; soldiers, 80; symbols and monuments, 208
Confucianism, 7, 99, 114
Congregationalists, 5, 44, 87, 100, 114, 142–43
Congress of Racial Equality (CORE), 160, 165
conservatism: political, 168, 183–85, 203, 207–8; religious, 8, 28, 57, 76–77, 184, 202, 215
conversion, 13, 19, 44; of African Americans to Protestant Christianity, 29–36; of Asian immigrants to Christianity, 136; and Christian missionaries, 113–14, 116; of Mexican Americans to Catholicism, 94; of Native Americans to Protestant Christianity, 22–23, 27, 38, 47, 123
Coolidge, Charles Austin, 150
Coolidge, Sherman (Etes-che-wa-ah), 148–52
Costo, Rupert, 149
Council of Conservative Citizens, 208
Council of Federated Organization (COFO), 173
Creeks, 46, 48–49, 51
Crummel, Alexander, 69
Cruz, Ted, 209
Custer, George Armstrong, 120

Davies, Samuel, 36
Davis, Jefferson, 105
Dawes, Henry, 117
Dawes Act (1887), 116–18, 132, 148, 152
Dawson, Joseph Martin, 109

Day, Mark, 178, 180
Death Comes to the Archbishop (1927), 97
Declaration of Independence, 57, 60, 65–66, 84, 116
Definition of Marriage Amendment (1996), 184
Delano grape boycott, 176–80, 191
Delany, Martin, 70
Delaware (Indians), 38, 40, 45
Deloria, Vine, 186, 196–97, 201
Democracy in America (1835), 44
Democrats, 105, 112, 167, 189, 202
Dennis, Dave, 173
de Otermín, Don Antonio, 17
de Tocqueville, Alexis, 44
A Dialogue Between a Virginian and an African Minister (1810), 43, 61–62
Diego, Juan, 123
Divided by Faith (2001), 211–12
Diwali, 203
Dixie, Quinton, 164
Dixon, Thomas, 132, 138–41
Douglass, Frederick, 45, 66–70, 84, 91
Dow, George, 136
Du Bois, W. E. B., 91, 107, 142

Eastman, Charles Alexander, 150
Edmund Pettis Bridge, 174
Edwards, Jonathan, 36, 37
Eistenstadt, Peter, 164
Eliot, John, 13, 23–25, 63
Elizondo, Virgilio, 179–80
Elliott, Stephen, 73, 78
Emanuel African Methodist Episcopal Church (Charleston), 60, 207
Emerson, Michael, 211–12
Emerson, Ralph Waldo, 73, 85, 89, 114, 136
Employment Division, Department of Human Resources of Oregon v. Smith (1990), 198–200

Enlightenment, 27, 65
Episcopalians, 78, 150, 168, 197
evangelical Protestants, 5, 14, 27, 41, 43, 88, 206; and civil rights activism, 167, 170–72, 182; and Pentecostalism, 146; and political conservatism, 184, 202–3; and race, 211–12, 214–15; and slavery, 35, 36, 44, 73–74, 76, 79–80, 82. *See also* Baptists; Great Awakening; Methodists; Presbyterians
Evarts, Jeremiah, 52–53

Falwell, Jerry, 183, 202
Fan, Chan Hon, 116
Fard, Wallace, 174
Farmer, James, 160, 161, 165, 166, 168
Fifteenth Amendment, 113
First African Baptist Church (Richmond), 102
First Amendment, 5, 7, 42, 110, 197, 200, 201
First Congregational Church (Atlanta), 142–43
First Congregational Church (Oakland), 114
First Presbyterian Church (Chicago), 130
First Presbyterian Church (New Orleans), 97
Flores, Patricio, 191, 192–93
Florida, 14, 33, 101, 161
Floyd, John, 74–75
Forman, James, 187–88
Forsyth, James, 120
Forten, James, 57
Fourteenth Amendment, 100, 112–13
Franciscans, 12, 14, 93, 178
Franklin, Benjamin, 35
Frazier, Garrison, 101
Free African Society, 58
Freedmen's Bureau, 101, 107
Freedom Rides, 165–66

Freedom Summer, 173
Free Exercise Clause. *See* First
    Amendment
Free Soil Party, 84
Free Speech Movement, 179
Furman, Richard, 73, 77

Gallatin, Albert, 51
Gam, Jee, 100, 114–16
Gambold, Anna Rosina, 48
Gambold, John, 48
Gandhi, Mohandas, 163–64, 176, 177
Garner, Eric, 214
Garnet, Henry Highland, 45, 68–70
Garrison, William Lloyd, 63, 82
Garvey, Marcus, 109, 143
Geary Act (1892), 116
Georgia, 48–54, 63, 80, 101, 103, 104,
    105
Georgia Baptist, 107
Georgia Equal Rights and Education
    Association, 107
Georgia Equal Rights League, 108
ghost dance, 111, 112, 118, 120, 148,
    197. *See also* Wounded Knee
    Massacre
Ginsberg, Allen, 136
God is Red (1973), 186, 196–97
Godwyn, Morgan, 28, 30–31
Goodrich, James, 87
Granjon, Henry, 123
Grant, Jacquelyn, 185, 188–89
Grant, Madison, 132–35, 141
Great Awakening, 35–42, 46
Great Migration, 143
Griffith, D. W., 140
*The Guadalupan Voice: Journal of
    Mexican Culture*, 155.

Hager, John S., 113
Haley, Alex, 174
Haley, Nimrata (Nikki) Randhawa,
    207, 208

Hamer, Fannie Lou, 160, 167–68
Handsome Lake, 45–48
Harding, Vincent, 185, 186–87, 188
Harlem Renaissance, 185
Harmony Baptist Church (Augusta),
    107
Harrison, William Henry, 46
Hart-Celler Immigration Act (1965),
    132, 183, 205, 210
Harvard College, 25
Heckewelder, John, 39, 40
Higginson, Thomas Wentworth,
    80–81
Hinduism, 8, 73, 85, 87, 88, 89, 92,
    111, 130–31, 137, 203, 206
Hobart College, 150
holiness movement, 132, 143–47.
    See also Pentecostalism
Hope, John, 108, 142, 161
Hope, Lugenia Burns, 109
Howard, Oliver O., 101, 107
Howard University, 162, 165
Huerta, Dolores, 178
Hughes, John, 78
Hurons, 19

immigration, 7, 127, 131, 138, 156,
    205, 207; from Africa, 210; from
    Asia, 91–92, 100, 113–14, 116,
    135–36, 205, 210; Catholic, 98, 112,
    123, 131, 152–54, 210; from Europe,
    98, 131, 136–37, 205; illegal, 205;
    Jewish, 98, 112, 131, 133–35, 152;
    from Latin America, 94, 123, 131,
    155, 195–96, 205; from Middle
    East, 204, 210–11; Muslim, 204,
    210–11. *See also* Chinese Exclusion
    Act; Hart-Celler Immigration Act;
    National Origins Act
India, 85, 87–88, 91, 92, 136–37,
    163–64, 205
*An Indian's Looking Glass on the White
    Man* (1833), 54

Indian boarding schools, 117–18, 148–49. *See also* Carlisle School; Pratt School; Wind River Boarding School
Indian Great Awakening, 36
Indian Reorganization Act (1934), 152
Indian Rights Association, 117, 150
Indians. *See* Native Americans
Internal Revenue Service (IRS), 202
Iroquois, 12, 19, 21, 46–47
Islam, 8, 12; black, 174–75. *See also* Muslims

Jackson, Andrew, 51–53
Jackson, Mahalia, 171
Jefferson, Thomas, 5, 47–48, 57, 85, 99, 110
Jemmy (slave), 33, 34
Jesuits, 12–13, 19, 21, 22, 34, 96, 193
Jesus and the Disinherited (1949), 164
Jews, 67, 76, 98, 112, 126, 131–36, 152, 156, 163, 206; Reform, 133
Jim Crow, 100, 108, 110, 121, 159–60, 164, 171
Johns Hopkins University, 129
Johnson, Lyndon Baines, 102, 167, 183
Jones, Absalom, 58, 60, 61
Jones, Charles Colcock, 81
Jordan, Winthrop, 76
Judeo-Christian tradition, 132, 135, 203
Judson, Adoniram, 88
Judson, Nancy, 88

Kennedy, Robert F., 178
Kentucky, 44, 102
Kerry, John, 184
King, Martin Luther, Jr., 107; assassination of, 185, 207; and "beloved community," 186; and Cesar Chavez, compared, 175–77, 180–81; and civil rights movement, 159–61, 165–66, 170–72, 188;

criticized by the Religious Right, 183–84, 202; and "I Have a Dream" speech, 170–71; influence of Howard Thurman on, 164
King, Mary, 172
King Philip. *See* Metacom
King Philip's War (1676), 13, 25–26, 55
Know-Nothing Party, 125, 210
Ku Klux Klan, 102–3, 105, 138–41, 156, 171
Kyi, Aung San Suu, 182

Lakotas, 111, 120, 148
Lamy, Jean Baptiste, 96–97, 121–22, 125
La Raza movement, 190–96
Las Hermanas, 192–95
Latinos, 7, 159, 211; and Catholicism, 7, 92–97, 100, 111–12, 121–27, 152–56, 160, 175–82, 190–96; and the civil rights movement, 175–82; and liberation theology, 190–96
La Verdad, 190
Lee, Robert E., 99
Le Jau, Francis, 14, 31–33
Lemon v. Kurtzman (1971), 198
The Leopard's Spots (1902), 138
Lewis, John, 174
liberalism: political, 184, 215; religious, 4, 84–85, 89, 91–92, 130, 132, 157, 161–62, 186, 191
liberation theology, 175, 184, 188, 203; and African Americans, 185–89; and Mexican Americans, 180, 190–96; and Native Americans, 196–97
Liberator, 63
limpieza de sangre, 13
Lincoln, Abraham, 99, 112
Los Angeles, 122, 125–26, 144–45, 153, 154–55, 191–92
Los Hermanos de Nuestro Padre Jesus Nazareno, 95

Lost Cause, 138
Lucey, Robert Emmet, 155–56
Lutherans, 197
Lyng v. Northwest Indian Cemetery Protective Ass'n (1988), 200

Madison, James, 110
Malcolm X, 161, 174–75, 186
March for Jobs, Freedom, and Justice in Washington (March on Washington), 165
Marshall, John, 52
Martin, Joel, 51
Martin, Trayvon, 214
Martinez, Antonio Jose, 96–97, 122
Maryland, 12, 29, 66
Mason, Charles Harrison, 144, 146–47
Massachusett Indians, 13, 22
Massachusetts Bay Colony, 22–25
Mather, Cotton, 23, 26–27
Matovina, Timothy, 94
Mays, Benjamin, 161–62
McGowan, Lucey, 156
McGowan, Raymond, 156
McIntyre, James Frances, 191
Melville, Herman, 92
Mennonites, 186
Metacom, 22–26
Methodism, 36, 43–44, 54, 57, 126; black Methodists, 102–7, 165; missionaries, 116; northern and southern, 83. *See also* African Methodist Episcopal Church
Mexican American Cultural Center (San Antonio), 192
Mexico, 7, 112, 123, 126, 131, 155, 178, 196, 205, 209. *See also* immigration
missionaries: in Africa, 59, 106; to African American slaves, 30–35, 81, 83; Anglican, 30–33; and Asia, 85–88; Catholic, 121–22; evangelical, 59, 107, 113; at home, Protestant, 153; Jesuit, 12–13, 19,
21–22, 34; Moravian, 38–41; to Native Americans, 12–14, 18–21, 22–23, 36–42, 45–56, 117; Quaker, 38, 47. *See also* American Board of Commissioners for Foreign Missions (ABCFM); American Home Missionary Society; American Missionary Association; Society for the Propagation of the Gospel in Foreign Parts
The Missionary Herald, 88
Mississippi, 102, 144, 146, 159–61, 167–73, 180
Mississippi Freedom Democratic Party, 167
Moby Dick (1851), 92
Mohawks, 13, 19–21. *See also* Tekakwitha, Kateri
Montgomery bus boycott, 164, 165
Mooney, James, 119–20
Moore, Russell, 208
Moravians, 14, 36, 38–41, 45, 48–49, 51
Morehouse, Henry Lyman, 106
Morehouse College, 106–7, 162. *See also* Augusta Baptist Institute
Mormons, 110–11
Morse, Jedediah, 88
Mosaix Global Network, 213
Mott, Lucretia, 82
Movimiento Estudiantil Chicana de Aztlan (MEChA), 192
Muhammad, Elijah, 174
Mundelein, George, 153
Murray, Pauli, 160–61, 167–70
Muskogees, 50–51
Muslims, 8, 203–4, 206, 209; racialization of, 209–11, 215. *See also* Islam

National Association for the Advancement of Colored People (NAACP), 109, 132, 141, 142, 165

National Baptist Convention, 106
National Black Economic
    Development Conference (1969),
    187
National Catholic Welfare
    Conference, 156
National Committee of Negro
    Churchmen, 187
National Convention of Colored
    People, 69
National Council of Churches, 180
National Origins Act (1924), 131, 156
Nation of Islam, 174–75
Native American Church, 111
Native Americans, 6, 13, 117–18,
    148; Euro-American conflict with,
    13, 25–26, 55, 112, 120–21, 148,
    197; missions to, 12–14, 18–21,
    22–23, 36–42, 45–56, 117; prophets,
    37–38, 45–51, 100, 118–19; and
    religious awakenings, 45–56;
    and religious freedom, 196–201;
    removal of, 45, 48, 51–53, 57. See
    also Indian boarding schools;
    Indian Great Awakening; Indian
    Reorganization Act; Indian Rights
    Organization; Native American
    Church; individual tribes
nativism, 7, 92, 125–27, 132–33, 138,
    141, 153, 156, 209–11
Naturalization Act (1790), 57, 137
Nazi, 163
The Negro Church (1903), 142
Neolin, 45
New Deal, 176, 183
New Divinity School, 36, 88
Newell, Harriet, 88
Newell, Samuel, 88
New England, 12, 13–14, 22–28, 36,
    42, 54, 57, 88–89
New Mexico, 12, 13, 14–15, 25, 95–96,
    121–23, 125, 149, 152–54
New Orleans, 99–100, 214

New Thought, 135–36
New York, 46, 58, 62, 64, 69, 78, 133,
    143, 150, 154, 162, 185, 187, 213
Nixon, Richard, 184
nones, 206
North Carolina, 48, 107, 138, 147,
    168, 172
North Carolina College for Negroes,
    164
Northern Arapaho, 150
North Star, 66
Nott, Josiah, 77
Nott, Roxanna, 88
Nott, Samuel, 88

Obama, Barack, 189, 208–9
O'Connor, Sandra Day, 199–200
Ohio, 40, 48, 61, 63
Olcott, Henry Steel, 136
Old Testament, 6, 64, 65, 75–76, 78,
    80, 166
Oregon, 111, 198–200
Organization of Afro-American
    Unity, 175
Our Country (1885), 153

Padres Asociados para los Derechos
    Religiosos, Educativos, y Sociales
    (PADRES), 192–95
Paiute Indians, 100, 118–19
Palmer, Benjamin Morgan, 97
Pang, Fung Chee, 113–14
The Panoplist, 88
Paradise Lost (1667), 23
Paramananda, Swami, 131
Parham, Charles, 144
Parks, Rosa, 165, 169
Parris, Samuel, 26
The Passing of the Great Race: The
    Racial Basis of European History
    (1916), 133–35
Payne, Daniel, 61
Pennington, J. W. C., 65

Pennsylvania, 12, 36–40, 48, 58, 66
Pentecostalism, 8, 132, 143–47, 215.
   See also holiness movement
Philadelphia, 57–58, 61–62, 80, 170
Pinckney, Clementa, 207, 208
Pinckney, Thomas, 51
polygamy, 110
Popé, 13, 16, 17–18
Pope Leo XIII, 176, 190
Pratt School, 117
praying towns, 13, 19, 23, 25, 28
Presbyterian, 5, 35–38, 81, 95, 97, 113,
   118, 130, 153
Priestly, Joseph, 85, 87
Proctor, Henry, 142–43
The Progress of Religious Ideas Through
   Successive Ages (1855), 89
Pueblo Revolt (1680), 13, 14, 15–18,
   25, 42, 122
Puritans, 5, 12–13, 22–28, 42, 44, 63

Quakers, 5, 12, 31, 35, 38, 47, 148

Ramadan, 203
Randolph, Peter, 81
Reagan, Ronald, 184
Reconquista, 18
Reconstruction, 6, 97–98, 101, 142,
   160; and African American
   Protestantism, 100–110; and Asian
   religions, 112–16; and the Ku Klux
   Klan, 102–5; and Latino Catholics,
   121–26; and Native Americans,
   116–21; religious freedom during,
   110–12
Redemption Church (Greenville,
   South Carolina), 215
Redstick Revolt (1813–1814), 50–51
Religious Ceremonies and Customs
   (1834), 87
religious freedom, 5–7, 42, 94, 110–12,
   159; and Native Americans,
   196–201. See also Employment

Division, Department of Human
   Resources of Oregon v. Smith; First
   Amendment; Lemon v. Kurtzman;
   Lyng v. Northwest Indian Cemetery
   Protective Ass'n; Reynolds v. United
   States; Sequoyah v. Tennessee Valley
   Authority
Republicans, 102–3, 105, 107, 112–13,
   120, 202, 203, 207, 208–9
Rerum Novarum, 155, 176, 190
Revels, Hiram, 102
Reynolds, George, 110
Reynolds v. United States (1878), 110
Rhodes College, 97
Rice, Luther, 88
Rice, Tamir, 214
Ridge, John, 51
Riverside Church (New York City),
   187
Rocky Mountain Presbyterian, 153
Roe v. Wade (1973), 202
Romero, Juan, 192, 193
Roof, Dylann, 207–8
Roosevelt, Eleanor, 168
Roosevelt, Franklin Delano, 168
Ruiz, Ralph, 192

Saffin, John, 27
San Francisco, 113–14, 123–24, 164
Santa Fe, 15, 95–96, 121
Sassamon, John, 25
Scalia, Antonin, 111, 199
Scott, Tim, 208
Second Great Awakening, 43
segregation, 101, 108–9, 125, 138, 141,
   144, 146, 153, 154, 164, 165, 166,
   170, 172–73, 175, 184, 201–2. See
   also Jim Crow
Selma, 174
Seminoles, 46
September 11, 2001, 8, 74, 209
Sequoyah v. Tennessee Valley Authority
   (1979), 200

Seymour, William J., 132, 144–47
Shawnee, 46, 50
Shelton, Charles W., 117
Sherman, William Tecumseh, 101
Shoshones, 118, 150
Shuttlesworth, Fred, 160, 165–66
Sikhs, 7, 92, 136–37, 206–7, 209
silent majority, 184, 188
Sisters of Loretto, 122
Sitting Bull, 120
slavery, 6, 43, 170; antebellum
     expansion of, 44–45, 61, 73, 97;
     black opposition to, 60, 61–70,
     82–85; Christianity among enslaved
     people, 79–82; debates over, 26–28,
     35, 57, 63, 75–79, 82–85; and race
     and religion, 28–32, 39; slave
     rebellions, 33–35, 60, 74–75. See also
     abolitionists; antislavery
slave trade, 66; internal, 73;
     transatlantic, 6, 35, 63, 66, 77
Smith, Alfred, 199
Smith, Christian, 211–12
Smith, Elias, 57
Smith, James, 57
Snyder, Gary, 136
social gospel movement, 138, 141–43,
     156, 159, 161–62
Society for the American Indian,
     149
Society for the Propagation of the
     Gospel in Foreign Parts, 14, 31
Son of the Forest (1829), 54
The Soul of the Indian (1911), 150
The Souls of Black Folk (1903), 142
South Carolina, 12, 14, 28, 31, 33, 35,
     63, 103, 202, 207–8, 215
South Carolina Baptist Convention,
     77
South Dakota, 120, 148, 197
Southern Arapaho, 150
Southern Baptist Convention, 83, 208

Southern Christian Leadership
     Conference (SCLC), 160, 164, 166,
     172
Southern Harmony (1835), 80
southern strategy, 184
Speer, William, 113
Spellman, Francis J., 154
Spiritualism, 91, 99
spirituals, 73, 79–82, 170–71
The Spirituals and the Blues (1972), 185
Springfield Baptist Church (Augusta),
     107
St. Basil's Church (Los Angeles), 191
Stanton, Edwin, 101
Stanton, Elizabeth Cady, 106
Stewart, Maria, 45, 64–65
Stono Rebellion (1739), 33–35
Stowe, Calvin, 84
Stowe, Harriet Beecher, 83–84
Strong, Josiah, 7, 113
Student Non-Violent Coordinating
     Committee (SNCC), 167, 172–74,
     179, 186–87
The Student Voice, 172
Sumner, Charles, 105
Supreme Court, 52, 54, 92, 105,
     110–11, 136, 165, 198–99. See
     also Brown v. Board of Education;
     Employment Division, Department
     of Human Resources of Oregon v.
     Smith; Lemon v. Kurtzman; Lyng
     v. Northwest Indian Cemetery
     Protective Ass'n; Reynolds v. United
     States; Roe v. Wade; Sequoyah
     v. Tennessee Valley Authority;
     Worcester v. Georgia
Syrian American Association, 136

Tagore, Rabindranath, 163
Tarango, Yolanda, 195
Tea Party movement, 207
Tecumseh, 50

Tejanos, 94
Tekakwitha, Kateri, 13, 19, 20, 21–22
Ten Great Religions (1871), 89
Tenskwatawa, 45, 46, 50
Terrell, Mary Church, 142
Thind, Bhagat Singh, 136–38
Thompson, Lewis, 103
Thoreau, Henry David, 73, 85, 114,
    178
Thurman, Howard, 160–65
Thurman, Sue Bailey, 163
Tijerina, Reyes Lopes, 177
Tillich, Paul, 198
Tippecanoe, Battle of, 46
Tituba, 26
Trail of Tears, 45
Transcendentalism, 85, 88–89, 91–92,
    135
Treaty of Guadalupe-Hidalgo (1848),
    121
Trump, Donald, 209
Turner, Frederick Jackson, 129–30
Turner, Henry McNeal, 100, 103–7,
    108, 109, 185
Turner, Nat, 44, 63, 73–75
Tutu, Desmond, 182

Uncle Tom's Cabin (1852), 83, 84
Union Theological Seminary, 185
Unitarianism, 57, 84, 85, 89
United Farm Workers, 176, 191
United States Constitution, 57, 68,
    110, 112, 167. *See also* Fifteenth
    Amendment; Fourteenth
    Amendment
University of North Carolina, 168
University of Southern California, 126

Varick, James, 58
Vedanta societies, 131
Vesey, Denmark, 60, 77, 103, 207
Vietnam War, 193

Virginia, 12, 28–31, 33, 63, 74–75,
    110, 168
Virginia Statute of Religious Freedom
    (1786), 110
Vivekananda, Swami, 130–31
Voltaire, 12
Voting Rights Act (1965), 171, 183

Walker, David, 43, 61, 63–65, 69
Wampanoags, 25
Washington, George, 133
Washington, Jesse, 109
Watson, Benjamin, 214
Watts, Isaac, 80
Wayland, Francis, 84
Webster, Daniel, 54
Wesley, John, 59
Wells-Barnett, Ida B., 109, 142
Wetherbee, Grace Darling, 150
Wheelock, Eleazar, 22
White, William Jefferson, 100, 107–8
White Citizens Councils, 208
Whitefield, George, 14, 35, 38
whiteness, 7, 13, 37, 100, 132–33,
    135–38, 141, 161, 189, 202
The Whole Truth, 147
Wilberforce College, 61
Wilmore, Gayraud, 189
Wilson, David, 118
Wilson, Jack. *See* Wovoka
Wilson, William J., 66
Wind River Boarding School, 150
Wind River Reservation, 150
Winthrop, John, 23
Wise, Isaac Mayer, 133
Woolman, John, 35
Worcester, Samuel, 53–54
Worcester v. Georgia (1832), 52
World's Parliament of Religions
    (1893), 129–30, 135, 138, 156
World War I, 133
World War II, 108, 132, 155, 176

Wounded Knee Innocent (1973), 197

Wounded Knee Massacre (1890), 112, 120–21, 148, 197. *See also* ghost dance, Lakotas

Wovoka, 100, 118–20

Wright, Jeremiah, 189

Wright, Richard R., 142, 161

Yale University, 168

Young Men's Christian Association (YMCA), 161–62

Young Women's Christian Association (YWCA), 162

About the Author

PAUL HARVEY IS PROFESSOR OF HISTORY at the University of Colorado, Colorado Springs. He is the author or editor of eleven books, including *Christianity and Race in the American South: A History*.